SPACE
WORKS

SPACE WORKS

A source book of design and decorating
ideas to create your perfect home

CAROLINE CLIFTON-MOGG   **JOANNA SIMMONS**   **REBECCA TANQUERAY**   **REBECCA WINWARD**

RYLAND PETERS & SMALL
LONDON • NEW YORK

Designer   Paul Tilby
Editor   Annabel Morgan
Picture research   Christina Borsi
Production manager   Gordana Simakovic
Art director   Leslie Harrington
Publisher   Cindy Richards
Text by Caroline Clifton-Mogg, Joanna Simmons, Rebecca Tanqueray and Rebecca Winward.

First published in 2008 as *Home Design Ideas*. This revised and updated edition published in the UK in 2017
by Ryland Peters & Small
20–21 Jockey's Fields
London WC1R 4BW
and in the US by Ryland Peters & Small, Inc.
341 E 116th Street
New York NY 10029
www.rylandpeters.com
10 9 8 7 6 5 4 3 2 1

ISBN: 978-1-84975-842-0

Printed and bound in China.

The publishers cannot accept liability for any injury, damage or loss to person or property, direct or inconsequential, arising from suggestions made in this book. The publishers recommend that any structural, electrical or plumbing work is carried out by a qualified professional.

A CIP record from this book is available from the British Library.

Library of Congress Cataloging-in-Publication Data for the original edition of this book:

Clifton-Mogg, Caroline.
  Home design ideas : how to plan and decorate a beautiful home / Caroline Clifton-Mogg, Joanna Simmons, Rebecca Tanqueray.
     p. cm.
  Includes index.
  ISBN 978-1-84597-750-4 -- ISBN 978-1-84597-751-1
  1. Interior decoration. I. Simmons, Joanna. II. Tanqueray, Rebecca. III. Title.
  NK2115.C735 2008
  747--dc22
                                    2008021895

CONTENTS

INTRODUCTION — 6

KITCHENS by Caroline Clifton-Mogg — 8

LIVING ROOMS by Caroline Clifton-Mogg — 50

BEDROOMS by Joanna Simmons — 90

BATHROOMS by Rebecca Tanqueray — 122

CHILDREN'S ROOMS by Joanna Simmons — 154

HOME OFFICES by Rebecca Tanqueray — 188

OPEN-PLAN LIVING by Rebecca Tanqueray — 210

OUTDOOR LIVING by Joanna Simmons — 224

Source lists — 240

Credits — 244

Index — 254

The way your home looks and feels is important. If you don't feel comfortable at home, you don't feel truly yourself, so reinventing your space to suit the way you want to live can have a profound impact.

INTRODUCTION

OPPOSITE **Achieving the right practical layout is just as important as the aesthetic choices you make when designing your home's interior (if not more so). Get both right, and you'll create a space that has a pleasing sense of 'flow', works for your lifestyle, and also expresses your personal style preferences.**

This book will help you with interior design challenges large and small, from big decisions such as choosing colours and flooring materials to the little details that make a house a home. This could mean having a strong-enough light to read your book by, adequate work space in the kitchen to enjoy cooking, and plenty of space to accommodate your shoe collection, among other things – and whether you are planning a major decorating blitz or just want to organize your space more efficiently, *Space Works* is here to help.

Every area of your home, including the outside space, is discussed here. Initial planning and thinking about what you want in each room is often the key to decorating success, so every chapter starts with thoughts on design, decoration and planning, and encourages you to analyse exactly how you want to live in every room in your home. Practical issues such as flooring and lighting are then discussed, including a section of helpful key points. At the end of each chapter you'll find a selection of styles for that room, offering an inspirational picture gallery and plenty of expert advice on how to achieve each look.

The book is designed so that each section is a complete resource. If you just want kitchen flooring, for example, you don't need to read the whole Kitchens chapter – just go to the relevant page. Whether you are decorating your first home or you're a serial renovator, enjoy putting your home together with *Space Works*.

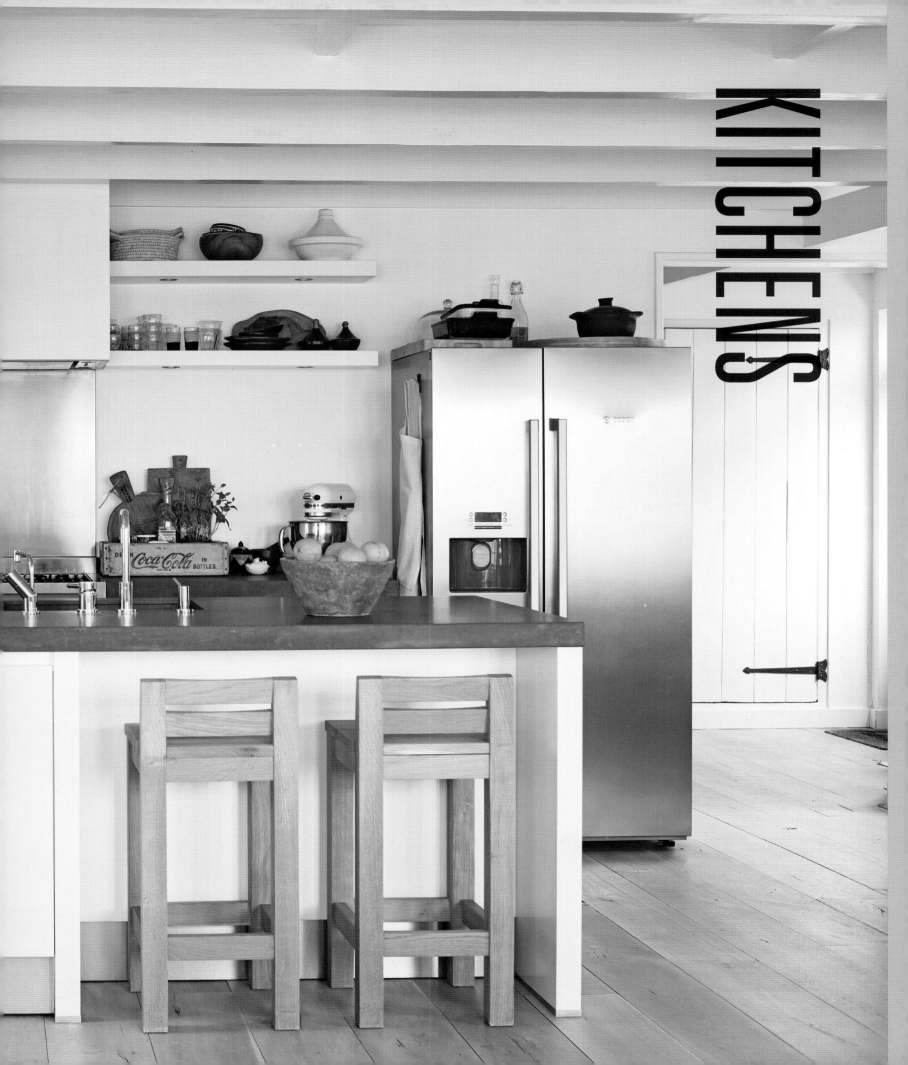

KITCHENS

BELOW LEFT **You can create coherence in an unusually shaped room through your choice of colour. Here the lower half of an island unit echoes the grey that's in evidence on the stairs, while a marble countertop offers flashes of the same shade (but without seeming heavy, as more of the solid colour might).**

BELOW **White on white is a timeless colour scheme, and equally suitable for contemporary or classic spaces. The key to success is to vary the textures – timber boards, tile and enamel all feature in this example – and to add definition with a stronger accent, in this case, the black of the range flue and wall lights.**

OPPOSITE **A country kitchen, complete with a cast-iron range, is decorated in a manner that is true to its origins, with shades of cream on walls and cabinetry, a mellow stone floor and natural wood worktops. Decorative details include still life paintings, decorated crockery and an oversized wicker hamper.**

ABOVE **In a compact room, sleek horizontal and vertical lines and a pared-down aesthetic help to evoke a feeling of space, while a neutral palette ensures a calm ambience. To avoid the look becoming clinical, choose surfaces with a subtle colour variation, such as natural stone and antiqued timber or metal.**

DESIGN & DECORATION

The design and decoration of what is often the most important, and certainly the hardest-working, room in the house is a matter to be carefully pondered; forethought is the answer.

The kitchen has long outgrown its original role as merely the place where food is prepared and cooked. These days it is a room for leisure and pleasure as well as the place where most informal entertaining is done, all of which means that its design and decoration are crucial. The kitchen is also a very personal room, in which you can spend a lot of time, so when you are there you should feel happy and at ease.

The actual design of your kitchen – the style of kitchen, units and appliances – will, to a certain extent, inform the decoration of the room, so it is sensible to think of these aspects at the same time, rather than superimposing one style upon another at a later date.

Many kitchens today are a smallish part of a greater whole. If that is the case for you, the design of the kitchen area must work with the overall design, and feel, of the larger room; a work area of metallic, minimalist design would look out of place in a room that was otherwise decorated with old pine furniture, for example. Even if the kitchen is a separate room, there should still be a stylistic link between it and the next room, to ensure continuity of design.

Planning is the keystone of successful interior design and nowhere more so than in the kitchen, where an efficient working system of some sort, no matter how loosely defined, is absolutely essential.

PLANNING

Getting the kitchen right is so important. Whether you are buying a complete kitchen from one company, or incorporating pieces sourced from different places, a kitchen is expensive to buy and install, and as you spend a great deal of time there it not only warrants, but really requires, effort during the early stages. There are professional kitchen planners, of course, but even the best of them needs help from the most important people in the equation – you and your family – for no one understands how to plan a kitchen better than he or she who will use it.

When thinking about how to plan for what you want, if it seems hard to decide exactly what you need, start from the other end of the scale and make a list of what you positively don't want, need or like. Everyone has strong views on kitchens – inadequate work space, refrigerator in the wrong place, small sink and so on – but you don't always remember such minus points when making your own plans.

Although it is often-repeated advice, the first step is to look at photos of kitchens online, in magazines, catalogues and, of course, in books. It is here that you will find not only the overview, but also the cunning solutions and clever details – the sort of innovative ideas, particularly in storage and arrangement of space, that have been thought through by professionals and described in detail on the page. These are the things you might not think of yourself, but once you know, many of them can be incorporated, even in modified form, into your design.

Another obvious but really useful idea is to look at friends' kitchens. Ask them why they like – or don't like – their own efforts and what they would change or never replace. Finally, if you can, get to some kitchen showrooms to inspect display layouts – you may pick up many useful ideas, not least in the area of finish and colour. The more of this research that you do, the clearer will be the picture in your own mind of what you want, and there's no better place to start than that.

ABOVE LEFT **In small spaces, there might not be much flexibility in where the key elements – sink, storage, cooking zones and preparation areas – are located. This makes the layout process easier in some respects, although for maximum functionality you may need to think creatively, and do plenty of research to find suitably compact appliances.**

LEFT **Sometimes there will be spatial challenges which have to be designed around when planning a workable layout, and you may even find that there's only one logical arrangement possible. Here, a steeply angled ceiling, and a supporting pillar of the building's timber frame, have dictated the placement of the kitchen cabinets.**

OPPOSITE **In a large room, an island unit is often the best way to maximize worksurface and cupboard capacity. Additionally, in open-plan spaces this type of installation not only marks the delineation between kitchen and living area, it can enable the cook to socialize while preparing food.**

ADAPTING AN EXISTING KITCHEN

Not everyone has the luxury of being able to design their kitchen from scratch, but the kitchen you've got doesn't necessarily have to remain as you found it.

OPPOSITE ABOVE **For a stylish kitchen update that doesn't require significant carpentry skills or budget, fix some wall-hung shelving above a freestanding sideboard or chest of drawers. Open shelves are particularly good for maintaining a feeling of space in narrow rooms, as they're visually less dominating than wall cabinets.**

OPPOSITE BELOW LEFT **There's nothing that says a kitchen island has to be fitted – the addition of a freestanding unit, sizeable butcher's block or even a table will provide additional work area, and perhaps also storage, if it's the type of design**

with shelving built in. You can even find trollies on wheels, if layout flexibility is required.

OPPOSITE BELOW RIGHT **If the design and layout of your kitchen is satisfactory, but the colour isn't to your taste, it's often easy to change. Solid wood cabinets and wrapped doors can be refinished (it's just a case of choosing the right paint), or you could consider replacing just the doors and worktops while retaining the carcases.**

 ABOVE **A small dresser/hutch might be all your kitchen requires for extra storage provision, rather**

than a total redesign. There are some great original mid-century kitchen cabinets available, ideal if you like the vintage look, but think creatively and you could repurpose other kinds of storage furniture.

ABOVE RIGHT **An attractive vintage railway luggage rack has been cleverly transformed into a wall-hung pot shelf and batterie de cuisine (with the simple addition of a few butcher's hooks to suspend pots, pans and utensils), while an industrial trolley makes for a handily moveable food storage solution.**

First identify precisely which elements of your existing kitchen don't work for you. They may be major disadvantages – poor siting of major or plumbed appliances – or relatively minor, such as ugly cabinet doors. Make a note of everything you don't like, then assess possible solutions. Major upheavals, such as moving cabinets, should be carefully costed first to see whether they are worth the bother and expense, or if it would be better to start from scratch.

Cosmetic changes are worth carrying out, even if only to alter your attitude to the room. First of all consider paint: wooden doors can be repainted in tough, good-looking finishes. New cabinet doors, either ready- or custom-made, come in materials from laminate and vinyl to painted MDF and solid wood, and in many designs; so do worktops and splashbacks. For a quick, easy transformation, fit new handles.

FITTED VERSUS UNFITTED

For many, the initial choice of kitchen is between the fitted
– a structured arrangement of built-in cabinets – or the unfitted,
a freestanding, less structured arrangement.

The kitchen usually has to be designed to fit the space allocated for it, rather than
vice versa, so in many cases a fitted kitchen is the only practicable answer. In
a larger space, however, a design of freestanding pieces – or one encompassing
both fitted and freestanding – may be preferred, particularly if the kitchen is to be
part of a living space.

Which direction you choose to go in may depend on the ease with which you
can combine the functions of a kitchen – preparation, cooking and cleaning – into
a sensible 'work triangle', the phrase used to describe the arranging of the separate
kitchen elements into a manageable, efficient layout that flows between the
different workstations.

Fitted kitchens might be a narrow galley kitchen, or a larger, rectangular version;
they might be L- or U-shaped, often with an island or peninsular unit, which can
add an unfitted flexibility to the design. Unfitted kitchens, because of their more
fluid perimeters, are often more successful as part of a larger space, where their
blend of styles works with a more eclectic mix of design and decoration.

OPPOSITE ABOVE **In this quirky space, freestanding pieces from a variety of periods have been combined with boldly painted fitted cupboards for a unique look – but the choice of vintage and antique furniture is far from haphazard, with the dimensions of each fitting its position perfectly.**

OPPOSITE BELOW **A fitted kitchen doesn't have to be a mass-market off-the-shelf option, or an expensive bespoke design. Here basic carpentry skills have been used to form base units from reclaimed timber, topped with a tiled worksurface, for just the right sort of vintage vibe.**

ABOVE **A fitted island unit can have services such as water, drainage and power supplied, increasing the layout possibilities for the space. Here a sink enables social interaction while preparing food or washing dishes – a hob/stovetop and extractor fan in the same place would allow cooks to do the same.**

ABOVE RIGHT **Fitted kitchens – especially those with a minimalist influence – are particularly practical and easy to clean, plus they can offer a blank canvas that allows artwork and accessories to come to the fore. Here a sleek white slab door provides a foil to the dark, dramatic wall colour and monochrome pictures.**

RIGHT **It's not only white kitchens that can offer a neutral background against which contrasting pieces can be shown to full advantage. Here moody black cabinetry creates the perfect backdrop to a white retro chandelier and a warm-toned hardwood dining set.**

OPPOSITE **Simple flush panel doors (preferably a handleless design) in a pale colour are the best way of giving a small space an uncluttered look – and if you match the shade of the cabinetry to the walls, then the effect is even more pronounced.**

ABOVE **If you don't have actual space, you can always create the illusion of it. Here a mirrored room divider reflects the other side of this studio apartment, not only giving the impression of a larger room, but screening off the messy working area (and providing more wall-hung storage on the kitchen side).**

RIGHT **If you're working with a particularly compact floor area, then full usage of every inch counts. Here a tiny sink and small hob/stovetop have been fitted into an alcove, with cupboards below and hanging storage on the back wall – where a small ledge also offers a place for utensils and glassware to perch.**

GALLEYS & SMALL SPACES

In converted flats or houses, in particular, there is often only a small or narrow space in which a kitchen can be installed, and it is here that the galley kitchen comes into its own.

At its most confined, the galley kitchen can occupy a single wall with all appliances, plumbing and storage ranged along it; at the next remove, there may be a further area or opposite wall where some elements can find a home. Often created from a corridor, the galley kitchen may seem small, but some of the most efficient and easiest kitchens designed are galleys – everything is conveniently within reach.

In such a confined space, it is important to use every inch of height and depth to create enough storage. If your kitchen is situated in a corridor, or an almost-corridor, extend shelves and cupboards right up towards the ceiling, to store what could be called the 'fish kettle collection' – those utensils you don't use every day, but are essential sometimes. And in a small area, remember that good ventilation is vital. Spend money on an efficient cooker hood and other feats of odour-reducing technology.

LEFT High ceilings and large room volumes require cabinetry of appropriate proportions – here, fitted cabinets are hung higher than usual, so there's not a large gap between their top and the ceiling, while a repurposed shop fitting makes for an island unit of suitable grandeur.

LARGE KITCHENS

A large kitchen might seem an unbelievable luxury, and in truth it is, but just as in a small kitchen, much care is needed to work out how best to use the space.

However large a kitchen, it is still important to keep the actual work area relatively compact and efficient; there is little point in having the cooking zone located yards from the preparation area. Instead, use the space for countertop features – a granite surface for pastry- and bread-making; endgrain maple for chopping; a small, inset sink for washing vegetables; or a specialist hob/stovetop. A larger room means that you can have bigger equipment as well – an oversized fridge-freezer, a wine cooler or a walk-in larder.

An island unit is a good idea in a large kitchen as it breaks up the space in a practical and aesthetic manner, creating a demarcation line between the functional and hospitable activities of the same room. The island can have stools against it facing the preparation area, and might even house a hob and sink so the cook can face the room.

ABOVE In a larger kitchen you might find that there is sufficient storage provision with base units only, allowing you to keep the walls free from bulky cabinets. The result is an open and airy space, with wall-hung shelves also offering the potential for decorative display.

OPPOSITE Period properties often feature large rooms with high ceilings, and there may be original architectural features to factor in to the design, too. Here, open shelves not only hit an appropriately historical note, but their placement works superbly with the decorative panelling, resulting in the perfect balance of traditional charm and modern convenience.

FITTING IN THE FAMILY

It has been interesting to see, over the past few years, the extent to which so many kitchens have become family spaces rather than merely rooms for the preparation of food.

The ideal family kitchen is one in which other activities can take place alongside the traditional kitchen tasks of food preparation and cooking. It is somewhere that all members of the family want to congregate and spend time comfortably – whether chatting, sharing a drink, reading or even doing homework. Where there is the space, the kitchen can be a real family room.

If your kitchen is a large one, then it is a question of dividing its functions in a way that is both practical and aesthetically pleasing, perhaps using an island unit to demarcate the different areas. If, however, the kitchen is relatively small, then – where it is feasible – think of bringing an adjoining room into play, either by removing an internal wall to make one large room or, less drastically, to enlarge the existing doorway between the two, and then visually linking the two areas with wall colour and co-ordinated flooring.

The best family kitchens have comfortable seating – an armchair, sofa or upholstered bench – with adequate lighting so books or the newspaper may be read without strain. Above all, they need lots of clever storage; if you want children to do their homework, or play, at the kitchen table, then they should be able to get at equipment they need easily and without fuss.

OPPOSITE **An island unit with an overhang creates the perfect perch for friends and family members who want to keep the cook company – or for those simply grabbing a snack or doing their homework. Folding bar stools are a great idea, particularly if space is tight.**

ABOVE **If you have young children, consider whether there's space for a pint-sized table and chairs in your kitchen – not only will they be delighted to share a meal or snack there with their little friends, but it's a good place for them to read or draw while you're preparing food.**

RIGHT **Whether you use it to keep track of important dates and special events, record 'must add' things for your next shopping list or as a doodling activity for children, a chalkboard is a fun and useful addition to any family kitchen.**

DINING AREAS WITHIN KITCHENS

With the gradual disappearance of the traditional dining room, more and more kitchens do double duty as places where food is not only prepared and cooked but also enjoyed.

The idea of eating in the kitchen can only be welcomed, bringing as it does traditional hospitality into the heart of the home. There may not be enough room in a small kitchen for a full or even half-sized dining table, but a little lateral thinking will often provide ideas for somewhere to sit and eat in comfort. This might be a small table in a corner, which is also used to display bowls of fruit or a vase of flowers; or perhaps a banquette seat, with storage beneath, built into an alcove, and used with a narrow table that is pushed into the wall when not in use.

The closer the dining area is to the kitchen proper, the more important it is that the style of the kitchen should work with that of the dining space: cabinet fronts that blur the line between function and decoration, and, behind the units, upstands in glass or wood rather than tiles or metal; open as well as closed storage so that utensils and artefacts can be on decorative display. Dining tables and chairs should also work with the kitchen. Finally, choose a dishwasher that is quiet!

OPPOSITE ABOVE **A compact space doesn't necessarily preclude fitting a dining area into the kitchen. The key is to find the right size and shape of table – a square or rectangular one, pushed up against the wall, is often a sensible choice. It's generally best to avoid round tables, which aren't so space-efficient.**

OPPOSITE BELOW **Coherence of aesthetic is particularly important in a small room, since a cluttered look can create a cramped ambience. Here the pale wood of the dining table top echoes the worksurface material, while the chairs boast a suitably minimalist look to chime well with the handleless slab-door cabinetry.**

ABOVE **Breakfast bar or island seating doesn't have to be minimalist in design, or even matching. Here, a row of four almost-but-not-quite-identical vintage factory stools are teamed with a couple of backless stools made from similar materials –** so the look still hangs together, but there's enough aesthetic difference to provide interest.

ABOVE RIGHT **In a small space a glass-topped table is a savvy choice, especially one such as this, with narrow wire legs – the design is visually quite light, and does not draw the eye. The limited colour palette in this kitchen, including matching the upholstery fabric to the fridge-freezer, also helps to avoid a fussy look.**

RIGHT **Lighting is an important tool in a kitchen dining space. Low-hanging pendants positioned above the table will provide enough illumination for meals, while the rest of the lighting can be turned down low (or even off), so that the room's more practical function can fade into the background.**

* The internet really comes into its own when comparing prices and styles of large kitchen appliances. Research takes time, but the benefit of all this choice is that there really is a combination of appliances out there to suit every kitchen and every pocket.

* Induction hobs can only be used with ferrous-based pans. If a magnet sticks to the base, they will work.

* Among the modular hob options now available are barbecues, woks, deep-fat fryers and steamers.

* Make sure that any glass-doored, built-in ovens are installed at a high enough level so that you can both see and move the contents with ease.

* Take precise measurements of the space available before you order a new appliance. Many of the new designs are super-sized and too big for a conventional fitted kitchen.

* In addition to a conventional upright refrigerator, an under-counter refrigerator drawer, used to store foods at a chilled temperature, can be a useful extra.

THIS PAGE Cast-iron range cookers are the classic kitchen workhorse. But there's no need to suffer the limitations of classic technology for the sake of style, as these iconic designs are now available in gas and electric versions, and even with options such as induction cooktops and fan ovens.

OPPOSITE ABOVE Built-in ovens are much easier on the back – and can be safer, too – since they can be installed at a height to suit you. There's no bending or crouching down to remove heavy (and piping hot) dishes from a low-level cavity, as with freestanding cookers.

OPPOSITE BELOW 'White goods' is a label that certainly doesn't apply literally any more – large appliances now come in a myriad of colours and styles, from classic cream to bright orange, gloss black to stainless steel. It's also just as easy to find retro designs as it is to track down an ultra-modern style.

If you are buying a large appliance such as a cooker or refrigerator, decide exactly what your budget is at the start, for this is an area where the cost can vary dramatically.

LARGE APPLIANCES

Widely available on the market are simple and functional appliances at very reasonable cost; also easy to find are designs with a higher price tag that have additional design and function details and are often better made. Finally, there are what one might term the supermodels – designs that incorporate sophisticated technological advances and combine them with aesthetic subtlety: wine coolers with separate thermostatic controls for white and red wines; giant side-by-side refrigerators; and freestanding freezer columns, with pillar-like freezer, refrigerator and wine cooler units that can be sited separately around the kitchen.

Cooking options range from a simple freestanding cooker combining a hob/stovetop and one or two ovens, to individual hobs/stovetops made in every size and every material from steel to ceramic, and individual ovens that possess an infinite variety of features and are powered by either electricity or gas. Range cookers vary from the traditional oil- or gas-fired designs to advanced semi-professional electric cookers disguised within an antique façade.

LEFT Sinks are often placed in front of a window, but if it makes more sense for the sink to feature elsewhere in the layout, then don't feel constrained by this convention. After all, dishwashers mean that much less time is spent looking at the view these days.

OPPOSITE Make sure you choose a sink that's big enough for your largest cooking pot or roasting tin, especially if you're looking at double bowl designs. More than one tap/faucet, as shown here on a double butler's sink, might not be necessary if you have a large, centrally positioned tap/faucet that can pivot.

LEFT A splashback will protect your wall from water ingress and can be chosen to make a striking style statement too. Here a beautiful piece of marble, which echoes the countertop, adds some natural beauty to a minimalist kitchen with a restrained colour palette.

Plumbing. The very word makes people sigh, but it is particularly important to get it right in the kitchen, where so much depends on where and how water is used.

WATER WAYS

The first thing to remember about any plumbing is that, once it is in place, it is difficult and expensive to alter, so think carefully about what you want before you embark on any work.

Every kitchen needs at least one sink; where it is positioned, and its size, is of vital importance to the layout. Choose as large and deep a sink as possible: so many items, from delicate china to roasting pans, can only be washed by hand. Plenty of draining room – preferably either side of the sink – is also a good idea. The best sink shape is based on the circular or the rectangular, depending on the configuration of the kitchen, and possible materials range from stainless steel to enamel (as in butler's sinks) or a composite.

A tap/faucet of fairly classical design with a single mixer spout works well at a kitchen sink, particularly if it has a movable spout or pull-down sprayer. Finally, a dishwasher is energy-efficient, cleans well and holds plenty of dirty crocks. This is not a luxury; this is a necessity!

* In a small kitchen, instead of making space for a traditional dishwasher consider dishwasher drawers, which are literally that: compact dishwashers housed in drawers that can be operated individually.

* When thinking about where to install the dishwasher, consider situating it at eye level, rather than on the floor, particularly if you include in the design a crockery cupboard above for everyday tableware and glass.

* If you choose a tap/faucet with a movable spout, make sure the spout is long enough to reach into the centre of the sink.

* Wooden worktops surrounding a sink should be kept nourished and water-resistant with oil.

* Double sinks work well as long as each sink is of a practical size.

* A movable over-sink vegetable drainer or colander is a useful accessory.

* A tap/faucet that dispenses boiling water is handy and more energy-efficient than boiling water in a pan or kettle. You could also look at a filtered drinking water tap/faucet.

* Traditionally, most sinks faced a window on an outside wall – both for the view and the drainage – but now it is possible to site a sink (or sinks) almost anywhere you need them.

OPPOSITE **Reclaimed timber – both in natural and limewashed tones – combined with painted wood and zinc metal touches gives a relaxed and rustic beach-house feel. If not protected by paint, wood can be given a coat of varnish, or oiled, to avoid water damage and help prevent staining.**

The choice of materials for the kitchen is just as much to do with the kitchen's style as whether you prefer wood or metal.

MATERIALS

The materials that you choose for cabinets and worktops will depend, to a certain extent, on your preferred style or design, for the options are almost endless. For many, wood is the preferred material for base units – either in its solid form, with many varieties to choose from such as oak, cherry and beech to maple, iroko and walnut, or as a veneered finish on a composite core. Wood can also be painted, laminated or lacquered.

There is a wide choice of other materials to combine with wood, used on countertops and working surfaces perhaps, but also as inset panels, upstands, screens and doors. Composite materials such as Corian are endlessly versatile, as are hard materials such as marble, slate and granite, which are useful next to a hob/stovetop for hot pans as well as inset where a cool surface is required for bread- or pastry-making.

❋ Technological advances mean that toughened glass can now be used as a finish in the kitchen, perhaps as a screen near the hob/stovetop, on a counter, or used over a laminated surface.

❋ Steel-fronted units give a professional finish and look best in a contemporary kitchen. Choose between matt brushed steel and more reflective stainless steel.

❋ Most kitchens look best with a combination of materials or, in the case of an all-wood kitchen, with different varieties and cuts of wood used in contrast.

❋ If you are linking a kitchen or cooking area with a dining area, rather than making one the mirror image of the other, just carry through one or two elements.

ABOVE **Even natural materials can boast strong tones that might be overpowering if not used with care. Here the warm appeal of hardwood cladding and a vintage industrial-style table and chairs are tempered by the cool, concrete-grey minimalist kitchen units and flooring.**

RIGHT **A white-on-white colour scheme benefits from the use of a number of different materials, ensuring that there is a variation in texture if not colour. In this kitchen, a luxurious white marble countertop is given a more utilitarian foil by the use of metro tiles on the adjoining wall.**

The ideal kitchen has light streaming through several large windows, with every surface lit to best advantage. But here in the real world most kitchens require some degree of help. Getting the lighting right in the kitchen must be a priority, to be considered from the first, as part of the design.

LIGHTING

Like the other rooms in the house, a combination of task and ambient lighting is best, from under-shelf strip lighting to illuminate the work surface below to adjustable swan-necked over-cabinet lighting. Task lighting should target specific close-working areas, with the light placed or directed in front of your body so that you are not working in your own shadow. Look at all the possible areas where light might be needed: directed onto the hob/stovetop perhaps, the worktops and towards the refrigerator; strip lighting beneath wall units is useful, as is track lighting, to be positioned where needed.

Press available natural light into service too (make sure blinds/shades or curtains are washable – even with an extractor, grease will coat them). If your kitchen has little or no natural light, use light-reflecting colours and surfaces to maximize what you have and use back- and up-lighters to create pools of light.

ABOVE **When you need to focus light directly over an island or table, low-hanging pendants are a practical – and rather chic – solution. Don't be afraid to choose oversized designs, not just because they will cast the light over a larger area, but because they have more visual impact.**

LEFT **Inset spots are a practical solution to task lighting. Remember, if you choose modern low-energy LED fittings, you will need to replace each unit when it eventually fails, rather than just the bulb – but the lifespan of this new technology is much extended compared to halogen or fluorescent lighting.**

OPPOSITE BELOW RIGHT
In a room without large windows, it's wise to opt for a pale colour scheme to help bounce around what natural light there is. Choosing sleek surfaces will also help, as will avoiding window dressings which cover any of the glazing.

ABOVE **Low-hanging pendants can work well as over-counter task lighting, just be sure to position them correctly – too close to the wall and they won't illuminate enough of the counter (especially if you choose small examples), but too far away and you risk having to work in your own shadow.**

❊ *Using dimmers on more than one lighting circuit can be very useful in the kitchen, allowing you to vary the mood and intensity of light throughout the room.*

❊ *If you have decorative displays of glass in the kitchen, consider backlighting the whole unit.*

❊ *Remember that even a room which receives enough natural light during the day will need specific task lighting in the evening, as well as ambient light.*

❊ *Lighting today is both a science and an art; experts can design ambient lighting schemes that can simulate natural light at different times of day.*

❊ *If you have a table in the kitchen, consider installing overhead pendant lights that can be dimmed and raised or lowered as necessary.*

* *Decide early on the flooring material. The best time to lay any floor is when the room has been stripped out and the plastering and electrical work completed.*

* *If you are combining a dining area with a kitchen, a sisal or seagrass square, rather than a more elaborate wool rug, would visually separate the eating area from the working one, without breaking up the space.*

* *There is no need to limit the flooring options in the kitchen to one material; very often in the immediate vicinity of cooker and sink, for example, a harder-working finish is needed than elsewhere in the room. Options might include linoleum combined with tiles, stone with wood or rubber with terracotta.*

* *Rubber flooring can be bought on a roll and is a good-looking, inexpensive option.*

* *Linoleum is available in a wide range of different colours. It can also be precision cut and inlaid to create simple or complex designs that could range from a geometric overall pattern to a design with a central motif and border.*

* *Poured, polished concrete that has been coloured is a relatively inexpensive hard floor finish and can look extremely striking.*

THIS PAGE **A seamless flooring material is definitely a hygienic choice, and it's so easy to clean – though do bear in mind that glossy products will often need polishing regularly to maintain their shiny good looks. Remember, for safety's sake, a non-slip product is a savvy choice in the kitchen.**

Flooring is an important element in the kitchen, so consider it in conjunction with all the other decorative options.

FLOORING

The kitchen floor must work with the materials chosen for the units and appliances; it must also be comfortable to walk on, easy to clean and hard-wearing, because kitchens are very high-traffic areas.

Wood is warm to look at and touch; it can be new or old, light or dark; it can be left in its natural state (but well sealed and finished) or stained or painted (this option requires particularly tough sealing).

Stone and marble, granite and slate look wonderful and last for ever, but they can be cold underfoot and over a large area underfloor heating might be a necessity. Ceramic tiles can also be cold. Terracotta, which works well in a country or traditional kitchen, looks and feels warmer than stone, is hard- and long-wearing and comes in machine- and hand-made versions. The latter is more interesting in appearance, while the former often emulates an antique look.

Other natural flooring options include linoleum, cork and rubber, while synthetic floorings such as vinyl can now emulate almost any other material from wood to marble to ceramic tiling.

FAR LEFT **In a timber-framed space, stone flags are a suitably traditional choice – and they're not only timeless but hard-wearing too. Remember, however, that stone is porous, and so will need to be sealed (and re-sealed periodically) with a suitable product to avoid staining.**

LEFT **In a room with neutral walls and furnishings, a patterned floor really takes centre stage and injects some unique character. Geometric designs can be achieved with square- and triangular-shaped tiles, while there's also a wealth of patterned tiles to choose from.**

ABOVE **Original floorboards can be an inexpensive and attractive flooring choice – but they may take a little work to look their best. You'll need to ensure the gaps between them aren't too wide, punch down any raised nails, sand well and finish them with a couple of coats of oil or varnish.**

Everyone needs storage, and everyone needs storage in a kitchen most of all; the application of logic is often the solution.

STORAGE

There is nothing more frustrating in a kitchen than not having a place for everything and everything in its place. Kitchen storage encompasses a variety of elements – there is food, fresh and dried or canned; cooking equipment and utensils; and china and glass.

Much of this can be accommodated in conventional cupboards, both floor-standing and wall-hung. In truth, good kitchen storage is as much about logic as cupboard space. Group different functions and store them closest to that point. Saucepans should be kept close to the hob/stovetop and oven, everyday tableware and glass close to the sink and dishwasher (a cupboard above the latter, perhaps), and perishable food should be ranged in a refrigerator and cabinets close to the preparation area. Large utensils not in use every day, and china and glass used for entertaining, can live in less accessible cupboards.

✳ *Many hobs/stovetops are situated on their own separately from the oven, and there is therefore often room beneath for one or two deep and capacious drawers in which to store saucepans and casseroles without stacking them.*

✳ *Rather than being kept in the refrigerator, root vegetables are best stored in a dark place in cane or wicker baskets, where air can circulate around them.*

✳ *A wide, shallow drawer close to the hob/stovetop, with permanent or movable divisions inside, is perfect for unwieldy but essential utensils such as spatulas, ladles and slotted spoons, and saves the worktop space a canister takes.*

✳ *Make sure you install enough power points/ electrical outlets to keep kettles and toasters neatly in a corner of the work surface and ready for action.*

BELOW LEFT **Open shelves allow very easy access, so are perfect for storing the sort of items that will be in daily use. Bear in mind than anything not required frequently may need a wash before it can be used, since inevitably there will have been a build-up of dust.**

BELOW RIGHT **Drawers can be a lot more practical and convenient than cupboards, since it's much easier to reach things stored at the back, thus maximizing genuinely useful storage space – this island unit with deep drawers offers lots of easy-access capacity for crockery, cutlery, pots, pans and other kitchen equipment.**

OPPOSITE **If the fitted units in your kitchen don't quite provide sufficient storage for your needs, consider augmenting them with some pieces of freestanding furniture – or even just a ladder, leaning against the wall, with butcher's hooks transforming it into a sort of casual batterie de cuisine.**

* *Finishing touches need not be tangible objects; bright accents of colour, like cabinet door panels painted in lime-green, yellow and orange, can personalize a working area.*

* *If you eat in the kitchen, consider a shelf or space for books – reference books, in particular. They not only look friendly, they also serve a purpose, as questions of the 'who-what-when' variety invariably come up over leisurely meals.*

* *If you hanker after an iconic bit of kitchen equipment – such as a Dualit toaster or a state-of-the-art coffee machine – bite the bullet and buy it. It will last for years, and give you pleasure every time you look at it, and that is really the best sort of finishing touch.*

* *Flowers in the kitchen are one of the most pleasing things, informally arranged and placed wherever there is room, whether on a shelf or a work surface.*

OPPOSITE ABOVE LEFT **Although the kitchen is a working area, it would be a shame to only include no-frills storage and practical objects. Here a small collection of useful, beautiful things – including a silver salt cellar, carved horn utensils and a stone pestle and mortar – creates a charming vignette.**

OPPOSITE ABOVE RIGHT **A flashy choice of splashback might be all that's needed to inject a glamorous, decorative touch to even the most understated of kitchens. Polished metal, mirror glass and metallic tiles all offer a luxe look – which is even more striking when used alongside minimalist-style cabinetry.**

OPPOSITE BELOW LEFT **If you're a keen cook with an exotic collection of ingredients, you're already halfway there to a decorative display – especially if the packaging they come in is colourful. If you need to decant from a box or packet, clip-top glass jars are both stylish and great for keeping foodstuffs fresh.**

OPPOSITE BELOW RIGHT **Even a collection of utilitarian items can be curated into a pleasing display with a little thought. Here old wooden chopping boards and a collection of treasured kitchen knives have been grouped together – crucially they all feature the same neutral tones of brown, grey and black.**

ABOVE RIGHT **You can't go wrong with fresh flowers, though be sure to place them where they won't interfere with the practical use of the room. This striking informal display of yellow blooms really zings out against the dark wall behind.**

RIGHT **Accessories that echo the accent colours within your kitchen's décor will always look more considered, and give the space a more polished, professionally designed feel. Here a simple bowl of lemons matches the yellow seating, which contrasts with the largely monochrome scheme.**

Finishing touches to the kitchen are those that make it individual, and set it aside from the showroom model; decorative and design extras that make a room stand out.

FINISHING TOUCHES

Finishing touches in this space are all a question of detail. They are the thought-out personal additions that mark the room as your own. Design details lift something standard to a different level; they are the carefully considered mouldings around an open storage unit, the bull-nose edging on a marble countertop, the metal rods for hot pans set into a wooden work surface next to a hob/stovetop, the standard wine rack cut down to fit into a dead space in a corner. Ideas such as these can be found in kitchen showrooms, magazines and – yes! – books, and are often worth incorporating at comparatively little cost.

Then there are the decorative details. Here is where it pays to be adventurous. Consider using unusual paint colours, or objects and pictures that you arrange with care around the room in unexpected corners; these are striking and unusual additions that not only stamp your personality on the room but also add an air of hospitality and welcome to others.

LEFT **Natural wood-panelled cupboard doors, adorned with blacksmith-made iron hinges and handles, offer a most rustic take on the country kitchen style – while the cosy warmth of the ochre walls in this example suggests a Mediterranean style influence, too.**

RIGHT **Chalky whitewashed walls and built-in concrete units are characteristic of old Greek cottages – what they lack in sophisticated convenience, they make up for in simple chic. Pared-down and basic, this utilitarian space is augmented with the cool greys of zinc and pewter, and the warm tones of old wooden cooking implements and chopping boards.**

The country kitchen could almost be called a state of mind. Espousing the traditional and the comfortable, it is just as at home in the inner city as down a country lane.

COUNTRY KITCHENS

When people say they want a country kitchen, what exactly do they mean? First of all, the materials used are important – in most people's minds, a country kitchen does not gleam with stainless steel and Perspex/Plexiglass (although state-of-the-art gadgets are definitely not banned; they are usually concealed behind cupboard doors). The materials of country choice are traditional – predominantly wood, used everywhere from floor to units and sometimes on the walls, as well as for many of the utensils. Stone in all its guises, from slate to York, is also employed for many of the hard surfaces, as are earthenware and enamelling.

A country kitchen is not a Luddite kitchen, however. There may be a dishwasher as well as a large refrigerator (which will often, if there is enough space, be kept in a pantry). Although there may be a contemporary hob/stovetop, for many people the country kitchen is tied up with the idea of a range cooker, with all its warm and welcoming associations. Traditionally heated by wood, solid fuel or oil, ranges are now just as often fired by electricity or gas, and many incorporate modern innovations (although all such are usually enclosed in a traditional outer case).

What there will also nearly always be in this country kitchen is colour, on the woodwork and on the walls. It will probably not be very strong or vibrant colour, even almost imperceptible colour, and if it is on the wood it may well be distressed either naturally or with the help of a little elbow grease. But it will be there and it will be accentuated by the colours of the objects that country kitchen owners, as a breed, like to collect – they will be both decorative and also useful, ranging from pictures to old metal pails, and sometimes old and sometimes new, but always with a traditional feel or appearance.

Above all, country kitchens exude a sense of cosiness– there really is no such thing as a cold country kitchen. When people wish for the style, they are saying that they want a kitchen that is friendly and hospitable, that emanates an air of comfort and, even more importantly, of warmth.

✳ *A country kitchen is the ideal place to incorporate old pieces of wooden furniture; a pine chest of drawers to hold pans and linens, or an antique armoire for just about everything from tableware and glass to food storage.*

✳ *Combine storage and display in open wooden shelving, with cup hooks for cloths, cups and utensils – a cheap and effective way to get the rustic look.*

✳ *For paint, go for either light, clear colours or shades taken from one of the many widely available ranges of historical colours.*

✳ *Collect odd and interesting bits to use as decoration – old kitchen utensils can be found in junk and antique shops, as can small, quirky pictures, vintage signage and eccentric prints.*

✳ *Rather than being hidden away, food is often kept out on display in the country kitchen, as are china, glass and equipment – a traditional dresser/hutch is the perfect display case for them.*

THIS PAGE Here white-painted wood-panelled walls and pale floorboards ensure a neutral backdrop for the natural tones of old timber — a vintage trolley table takes centre stage, while the distressed finish on the panelled cabinet doors provides textural interest. Metal accents, both painted and polished, add definition.

Can't commit to a single aesthetic for your space? The good news is that you don't have to. Follow a few simple rules, and you can create a unique yet coherent look.

ECLECTIC KITCHENS

One person's idea of a stunning eclectic kitchen is likely to be very different to another's – that's the beauty of this mix-and-match style, pretty much anything goes. Well, not quite anything. In order to maintain a sense of consistency and balance, there are a few basic guidelines to follow.

Firstly, it's important to choose pieces that are in keeping with the proportions of the space (though a little deliberate oversizing, say, of a statement light, can have a stunning decorative impact). It's also critical that you select furniture, surfaces, appliances and accessories which have some harmony with each other in terms of scale or colour.

That said, contrast is an essential element of the eclectic look, especially if you're looking to create a dramatic effect. Don't group elements together that are subtly different; instead make sure the pieces are at opposite ends of the style spectrum – for example, a crystal chandelier might be suitably offset by the utilitarian feel of concrete worktops, while an antique dining table might come into its own set against a largely minimalist scheme.

If you're concerned about whether you'll be able to create an eclectic space that works, the simplest approach is to opt for a restricted colour palette, especially if you choose a white-on-white or monochrome scheme. It's also a good idea to stick to combining just three distinct decorative styles, to avoid the finished space looking muddled and fragmented.

* *The simplest take on the eclectic kitchen is to use varying shades of paint, or different materials, for the cabinetry. The same style units, painted in three complementary blues, for example, will shift a matchy-matchy aesthetic up a gear.*

* *Don't be afraid to mix traditional pieces with contemporary décor. The sleek lines and plain surfaces of modern design can be the perfect foil for more decorative, classic shapes and the rich patinas which are often built up with age.*

* *Pops of brights or flashes of luxe materials can be an easy way to add a little eclecticism. Choose an unexpected colour or an unusual finish for one element of the kitchen, and keep the rest of the space fairly restrained.*

* *Reclaimed shop and factory fittings, repurposed as kitchen storage, offer huge potential to create a unique look. They pair well with minimalist fitted units and neutral colour schemes, which throw the emphasis onto the character of the vintage pieces.*

OPPOSITE **With walls in boudoir-pink, paintings, ornaments, perfume bottles and an oval mirror, this kitchen is marvellously un-kitchen-like. The polished chrome, marble and gilt elements mean it's definitely got a luxe look, but it's also thoroughly practical, with a stainless steel sink, drainer and splashback.**

RIGHT **Quirky vintage style meets industrial chic in this cheerful kitchen-diner. A table with a classic 1950s shape is teamed with a set of painted metal Tolix-style chairs, while an ultra-modern tap/faucet in bright yellow echoes the zingy shade of the internal window (as well as a number of accessories).**

FAR RIGHT **Here the tension between the beautifully imperfect moulded-front cabinetry, which likely has an 18th- or 19th-century origin, and the industrial aspects of the space – including the concrete floor, metal furniture and brick wall – creates an interesting aesthetic. A monochrome colour scheme of grey and white ties everything together.**

RIGHT **You might assume that the industrial look is likely to appear heavy, but this clever stainless steel design gives the impression of being feather-light, as it almost floats above the polished concrete floor. Partly supported by the original iron column, the counter has been cleverly designed to conceal the services, including gas and plumbing.**

OPPOSITE **Industrial finishes can work just as well in a compact kitchen as they can in a warehouse space. Here stainless steel and concrete are contrasted against flat white plaster, while utilitarian crockery displayed on open shelves adds complementary tones of blue and green.**

Utilitarian, hardworking and durable — the industrial-style kitchen isn't just a style statement, it's an extremely practical choice of aesthetic for the serious cook.

INDUSTRIAL KITCHENS

The popularity of industrial chic has never been greater, and you can see its influences popping up all over the home — but arguably nowhere is this style as appropriate as in the kitchen. With its resilient surfaces and practical, unfussy designs, this aesthetic is the perfect choice for such a hardworking area.

Taking its cues from 19th- and 20th-century factories, the industrial kitchen is characterized by the use of brick, concrete, steel, ceramic tile and timber, and the sort of utilitarian designs that boast no unnecessary frills — think trestle tables, metal or prismatic glass pendant shades, metal trolleys and freestanding shelves, and vintage-style stools in steel and timber.

Properties such as warehouse apartments might boast large room volumes, and appropriate internal architecture such as exposed ducting (in a fashionable zinc or stainless steel finish), raw brick walls and concrete floors, but in fact they're not the only type of home that can suit the industrial-kitchen treatment — this efficient, frugal style is just as suitable for small kitchens in modest homes, too.

For the most contemporary take on the industrial look, inject a bit of a contrasting stylistic foil. You could aim for a balance of raw industrial beauty with some luxe finishes, or you could temper the homespun vintage look with some harder-edged utilitarian pieces.

* *For a budget-friendly take on the look, you could opt for freestanding stainless steel kitchen furniture – the units made by commercial kitchen fabricators can represent great value, and are authentically industrial.*

* *If a polished concrete floor isn't practical or within budget, there are plenty of ceramic tile options that can offer a comparable texture and tone. Similarly, you'll find reproduction accessories and furnishings that channel the same style influences as harder-to-find originals.*

* *When cleaning stainless steel, avoid abrasive products as they will scratch the surface. Diluted white vinegar or soapy water should do the trick (or invest in a specialist stainless steel spray), then dry the steel with a microfibre cloth to avoid water spots.*

* *Hardware matters. From cage lights to cup-shaped drawer pulls and visible hinges, these metallic details – whether they're '50s-style chrome, rustic wrought iron or a more modern-looking matt bronze – really do contribute a great deal of authenticity to the look.*

White is infinitely adaptable. It works with small kitchens and works with large. White works with old kitchens and, yes, it also works with new!

THE WHITE STUFF

When the first fitted kitchens were introduced, they came – rather like Henry Ford's first cars – in one colour only, but unlike the famous black cars, these early kitchens were white. White was the colour of modernity and of progress; it represented cleanliness, efficiency and hygiene.

With time came choice and change, and kitchens, fitted or unfitted, began to be produced in many other colours and finishes; but, for many people and in many settings, the white kitchen still reigns supreme.

The thing about white is that it is a style, not a colour; far from being fashionable, and therefore in or out, white is beyond fashion, and its very versatility gives it the edge over many other styles and designs.

White is right for a super-contemporary, high-lacquered, technological dream kitchen, and it is just as right for a classic, functional, practical room. It works admirably in a comfortable country kitchen that is part living room and part cooking zone, and it is the perfect way to tie together all the disparate elements of an unfitted kitchen, where you may have some freestanding pieces of furniture mixed with more conventional fitted units.

White has an easy ability to blend into the background when required, and for that reason it works very well as part of a larger open-plan living space where it will not vie for attention with stronger architectural elements. It also, conversely, is often the colour of choice for a small kitchen, where it opens up the space and makes it appear larger. For the same reasons, white is the ideal colour for a dark kitchen; white's light-reflecting qualities mean that it collects all available natural light and throws it back into the room. A glossy reflective finish will obviously bounce back more light than a matt texture, and a light-toned floor will take the process further.

If you are updating an old or tired kitchen, one of the simplest and cheapest tricks is to buy replacement doors for base and wall-hung cabinets; if they are painted white wood, the improvement will be tangible.

OPPOSITE **A very pale scheme doesn't have to be stark and minimalist. Here shades of white and grey have been used to create a welcoming country-style aesthetic that channels Scandinavian influences, with painted tongue-and-groove doors, open shelves displaying everyday crockery and glassware, and accents of metal and natural timber.**

RIGHT **Here a white dining table and chairs almost disappear into the background of white walls, white floor and white cabinetry – this is a handy visual trick to use if you're trying to make a small room feel more spacious.**

BELOW RIGHT **A beautiful powder-blue range cooker takes centre stage in this kitchen, as its colourful enamel contrasts against the white-on-white backdrop. Touches of chrome and zinc, as well as the styling of the pendant lamps and cabinetry metalware, lend a retro feel.**

BOTTOM RIGHT **Pale wood can be the perfect partner for a white-painted kitchen. With just enough warmth to enliven the ambience, without being overpoweringly strong, birch, beech, elm and paler types of oak can all work well. In this kitchen, a display of pastel casserole dishes also adds a touch of colour.**

❋ If you are installing a new kitchen on a tight budget, a simple white kitchen will make the most of your money as well as look good. Go for plain cabinets without excess decoration, keep details such as handles and taps/faucets as simple as possible and choose a warm wooden work surface.

❋ Make sure that any dining table and chairs work with the style of the white kitchen; polished wood is a perfect foil for an otherwise white background.

❋ There are cool whites and there are warm whites, with many variations in each group. Your choice of palette might well be influenced by how much sun your kitchen gets each day.

❋ If the kitchen leads into a dining area, continue the white palette through but use different, richer tones within the same palette. You can also add textural interest with fabrics and furnishings, to mark the contrasting functions of the spaces.

The concept of the kitchen as the heart of the family home is not a new one. From medieval Great Halls to farmhouse kitchens, for centuries family life has centred here.

FAMILY-FRIENDLY KITCHENS

It was the rapid growth of cities in the 19th century that saw the kitchen relocated to somewhere below stairs in the new, narrow houses built in long terraces in every town. Now, two centuries later, new living patterns and a generally more informal way of life mean that once again the kitchen is being seen as a room that should play a central role in the everyday life of the family.

It makes sense, in so many ways, for the kitchen, particularly a larger kitchen, to be the centre of the domestic web. Few of us want separate dining rooms, so moving a table into, or just beyond, the kitchen makes sense. Once there is a table, what better place to do homework, read the paper or sit and chat? In a kitchen that cannot fit in a conventional table, an island unit or bar with stools at one side facing into the cooking area play much the same role, connecting the functional and social aspects of the room – both a vital part of family life.

A family-friendly kitchen should not be too clinical in design; colour and decoration make it a welcoming place. If there is enough space, some of the accoutrements of the traditional living room could be included – not to replace the living room, but to extend it – such as a comfortable armchair or, even better, a small sofa and shelves for books. All these things bring people together, and that surely is what being family-friendly is all about.

❋ Enough storage for non-cooking equipment is important in a family-friendly kitchen – drawers where paper, pens and pencils can be kept, shelves where books and magazines can rest undisturbed.

❋ Adaptable, portable storage is useful when a room has several different functions and uses: deep baskets are a good idea, where toys and other necessities can easily be stored when the function of the room changes at different times of day.

❋ The right lighting is important – you will need adjustable, specific task lights, but also enough ambient lighting to change the mood from that of function to that of leisure.

❋ Make sure there is easy access to everyday glasses, cups and mugs that does not necessitate general upheaval in the food preparation area.

❋ The family-friendly kitchen is always a place for pictures and photographs, whether they are hung on walls or propped on shelves.

LEFT **Hardwearing, easy-clean surfaces are a must for a family-friendly kitchen – and it's best to choose an aesthetic that won't be ruined easily by a little wear and tear (think the forgiving distressed look of vintage chic, rather than the sleek, highly polished surfaces of luxury minimalism).**

OPPOSITE **The eclectic look – especially the bright-on-white variation – is particularly suitable for those with young children, since all their belongings will then fit in easily with the space. For example, here a couple of child's adjustable high chairs look perfectly at home within a set of mismatched seating at the dining table.**

LIVING ROOMS

THIS PAGE **A collection of books and selected decorative pieces can make for an eye-catching display – it's just a case of carefully curating the elements for a balanced, yet not-too-regimented look. Don't over-fill your shelves, since sufficient blank space will allow each object to make an individual impact.**

ABOVE **For a cheerful modern look, give a neutral room a lift with some key pieces in vibrant, complementary shades. Here the tan-coloured chairs contrast with the teal sofa and cobalt armchair, with green-blues and warm tones also picked out in some of the room's decorative accessories.**

ABOVE RIGHT **A room flooded with natural light is always going to be a congenial space but if the room is south-facing, then you'll need to consider a way to mitigate excess warmth and bright light. Sheer curtains not only perform this purpose, but look stylish, too.**

DESIGN & DECORATION

Ideally, the living room is the place where all the family comes together. It is neutral territory – somewhere all can spend time, either together or alone, and the room's design, decoration and arrangement should reflect its multi-faceted nature.

The design of this central room is very important, for the living room, for better or worse, makes the strongest impression on others. Gimlet-eyed visitors will notice the colours that you have chosen, the pieces of furniture you have bought and the way that you have arranged them. They will look at where you have put your pictures, books and music. In short, they will check out how you live.

To make matters more complicated, it is essential that the design of the living room represents, as well as the views of others, the likes and dislikes of the people who use it most. It should accommodate the daily needs of all its occupants, and be somewhere both peaceful and convivial pleasures can be enjoyed, from reading to giving a party. It may also double as a study and eating area, all of which is a great deal of work for one room.

The essence of good design lies in careful planning, which we explore over the page, but in general terms both the design and decoration of a living room should be neither too dramatic nor too specific; interesting, of course, but above all both comfortable and welcoming.

ABOVE **If you regularly entertain a lot of people, it's wise to choose seating that will be flexible. These built-in benches can accommodate quite a crowd, but, with the addition of cushions, are also perfect for lounging around solo, or with a loved one.**

Before you immerse yourself in choosing the colours and materials, furniture and furnishings for your new living room, the first and possibly most important task is to plan the room, both in the broadest of terms, as well as, if possible, the finest of details.

PLANNING

Whether your living room is pint-sized or oversized, getting the proportions and scale right are all-important. This means choosing correctly scaled furniture for the room, and arranging both the large and the small pieces in the most pleasing and practical way. Decide on what functions the room will have. What sort of furniture will you need? What seating? What tables? What storage and what decoration? Everything in the room should balance; there should be equal densities, equal masses of weight.

Every room needs a focal point – possibly two if the room is large. The fireplace is a traditional and natural focal point, and still works well. Be wary of designating the TV a focus – rather, use a round central table with one or two chairs, or a sofa and armchairs around a lower table. Other areas should be linked to the focal point, both visually and practically – you must be able to walk through the room without bumping into anything.

If you are of a practical nature, make a floor plan showing any built-in features, then use approximate shapes to plot the best positions for furniture. It's easy to do and gives a visual sense of the room in a way that is difficult to achieve by writing things on a list.

ABOVE RIGHT **This living room has been arranged as the perfect space for media consumption – inset spots above the sofa provide illumination for reading, while the sofa itself has been positioned opposite a wall-mounted flat-screen television (hung in just the right spot to avoid screen glare from the large windows).**

RIGHT **A very large room can benefit from the addition of some kind of room divider, to create cosier areas – no-one likes to snuggle up and relax in a space that feels more like a hotel lobby than a living room. Open shelves offer a triple purpose, since they provide useful storage and display capacity, too.**

OPPOSITE ABOVE LEFT **Opening up a space can transform two cramped rooms into one comfortable one, but whether it's possible to remove walls will depend on the construction of your home. With a timber-framed building, such as this period example, it might be that the original woodwork needs to be left in place.**

OPPOSITE ABOVE RIGHT **Furnishings should always match the space proportionately, but in terms of style you have much more flexibility. Here a grand period room, complete with moulded plaster ceilings and ornate architraves, has been furnished with a pair of iconic sofas in the Modernist style.**

OPPOSITE BELOW LEFT **Siting a pair of matching sofas opposite each other not only creates a sociable seating arrangement, but also provides a visually appealing arrangement. Here the effect has been heightened by lining up the pair with the window, and placing them in the centre of the room.**

OPPOSITE BELOW RIGHT **In a living room predominantly used for socializing – rather than reading, creative hobbies, watching television or indulging in other screen-based media leisure activities – then a group of comfy sofas and chairs, arranged around a large coffee table, is a most agreeable arrangement.**

LEFT **Timber-framed period properties often feature smaller windows than their more modern counterparts, so consideration should be given to maximizing the natural light in such a space. A pale colour scheme and glazed internal doors will help to ensure that the room is as bright and welcoming as possible.**

ADAPTING AN EXISTING LIVING ROOM

When an existing, not-quite-perfect living room has to be adapted to suit different demands and needs, lateral design thinking is often required.

How nice it would be if every living room were exactly the right size, the right proportions, with a place for everything and ready for instant occupation – but that is rarely the case.

The first thing to do is to evaluate what cannot be changed, whether for reasons of finance or structure; these will usually be architectural features such as windows, doors and load-bearing walls. Although you may not be able to change them, you may well be able to disguise, hide or adapt, and this is where the lateral thinking comes in.

Doors, for instance, that lead nowhere or are too numerous can be permanently closed, and hung with pictures or hidden with a piece of furniture in front; windows can appear smaller or taller with the clever use of blinds/shades, or curtains that are hung beyond or within the area of glass. Difficult corners and angles can be made into shelved areas or cupboards, which can be built to correct ungainly proportions. Furniture also changes the visual proportions of a long thin room; for example, if pieces are arranged across the width of the space, rather than down its length. Lastly, do not underestimate the importance of an unbiased eye: a friend, whose taste you rate, will often point out a new way of dealing with a problem.

OPPOSITE ABOVE **In an unusual conversion, particularly one with a small floor area, you might need to think more creatively. The focal point in this room is the wood-burning stove – but the constraints of the space means it can't feature in the traditional central position, and in fact if it were, the furniture would be more difficult to arrange around it.**

OPPOSITE BELOW LEFT **In a narrow space, which can't be opened out in any way, the furnishings need to be chosen and arranged particularly carefully. Here a comfy corner sofa provides the majority of the seating, while a small armchair allows face-to-face conversation too (without impinging on the through-flow of the room).**

OPPOSITE BELOW RIGHT **Pushing furniture back to the walls will help maximize the feeling of space within a small room – just make sure that you leave sufficient leeway for through-routes to be unimpeded. Here a chest, used as a coffee table, is placed asymmetrically between a pair of sofas so that the balcony can be accessed with ease.**

FITTING IN THE FAMILY

Family life means family compromise and a willingness to be adaptable – virtues that are necessary not only in personal relations, but also, more prosaically, in practical living terms.

It is likely that this room must encompass the varying interests of several family members – which can seem difficult. But with a bit of thought most rooms can work very successfully in more than one way. This doesn't mean a corner for each person like a giant game of forfeits, but planning the room around everyone's preferences.

Flexibility of furniture and the arrangement of space is part of the answer; tables that are the right height to work at, modular seating units that can be reconfigured to suit the occasion, and low upholstered units that can work as stools or low tables are some of the possible options.

Furniture solutions should be coupled with the right storage, which can be as simple as boxes and baskets, or as complicated as custom-designed show pieces. Open units that are deep enough to hold books, DVDs and CDs, perhaps with adjustable shelves, are relatively simple to find. Another idea is to group similar elements together – toys, for instance, are best kept in one place where they can easily be found and put away. Such small things bring continuity to a space and mean that the room works as one whole rather than several disparate parts.

OPPOSITE ABOVE **Choose the right toy storage and it'll be easy to reclaim a family room in the evenings, when it's more of an adult zone. Soft fabric baskets not only allow small children to choose their own toys at playtime, but even the youngest can help with tidying up – then the baskets can be placed out of the way.**

OPPOSITE BELOW **Furniture for children doesn't have to be chunky and practical – there are plenty of design-led options, including pint-sized versions of mid-century designs (and they're not as expensive as you might think). Alternatively, you could take a small-scale piece of furniture and customize it with a lick of paint.**

THIS PAGE **Kids will be delighted to have a spot to call their very own within a communal area like a living room. Here a homemade teepee provides a private reading nook in the corner, though it can be easily placed more centrally for playtime.**

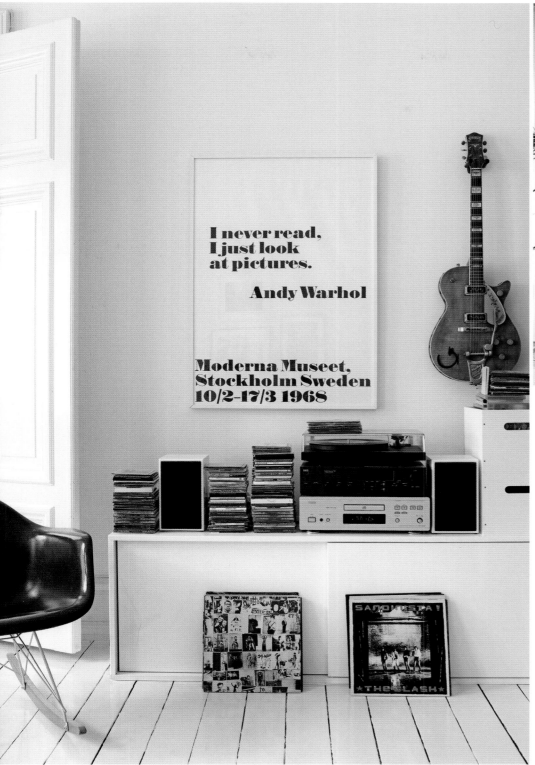

There is no escaping technology in the 21st-century home. The only question is how to house it and use it.

TECHNOLOGY

The good thing about what one might call leisure technology today is that the designs themselves are so much better-looking than they once were: television screens are flatter, thinner and less obtrusive; CD and DVD players are neater and smaller. The bad thing is that there is far more of it about and many of us want our living rooms to be the home for the screen, DVD player and games console as well as some sort of music centre.

The decision, which ideally should be made when you are planning the room so that all necessary cables can be discreetly hidden, is whether to reveal or conceal and, if so, how? Concealing a television screen is simple – install it in a cupboard, either especially made or an old piece converted, or – a decorator's trick – by installing a hinged or sliding mechanism that suspends a painting in front of the screen and pivots or slides to reveal the screen.

The other (easier) option is simply to install it unapologetically, on a wall, set into a storage unit or sat on a surface of the right height. Ensure that wherever and however you place it, it is easily accessed and watched. No one wants to move furniture to get to the television.

OPPOSITE **When a work area needs to be incorporated into a living space, it helps to choose a computer that is unobtrusive and sleek in its design, rather than a bulky unit. Alternatively, why not opt for a laptop, and simply put it away when it's not required?**

ABOVE **There's no rule that says tech has to be hidden away – it can make a statement about the residents' tastes just as strongly as artworks. Here a collection of CDs and vinyl sits alongside a stereo system, while a wall-mounted guitar underlines the homeowner's passion for music.**

RIGHT **Now that televisions are thinner and lighter than ever before, it's become easier to find a way to conceal the screen when it's not in use. You can invest in sliding screens, or units that descend from the ceiling, but a simple curtain is an effective, budget-friendly option.**

FURNITURE

All living rooms need furniture, but that does not mean that any old thing will do. Some unfortunate examples, instead of appearing welcoming and comfortable havens, seem on first glance more like burial grounds for unwanted and unloved pieces.

Of course it is essential to have furniture, but it is also essential to have the right pieces of furniture – from the seating and occasional tables to lamps and objects – and all must be chosen with due regard to their place in this most important of rooms.

Seating comes first, naturally, and what works best here is usually a combination of styles and designs, to accommodate different situations and people. Personal preference should be taken into account – people often have strong opinions about what sort of seating they like. Many people like to sink into a squashy, cushioned easy chair or sofa to read or chat, but there are others who are only comfortable in an upright upholstered chair, so there should always be a choice available.

Chairs that can stand against the wall and be brought into play when they are needed are useful, as are low stools that can be sat on or drawn up to a chair, as well as doubling as a table for drinks and books. Whatever you choose, remember the overall design plan that you conceived for the room, and into which the separate pieces must fit. Scale and proportion should especially be taken into account; sofas in particular should be large enough for the space that they are going to occupy, for nothing looks more uncomfortable than a small sofa in a large room.

Where there are chairs, there should be tables – or other flat surfaces – to hold drinks, lamps and books. They must be within easy reach of chairs and sofas, but avoid the Victorian parlour look; choose pieces of different heights and shapes, mixing side tables with chests, low tables and even small cupboards to stand against the wall, beside a sofa perhaps.

ABOVE RIGHT **There may still be a place for the three-piece suite in the contemporary living room, but there's nothing to say that your seating must stay in this conventional mould. Built-ins, floor cushions, daybeds and even hanging chairs all have their benefits (and striking style potential).**

RIGHT **Benches made from wood or metal can serve more than one purpose. They're great as occasional seating if you're entertaining a crowd (just be sure to top the seat with a cushion or two, for comfort's sake), and they can also be pressed into service as a side table.**

OPPOSITE **If your chosen aesthetic is mid-century, then a three-piece suite arranged around a coffee table would definitely be an authentic choice. This set features two slightly differently designed armchairs, to avoid the monotony of closely-matched pieces, while the '50s-style fluid lines contrast beautifully with the geometrics of the architecture.**

COLLECTIONS & DISPLAY

One of the pleasures of building a collection is enjoying it on a daily basis, and where better to display a collection than the living room? Not just a place to sit and relax, it is also a room with interesting and pretty things to look at.

As the principal reception room, the living room is the perfect place to display and arrange pictures as well as other collections of objects and pieces. A collection can be amassed over the years, and become an important part of your daily life, or it can simply be a group of things that you are fond of and which are connected to each other in some way – through design, perhaps, or theme, or material. The important thing, no matter what the basis of your collection, is that they be grouped and displayed together in a way that shows them in the best possible light.

Good display does not have to be intricate, elaborate or expensive; all it needs is careful consideration of how to show off what you have. Some objects look their best in open display cases or shelves; others are most appealing set out on low surfaces. Almost every collection that numbers more than two looks better in a close-knit arrangement, whether on a surface or the wall. Judicious lighting can be helpful, but most effective groups rely just on pleasing arrangements, balancing height and shape to best effect.

The hanging of pictures and photographs together is not difficult, but can require practice to achieve a pleasing result. You may find it helpful to position the group on the floor first, moving pieces and experimenting with what works best together, before committing to hammer and picture hooks.

OPPOSITE ABOVE **If you've got a collection of artwork, why not display it in a way that will allow you to ring the changes periodically? Here a picture ledge behind the sofa allows the large canvases to be switched out whenever the homeowner's mood takes them.**

OPPOSITE BELOW LEFT **Glass-fronted cabinets can be the best option for any truly committed collector of ceramics, glassware or other decorative pieces. Not only does the visual impact of the display benefit from the items being grouped together, but on a practical note, the need for dusting is much reduced.**

OPPOSITE BELOW RIGHT **Hanging art salon-style isn't as difficult as it might appear – especially if you use paper templates to work out a balanced configuration before committing to fixing up the picture hooks. Using frames that have similar aesthetics (even if they don't match exactly) will help create coherence.**

BELOW LEFT **Grid-style picture hanging is a strong look which emphasizes the similarity between artworks. It works most effectively where pieces share a common style and maybe subject matter, and are displayed in matching frames – it's perhaps best used within a scheme that boasts strong symmetry in other aspects of its design.**

ABOVE RIGHT **Collections don't have to be of fine, beautiful objects to have aesthetic value – and even workaday items can add a decorative touch if they're carefully chosen and curated. Here, very appropriately, some old crates have been upcycled into a display unit for an eclectic selection of vintage things.**

RIGHT **With a little creative thinking, you can come up with all sorts of quirky and imaginative ways to present small items. This glass tazza elevates a heap of sea urchins and coral, giving the mixed display of decorative things a bit of height, as well as a touch of glamour.**

FAR LEFT In a period home, a colour scheme that reflects the heritage of the building can be the most fitting option – but don't feel you have to recreate an authentic historic look. Here exposed plaster and wood add the warmth you might expect from a grand Italian interior, but without subscribing fully to tradition.

LEFT A living room should be relaxing in its ambience, but don't take that objective too far and end up with a dull space. Here greys and creams make for a restful scheme, while the lustre of luxurious fabrics and gilded details ensure that the restrained colour choice doesn't come across as flat and boring.

BELOW LEFT In a neutral scheme, a shot of bright colour can be just what's required to enliven the mood – and the best news is that you can instantly update the look of the space by replacing a vibrant accessory or two with a new alternative.

OPPOSITE Repeating the same accent shade in different parts of the room – such as the yellowish tones of natural wood that are echoed by the New York cab in the wall-hung collage – will give your scheme a sense of balance and togetherness.

LIVING ROOM PALETTES

A successful palette of colours for a living room has to be just that – a colour scheme easy to live with in all situations and at all times.

As perhaps the most important room in the home, or certainly the room that has to work the hardest in many different ways, the colours and textures used in the living room are all-important. They should make the room a pleasing place to spend time: somewhere to sit and read, watch television, listen to music or talk; a place also, perhaps, in which to work or to eat. The room should exude not only an air of pleasant comfort and relaxation, but also a sense of purposefulness. All these different and sometimes conflicting aspects can be encouraged by the choice of colour – and also texture – throughout the room.

The colour palette should suit all those who use it, so in a family home should not be over-feminine or unduly masculine, as well as being easy to live with and welcoming to guests, easy to dress down, as well as up. It sounds a tall order, but look to outside factors, the most important being quality of light, to inform your choice and find the right shades. Which way does the room face, how much natural light does it get, is it naturally warm or cold? A north-facing room will benefit from warm colours; a south-facing, many-windowed room can take cooler tones.

OPPOSITE **You might think that floral cushions would never go with an ethnic-patterned rug. But here the combination works because the colours are similar tonally (knocked-back, almost faded shades), plus the rest of the room has been kept plain and neutral, so there aren't too many elements fighting for attention.**

LEFT **Don't skimp on cushions – too few will always look mean and meagre, and comfort levels may be compromised. It's best to introduce a little variety, while ensuring coherence, by choosing complementary patterns, colours, shapes and sizes rather than a matching set.**

RIGHT **As well as cushions, a blanket or throw will help to up the cosiness factor in your living room – they're not just a decorative way to cover up a less-than-perfect sofa or armchair (or to protect furniture from small children or pets), they're great for snuggling under, too.**

SOFT FURNISHINGS

Individuality can be easily expressed in a living room with clever choice of soft furnishings, and the right material can add colour and pattern in an instant.

Next to the colours of the papers and paints that you choose for the walls, the quickest, most effective and often cheapest way to bring personality and comfort into a room is with the soft furnishings. Old pieces of furniture can be transformed, new pieces made unique, for fabrics are the icing on every decorative cake. The price and design ranges are so huge, the patterns so numerous, the colour spectrum so wide that choosing the upholstery fabric on the sofas and chairs is one of the most enjoyable aspects of designing any room.

As far as the design of the fabric is concerned, the scale of the pattern in relation to the size of the piece to be covered is a factor to take into account; a large-scale pattern will look wholly out of proportion on a very small chair seat. Think also of the other colours in the room, such as the walls and windows; it is important that soft furnishings work with these, although a decorative scheme is always more successful if there is harmony rather than an identical match. If you prefer to keep the colours of the larger pieces of furniture subtle in tone, stack them with contrasting cushions in new and old fabrics to add interest.

* *Where soft furnishings are concerned, cheapest is not always best: on a single chair, for example, a really fabulous, beautiful fabric that costs a little more per metre will transform a chair into a showstopper and give you pleasure for years, long after you have forgotten the extra cost.*

* *Trimmings – from elaborate passementerie to simple braid, piping/cording and ribbon – can do wonders for a plain upholstered or loose/slipcovered chair or sofa.*

* *Old textiles can be used to great effect as soft furnishings. If you do not have quite enough to cover a whole chair, consider just covering the seat, or even using a piece as a central panel running the length of back and seat.*

* *In the same way that cheap clothes look better when simple, if you are opting for less expensive furnishing fabrics, look for simple colour combinations – two or three tones at most – and simple patterns, such as stripes or checks, which always look better than an elaborate, over-coloured design.*

* *Like a different lampshade, a new and unusual cushion cover can rejuvenate a room in an instant.*

* Shutters can be used either on their own or in conjunction with curtains; if the latter, the curtain pole will need to be set at a reasonable distance from the window so as not to impair the shutter workings.

* The choice of curtain poles is wide indeed, and ranges from antique reeded brass poles with elaborate finials to simple polished wooden rods. Many wooden poles can be painted to work with the rest of the décor.

* If you choose to curtain tall windows, ensure that the curtain headings are deep enough to look in proportion.

* If you have tall windows, and even in a room that is otherwise subtly decorated, do not automatically reject the idea of curtains or blinds/shades in a bold, large-scale design (small-scale designs will not work well in a large room.) The contrast that a bold design adds can lift the entire scheme.

* As a general rule, the cheaper the curtain fabric, the more metres you should use – a full curtain appears a generous one and makes the room feel warm and welcoming.

ABOVE **Always ensure that curtains are hung on a sufficiently long pole or rail that they can be fully drawn back from the window, and don't obscure any of the glazing when open. This ensures that the maximum amount of natural light can pour in and illuminate the room during the day.**

BELOW RIGHT **Blinds/shades are a great window treatment option for a bay, which can prove awkward and perhaps a little fussy, aesthetically, to dress with curtains. Roman, Venetian or roller blinds/shades (or perhaps louvred shutters) offer a sleeker look.**

OPPOSITE **Never skimp on the fullness of curtains, especially if you're looking to create a sumptuous interior. The ratio of the finished width of the curtains to the pole or track length is typically 2 x or 2.5 x for pleated and gathered headings, while eyelets/grommets or tab-top headings are less full (1.25 x or 1.5 x).**

WINDOW TREATMENTS

The living room needs as much natural light as can be collected. It also needs to be a warm and comfortable space; how you dress the windows is the key.

Once windows were hung with layer upon layer of curtains of different weight; today's windows are carefree in comparison. Simplicity is the answer: gone are heavy pelmets, swags and drapes; now curtains are hung from poles or neat, near-invisible fixtures. Blinds/shades, both narrow and wide, are in evidence and in many period houses shutters are being restored and used again.

The key to successful window treatments is making sure that all is balanced and kept in proportion. If you are buying curtains, for example, make sure that their dimensions neither overpower the window by being too long or wide, nor appear mean, by skimping on material, or being hung too short.

Blinds/shades give a clean, pared-down look. The best styles are the roller blind/shade and the flat, pleated Roman blind/shade. Roman blinds/shades look better where there is enough width to show off the design and the pleats; rollers work well on smaller windows or where there are several windows of differing sizes.

* If you use table lamps, make sure that they are of different heights, so there are varied pools of light through the room.

* Pairs of lights arranged with geometric regularity can look monotonous; if you do have some pairs, break them up around the room, so that it is not immediately obvious.

* Do not despise the humble uplighter, which ranges from a simple cylinder to a statement piece. Hidden in dark corners, they can add depth to a room as well as subtly increasing its size.

* Dimmers are not difficult to install and are essential for living-room lighting, allowing you to vary the mood at the turn of a switch.

* Chandeliers, in every shape and size, are once again in fashion and fun to have hanging overhead; make sure, however, that they work as part of an integral lighting scheme and are not used as the principal source of illumination.

* Include beautiful or statement lamps. Their presence will be much appreciated and will bring personality and individuality to any living room.

OPPOSITE **An oversized light fitting can make for an impactful centrepiece – but it's wise to ensure that any such low-hung pendant is above a table, to avoid accidental collisions. Where a lamp is at eye level, and the shade isn't opaque, the bulb should be chosen carefully to avoid dazzling the room's occupants.**

RIGHT **The standard lamp has come a long way since the turned-wood-mounted lampshade that stood in the corner of your grandmother's living room. Designs with multiple lamps, and flexibility in terms of their positioning, can be great task lighting options.**

ABOVE RIGHT **Counterweight designs are an ideal choice if you'd like to illuminate a spot with a lamp, but need to position the base in a different location. They often feature a very heavy base made from stone or metal, or in some cases a hanging weight to counterbalance the shade.**

Using a living room well is about using it to its fullest extent and lighting is the key to achieving that. Lighting should be individual and personal and, of course, effective.

LIGHTING

As in every other room in the house, a combination of lighting is what works best, and the ideal way to work out what might be needed is to write down exactly what activities might be taking place in the room. There will need to be task lighting – a bald way of saying specific lights for reading, writing and so on. These can be a mixture; some table lamps, some floor, some directional. Old lights as well as new, floor lights as well as table – it is the combination of styles and designs that gives a room character.

Then there should always be ambient or mood lighting to create the atmosphere that you want at different times – a mixture of options that could be suitable both for cheery parties and cosy evenings. Don't forget that many lamps and lights are objects of beauty in their own right; there are both contemporary and traditional shapes that should be appreciated in their full and bright glory, so do not hesitate to include pieces that you really like, even if they do not do much for the practical aspects of lighting the room.

The floor is the canvas on which you paint the room. If it is right, it may go unremarked; if it is wrong, it will be noticed by all.

FLOORING

The right flooring for a living room is a question both of personal preference and practical issues. The main questions are whether the floor should be hard or soft, and what options are available. If you live in an apartment, does the lease require that you have a soft floor, rather than wood or tiles? Is warmth an issue? Or small children?

For many people a wooden floor is the only floor, and indeed its virtues are many. It is warm underfoot, the range of available woods is large – from glossy dark mahogany to pale scrubbed pine – and if chosen with care, it will last a lifetime. Existing wooden floors can be refurbished if necessary, then painted, stained and embellished.

But wood is not suitable for everyone. Many decorators prefer, particularly where laying or repairing a whole floor would be costly and disruptive, to choose either a natural floor covering such as sisal or seagrass, or a flatweave, looped wool carpet that simulates the natural look. Both make very good backgrounds for rugs.

If you have free rein, the many other options range from rubber, linoleum or cork to polished concrete, stone and terracotta.

* Remember that if the existing floor is uneven, you may need hardboard laid before installing either a natural floor covering or carpet.

* Sisal, seagrass and other natural coverings should be coated with a stain-protective covering before being laid, as they are difficult to spot-clean.

* For lovers of traditional floors, reclaimed floorboards and parquet flooring can sometimes be found. Search the internet and architectural salvage companies. You can also find reproduction floorboards, carefully distressed to look just like old.

* If your existing wooden floors are in reasonable condition, they can be sanded, although this is something that is best done before moving in. Old boards can also be stained or painted, which is a quick and easy way of updating a room; the range of oil-based floor paint colours available is now as wide as that for the walls.

* If a new floor has to be laid, investigate the possibilities of underfloor heating, which renders previously hard, cold floors warm and welcoming.

OPPOSITE ABOVE **A pale carpet is the perfect blank canvas for a pared-down scheme, particularly if it matches the colour of the walls. However, it's not the most practical of choices, even with a stain-protection treatment, so if you have small children – or a predilection for red wine – think twice.**

OPPOSITE BELOW LEFT **Tiled floors don't have to only be reserved for kitchens and bathrooms, it's just a case of choosing the right option in terms of texture and colour. Here pale, pinkish-beige mottled tones add warmth to a high-ceilinged space, and complement the natural wood of the chair and panelling.**

OPPOSITE BELOW RIGHT **Polished concrete has become a popular option for contemporary minimalist interiors, especially those with an industrial vibe. Here it suits the pared-down aesthetic very well, even though the internal architecture suggests a period conversion more likely to be a chapel or village hall than a factory.**

ABOVE LEFT **A statement rug can make or break a scheme – especially if you're using strong colour and pattern. This bold and bright example works beautifully, thanks to the fact that the colours and some elements of the design are echoed in the cushions upon the sofa, giving aesthetic coherence.**

LEFT **Original floorboards are beautiful, but a rug will help prevent draughts and create a cosier feel in the space – as well as being perfectly in keeping with period style. Oriental rugs are an investment, and quality (hand-knotted, wool and silk) examples keep their value; just make sure you look after them well.**

A living room without storage would actually be a room in which no one could easily live. Consider what you will need in order to enjoy this space, where so many diverse activities might take place.

STORAGE

Storage is a word that can imply things set apart, hidden away until they are finally needed. But living-room storage is not like that – it means finding the best way to look after the things you need in this most companionable and personal of rooms. Yes, there can be discreet storage here – cupboards that hide a multitude of things – but there can also be storage that serves a dual purpose, such as an open unit that divides the room as well as housing essentials. A combination of built-in and freestanding pieces may work best, and the freestanding might be old or new, or a mix of both; this could be the place for a fine bookcase or old dresser/hutch or sideboard/credenza.

Custom-built fitted storage looks best when designed as part of an overall concept. Should you have them, the obvious sites are the alcoves beside the chimneybreast. The conventional design is one of open shelves above a cupboard, but consider extending the cupboard depth into the room, to allow a more generous storage space, as well as creating an extra surface for lamps and objects.

ABOVE **Wall-mounted shelves are a good option for a large collection of books, as you can utilise the whole space between floor and ceiling for maximum storage capacity. Make sure you choose a design with a large, sturdy bracket, to ensure solid support for the heavy load.**

FAR LEFT **Make your furniture work harder by selecting pieces which fulfil both the storage and display functions. The glossy black finish of this glazed cabinet really makes it stand out against the pale background of white walls and grey floorboards, and neatly frames the objects kept inside it.**

OPPOSITE BELOW RIGHT **There's a reason that the traditional configuration of cupboards with shelves above, built in either side of the chimney breast, has become a classic – it's not only beautifully symmetrical and so pleasing to the eye, but it makes great use of the available space.**

ABOVE **Usually more associated with the dining room, a sideboard/ credenza can be a great option for a living room, offering plenty of display potential for family pictures and decorative objects, as well as capacious storage in its cupboards and drawers.**

❋ *That all-purpose and attractive piece of furniture, the French armoire, either painted or in a wooden finish, comes into its own in a country-style living room. Adaptable and commodious, within its cavernous depths it can store anything from books to bottles.*

❋ *Freestanding storage options include a sideboard/credenza or chest of drawers; instead of a low table, try an ottoman or chest for last-minute clear-ups.*

❋ *Keep media players and games consoles out of sight with a cabinet repurposed as an entertainment centre. Glazed examples can be a boon, as remote controls can be used without opening the doors, but make sure there is sufficient ventilation to avoid overheating.*

❋ *Built-in furniture usually looks best painted the same colour as the rest of the woodwork in the room, but consider picking out any mouldings or decorative features in a slightly deeper shade or shades.*

❋ *Good-looking baskets can be the ultimate quick storage fix, either ranged in sets on open shelves, or strategically positioned in corners and under windows for magazines, papers and general junk.*

❋ *Books really do furnish a room, and the living room is the ideal place both to store and display them. Decorative as well as essential, try to fit shelves with adjustable fittings so that volumes of all sizes can be accommodated.*

OPPOSITE ABOVE **For extra impact, consider choosing a theme for artwork – this will give a polished, curated look that really ups the style stakes. Here three pictures have a common thread of subject matter, and a largely monochrome colour profile, even though they vary considerably in medium and aesthetic.**

OPPOSITE BELOW LEFT **The most successful groupings of decorative objects usually have enough coherence to look deliberately put together, but enough variety to inject a little character. Here stone carvings with similar lines are grouped on a marble-topped table, contrasted against an abstract painting (which has been carefully chosen to tone in with the table base).**

OPPOSITE BELOW CENTRE **Less is often more – but make sure your decorative touches are suitably proportioned for the space in question. This ornate mirror adds an opulent touch to a fairly neutral, pared-down room, but its impact wouldn't have been nearly so successful if it didn't dominate the wall above the mantelpiece.**

OPPOSITE BELOW RIGHT **Even the most mundane, practical of items can have decorative potential. Here a collection of paperwork is being kept in brightly-coloured box and lever-arch files, meaning it's not only well-organised and easily to hand, but the pops of red, pink and blue give the largely monochrome space a lift.**

ABOVE RIGHT **If you're looking to create a calming ambience, then choose finishing touches that don't introduce too much stylistic tension. Here a rustic timber chest is given added interest with statuesque dried plants, which are in keeping with the natural theme of the space, with its neutral linen-upholstered chair and natural fibre floorcovering.**

ABOVE FAR RIGHT **It's perhaps more usual to dress a room with cut flowers – but why not consider the beauty of other plant-based decorative choices? Here the beautifully haphazard natural form of a dried branch adds organic beauty to a very pared-down space with strong horizontal and vertical lines.**

* *Mix pieces together from different worlds and different periods – old and new can be tied together by colour or shape.*

* *Use a flat surface – a table or the top of sideboards/ credenzas – to form a horizontal composition, mixing vases and bowls of flowers with interesting pieces of decorative glass and a picture or two hung low, or propped against the wall.*

* *To create pleasing arrangements, go for textural contrast – rough and smooth, metal and glass.*

* *Lighting is important; use either a striking lamp or a cluster of candles to add depth to a display.*

* *Never underestimate the power of the unexpected – a visual jolt, like a flash of colour in an otherwise neutral colour scheme, always adds interest.*

* *The secret of a good decorative grouping is proportion and scale. A group of objects all of the same dimensions and height will not work. The eye must be drawn vertically upwards as well as horizontally in order to achieve visual harmony.*

* *Anything and everything that gives you visual pleasure can be added to the living room as a finishing touch.*

FINISHING TOUCHES

The finishing touches to a room are the fun bits – the decorative additions that give a room an extra layer of interest.

Every room needs finishing touches. They are the things that distinguish a loved and lived-in room from a property developer's bland show apartment or a hotel room, so it is worth thinking how to display the things you love to best effect. A room's finishing touches need not be what the auction houses describe as 'important' pieces, but they are the decorative details, the things you like and which give a room personality – your personality.

Such details might range from pictures to old plates or pieces of material; cushions are finishing touches, as are antique mirrors, pictures and flowers and plants. Objects both old and new finish a room, as do books and pieces of china, glass and wood, photographs (both framed and unframed), table lamps and candlesticks and candelabra.

The late David Hicks probably invented the concept, and name, of 'tablescapes'; clever groupings of objects that draw the eye to points of interest throughout the room. Arranging disparate objects, combining them harmoniously, is a pleasing one, and it is also a very satisfying pastime – instant interior decoration, in effect.

❋ *Curtains are not a necessity where modern country style is concerned, even at French windows, and particularly in a setting of natural charm, but windows that have been well draught-proofed certainly are.*

❋ *Do not overplay the decorative accessories; the country living room is no place for sophisticated and overly stylized works of art. Concentrate on the natural and the appropriate, which enhance rather than contrast.*

❋ *Mix old and new furniture together; although simply made and simply styled furniture works well in a country setting, so does the odd contrasting piece – an elaborate or fancifully decorated chair, desk or table, say.*

❋ *Make sure that the room is warm and cosy. Make use of existing fires and stoves, and consider installing underfloor heating or chunky, old-fashioned radiators.*

BELOW LEFT **In a room where natural shades predominate, the layering of textures is essential for creating interest. Here the earthy tones of natural timber and organic fibre flooring have been combined with white-painted elements, while a sheepskin adds a luxurious touch.**

RIGHT **Just because the interior architecture is rustic doesn't mean that modern country style has to be rough and rugged. Here blonde wood and sleek mid-century shapes add a slightly Scandinavian feel to a relaxed living space.**

OPPOSITE **Playing up the contrasts will elevate the country look from pleasant to super-stylish. Here richly embroidered cushions still fit with the country aesthetic, but really stand out against the rough-hewn timber panel walls and natural fleeces.**

Modern country style combines old favourites and new thinking. Relaxed and simple, yet stylish and comfy, it works just as well in town as on the village green.

MODERN COUNTRY

It would not be an exaggeration to say that there is a fresh new feeling to the country-inspired living room. The uncluttered and (generally) spider-free modern country style is a contemporary take on the traditional rural genre – an easy, relaxed and welcoming look that works not only in its spiritual home, the countryside, but in many city spaces as well.

Although the variants are as many as the locations are numerous, modern country style has a certain number of givens – points that are relevant to all those who espouse to a contemporary country look. First of all there is always a simplicity; simplicity of setting and style, simplicity of textiles and pattern, and simplicity of colour and material.

Rather than having fitted upholstery covers on all the seating, choose a mixture of some fitted seats and others dressed with loose, unfitted covers that are not too closely tailored; the effect that you are aiming for is the look of loose, barely fitted old country-house slipcovers – often originally made in chintz or cretonne or natural linen – that protected the grander fitted covers when the room was not in use. Modern loose/slipcovers can be very pretty made in light, clear-coloured plain fabrics that can be easily washed – another reason for going for the relaxed, baggy look, which gives more leeway should there be any shrinkage or distorting of shape.

Throws, now a classic decorating staple, come into their own in modern country style. From new cashmere to old Paisley shawls, tartan rugs to windowpane-check Welsh blankets; old and new, they add a splash of colour and pattern as they cover sofa backs and seats as well as chilly feet and shoulders. The colour schemes that work best in modern country living rooms are usually soft and harmonious; flat and eggshell finishes usually work better than high gloss.

Although this is not necessarily an expensive look to get right, modern country requires at least as much care – if not more – than a more extravagant style. On the floor, for instance, no covering may be needed, except perhaps a rug in front of the fire, but the floor that is there, be it wooden or tiled, must be in as good condition as its age and your handiwork allow.

❊ Less is definitely more when introducing unusual elements into a room; it is the surprise of the contrast that works, rather than the overall blanket effect.

❊ Many of the most innovative 20th-century designs were created in glass and ceramics and a collection can still be formed relatively easily, albeit not quite as cheaply as 10 or 20 years ago. The angular, exuberant glass vases and figurines in reds, oranges and yellows have great decorative charm and look wonderful grouped together on a surface or against a window.

❊ The best 20th-century furniture designs, of chairs in particular, often had a sculptural quality and will therefore benefit from being displayed in comparative isolation – in a corner or beneath a window – where they may be clearly seen and appreciated.

THIS PAGE **Mid-century sofas with a wooden frame are particularly good for compact spaces, and they're fairly low-budget too – but they're not as great for lounging as many modern designs, so it's a wise idea to pile them high with pillows and cushions (those made from vintage fabric would be particularly in keeping).**

OPPOSITE ABOVE RIGHT **You can combine a variety of different vintage styles, provided you pay attention to creating coherence with colour and proportion. Here the warm tones of ochre in the coffee table and chest complement the patterned rug, while yellow chairs add a shot of sunshine.**

The living room is the ideal place, in decorative terms, for old to meet new, get tipped into the decorative blender, and emerge as something original and fresh.

VINTAGE-INSPIRED STYLE

The term 'vintage' is sometimes rather bandied about in books and magazines, often seeming to be used as a synonym for the slightly less glamorous term 'second-hand' and often seeming to mean, in some contexts, almost anything that is not absolutely straight-from-the-box new.

But for most interior decorators, the term translates into something slightly more precise – those patterns and designs that are not yet antique (in the auction house definition of being over 100 years old) but are not band-box new either, with particular reference to the designs of the mid- to late-20th century.

Like any period of decoration there is both good and bad to be found here, but the 20th century was a period in which some furniture and textile designers produced highly original and brilliant work, much of which is not only highly collectable today, but also has a strong influence on much modern design. Many of the fabric and paper designs, in particular, have an exuberance and an originality that make them stand out, and it is these pieces that can add a huge amount to an otherwise contemporary living room.

The trick, as with all attempts at mixing styles and periods, is first, obviously, to pick the right designs, and second to use them with considered care – not to create a retro pastiche, but to inject some of the unusual colours and patterns of previous decades into the rest of the existing scheme, adding bold, contrasting shots that throw the other elements into relief, and add an individuality and sense of novelty into the room.

The preferred colours of the 20th century were often bold and deep, and often veered towards the sharp – all of which is great in relatively small doses. Instead of covering every wall in a vintage colour, consider painting just one wall of your living room – a device very popular 50 years ago – or even using the contrast colour for the doors and windows.

RIGHT **Though it's easier to create an eclectic space by sticking to just two or three distinct styles, you can throw out the rule book entirely and just rely on instinct. Here a Eero Aarnio Ball Chair sits alongside a couple of contrasting cabinets – a nondescript white-painted example and a grander piece with ornate carving.**

FAR RIGHT **Veneered in hardwoods such as teak and rosewood, 1970s furniture offers a sleek look that combines just as well with minimalism as it does with a busier, homespun vintage look. There's a good choice of price points, too, depending on whether you opt for a designer original, or a manufacturer such as Ercol or G-Plan.**

* *Hang only those pictures that have a definite part in the overall scheme. This is not a look where every wall should be densely covered with art.*

* *Alternative loose/slipcovers that can be easily replaced are a good solution to the inevitable wear and tear of elegant, pale-coloured furnishings.*

* *Instead of a coffee table, choose a chest with a flat top – ample storage is key to this look, which should be clutter-free.*

* *Lighting is very important in this style of room: use table lamps of different heights and styles as well as ambient background lighting that can be adjusted to alter the mood, depending on the occasion. Natural light also is important and should be emphasized; curtains should not be heavy and light-excluding.*

* *Flowers, simply arranged, are always welcome in this room, adding the right note of decorative welcome.*

Simplicity is something we all desire in our lives, and nowhere more so than in our homes. Yet simplicity does not have to mean scruffy, and the simple, elegant living room is a case in point.

SIMPLY ELEGANT

To the relief of many observers of the interior scene, we have moved – in contemporary decorative and design terms – from the rigorous and often taxing minimalism of twenty years ago, where hard, often uncompromising elements were used in abundance with statement-making glee, to a look that, although it is still edited, pared-down and unfussy, also includes a palpable degree of comfort and warmth. Is this a description of the perfect living room, perhaps? It is certainly one that many will comfortably identify with.

There is an elegance in this style of room, but it is not a fussy, nor contrived effect. It is an elegance that is easy, a style that comes through the careful selection and even more careful editing of pieces put together after time spent judging how the look will work. Everything, from sofas and chairs to pictures and decorative objects in the simple, elegant living room will be chosen because they work on their own as well as with the other elements, which means that the way that objects and decorative accessories are displayed is important.

Texture is also important, both in furnishings and on the floor; the cleaner the lines of the furniture, the more inviting should be the texture of the covers. Floors – with wood or natural finishes – are often uncovered, or finished with one or two simple rugs, which are rarely bright in colour or highly patterned.

As well as texture, the choice of colour is also relevant. A calm atmosphere is a vital part of the simple, elegant living room and there is something about pale colours in a neutral palette that soothes the eye; the trick is to choose a neutral spectrum – colours with a grey, pink or yellow cast, perhaps – and to combine various different shades together within that group, adding just a little contrast, either in an area of sharper colour or an unexpected object.

Above all, this living room is one where order reigns; there is nothing at all simple about mess, and unnecessary or unwanted pieces should be kept out of sight in cupboards or, in extremis, a large basket or box.

LEFT **A fairly grand period room has been given the white-on-white treatment, with walls, woodwork, flooring and chimneypiece all in the same pale shade. Against this blank canvas the rich shade of the 1970s leather chair really comes to the fore, while echoes of the same chocolate brown are in evidence in some of the room's few decorative accessories.**

ABOVE LEFT **Here a simply decorated room, in a restrained colour palette of neutrals, avoids seeming sterile through the use of texture – a tactile velvet sofa boasts details including brass and rich timber, the parquet floor exudes elegance, while the walls feature a soft patina.**

LEFT **Symmetry can be an important tool when it comes to creating a pared-down space, since the polish it affords ensures the look never appears thrown together or lacking in charm. Here a pair of low-hanging pendant lamps are positioned above the coffee table, perfectly in line with a pair of matching sofas placed opposite each other.**

ABOVE **For the ultimate in simplicity, a monochrome palette is hard to beat. Here, the only hints of colour come from the books on the coffee table and the warm-toned rattan lampshade – everything else is black or white, with the textures of different materials giving the look some variation.**

White is the subtlest of options for a living room; cool or warm, it is adaptable, flexible to your needs and can be as sophisticated or as simple as you wish.

WHITE AND LIGHT

An all-white living room sounds wonderful, but achieving the perfect white room requires thought and application. The most effective way of achieving a pleasant room is to create one that is white in feeling rather than in actual colour, with a mixture of white-based shades and tones subtly combined.

White is not a single colour, nor a single tone; every paint card tells you that. There are cool whites – like pearl and alabaster – and warm whites, such as buttermilk and ivory. It is important to decide, early on, which particular palette suits your style and, having done that, to broaden your palette, to include two, three or even more shades of white within the final scheme. The finishes should be varied too, with matt, eggshell and even a couple of points of high gloss used in the same room. Most white rooms look better when highlighted with small accents of colour – no sharp contrasts, rather subtle pointers, used in cushions, curtains or even flowers.

White is of course light, and its reflective qualities mean that it bounces back any available natural light – a good thing in principle, but in southern countries, where the natural light is far brighter than it is in the north, white needs to be subdued, used with caution, with soft tones prevailing. Artificial lighting in a white room is therefore perhaps even more important than in other colour schemes. A variety of different light fittings can temper and direct the light in a white room, giving it areas of warmth and comfort.

White living rooms respond to textural subtleties – architectural finishes in various materials, and textiles in a number of interesting finishes – so think about what floor surface and upholstery will look best. In a white room, the furniture is very important, as it must be neither overpowering nor invisible, particularly if you are using tones of white for covers. Painted furniture works well in a white living room and brings a new element into the mix.

It goes without saying that a white living room should look tidy. Clutter does not equate with the atmosphere of cool and calm that should emanate from a white room.

OPPOSITE In this white-on-white room, the traditionally shaped upholstery, distressed paintwork and touches of grey-green – both in the ticking stripe and original fitted cabinet – prevent a minimalist colour palette from feeling too contemporary for a period home. Additionally, an antique chandelier adds a luxurious touch.

ABOVE Warm shades of white, plus the soft shimmer of mother of pearl and occasional gleam of a metallic accent, prevent this living space from seeming anything other than welcoming and comfortable. The blank walls, devoid of artwork, help to maximize the feeling of space and calm.

* The decorators' favourite, all-purpose white is not the blinding 'brilliant white', with its detergent-like optical brighteners, but a soft white that has been mixed with a hint of yellow to give a warm hue. Look for it in paint colour cards labelled 'historical' or 'heritage'.

* A white-toned room is the perfect background for contemporary furniture – the clean, sleek lines of materials such as laminates, glass, polished wood and plastic will all stand out against a cool, neutral background.

* White is also a perfect background against which to display objects or pictures; simple white shelves become an almost professional setting.

* The successful white room is one where decorative accessories have been carefully selected. Start with an empty room and then add things one by one, gauging the effect after each addition.

* Unless you're deliberately aiming for stark minimalism, be careful with white high-gloss finishes, as they can easily appear too cold and clinical.

MASCULINE MONOCHROME

The living room need not be slanted towards family or female taste; many successful schemes are based on a simpler, more assertive look – masculine, in fact.

Perhaps it is a hangover from the glory days of gentlemen's clubs and the idea of the out-of-bounds inner sanctum or study, but there is something in the idea of a living room geared towards masculine taste that still touches a chord with even the most metrosexual of modern men.

Stereotypes apart, the main difference between a living room aimed to please the taste of a man and that which appeals to more feminine desires is probably the absence of soft decoration – not too much patterned chintz, and a distinct lack of ruffled, floor-flowing curtains – combined with clean lines, no mess and everything in its place. Add to this a relatively sober palette – though not a boring one – and sharp definition in pattern, design and textures, and you have the perfect masculine room, one in which others might also wish to spend time.

The ideal contemporary, masculine look focuses on a space that is well defined: one that has clarity of purpose as its overriding theme, in which every object looks as if it belongs. So thoughtful planning

is essential, with enough storage for everything that needs to be there as well as maximum space for any necessary gadgets, and the wherewithal to use said gadgets – enough flexible power points and fixtures to allow all technological pieces of equipment to function.

The design of this type of room is not just enhanced, but completed by the right selection of furniture: there must be somewhere pleasant to read and sit, such as sofas and chairs with deep enough seats and tall enough backs. Wall and upholstery colours should be rich and deep or cool and sharp, but never bland and boring, and whatever is on the floor should act to unify the whole room. In a setting that relies on design and colour rather than on decorative accessories, a focal point is always a good idea – the fireplace if there is one, or perhaps a sociable grouping of sofas and chairs around a low table.

Combine these elements and it will be evident that all is united by one factor: utter comfort. In the end, it is that which defines the perfect masculine living room.

ABOVE LEFT **With its strong, earthy colours and sleek shapes, 1970s style is ideal for spaces where you wish to create a more manly appeal. Here a palette of olive green and orange, with black accents, is the antithesis of the soft, muted shades you might associate with a more feminine style.**

ABOVE **The masculine aesthetic doesn't need to be ultra-modern, or avoid classic shapes or comfy soft furnishings – it's just a case of being sparing with the decorative detail, and focusing on strong geometric shapes and plain colours (or simple patterns). Here a pair of classic armchairs and a squishy sofa are offset with an angular coffee table and minimalist chimneypiece.**

* *A wooden floor, which is warm both to look at and to walk upon, is often a perfect solution for a room that combines different activities and pastimes, as it unifies the room and extends the feeling of cubic space.*

* *When adding colour to a masculine scheme, consider an autumnal palette – the deep tones of autumn fruit and the rich colours of changing leaves – rather than one inspired by spring or summer.*

* *A simple, well-designed space is the very place to include one or two pieces of furniture that are modern classics – sculptural, contemporary designs of chairs and lighting that have been tried and tested over the last 50 years or so and found to be very fit for their purpose.*

* *Lighting should be ubiquitous and varied, with enough task lighting to allow many different activities.*

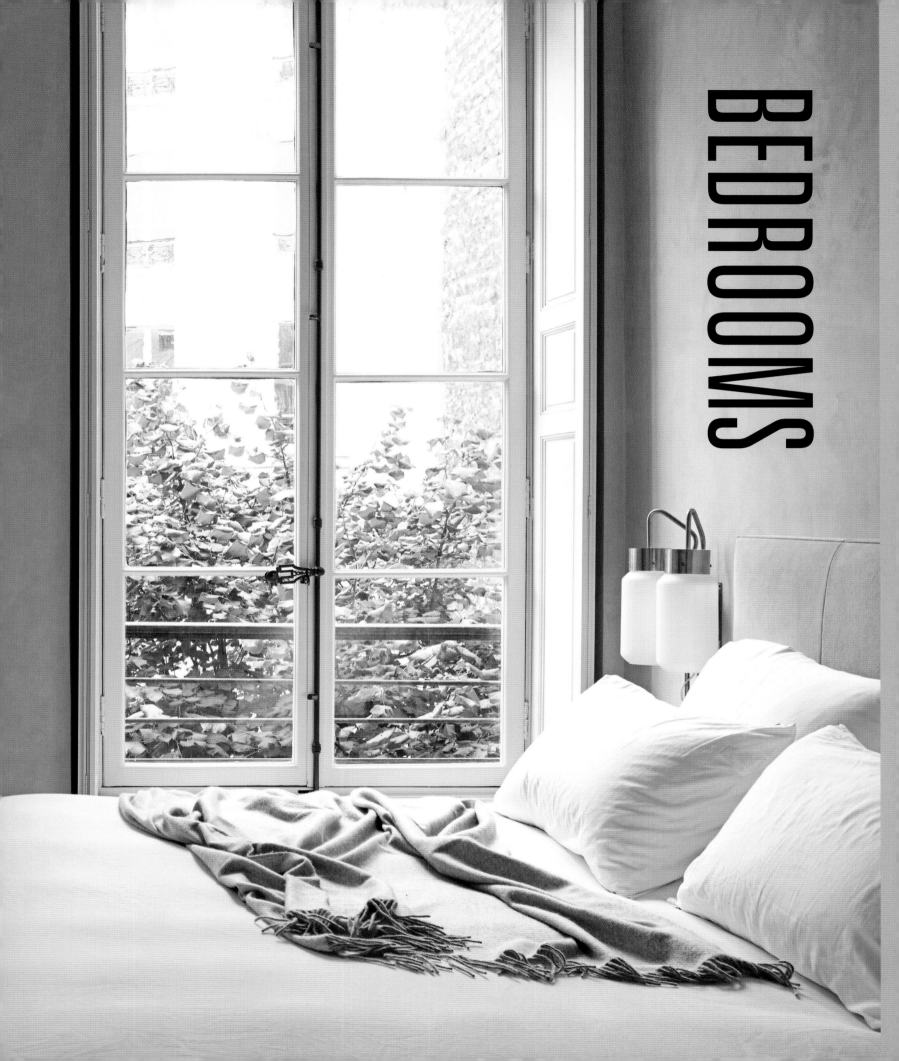

BEDROOMS

OPPOSITE **In an ultra-modern building, the charming vintage style of this bedroom contrasts beautifully with the interior architecture, which is comprised of sleek minimalist lines. The unusual glass partitions offer tantalizing glimpses of what is usually an intimate, personal space – but curtains may be drawn when privacy is required.**

RIGHT **In this traditional bedroom, luxurious textures – such as jacquard fabric, leather, tapestry and sheepskin – have been layered together to create a sumptuous effect. The rich autumnal shades of the rug, bedspread, curtains and antique furniture both enrich and soften the powerful dark green of the walls.**

BELOW RIGHT **The décor of your bedroom can help you to get a good night's sleep. A pared-down, neutral scheme creates a calm atmosphere, so focus on plenty of sleek storage to hide the clutter, and pick a palette of complementary shades that recede rather than draw the eye.**

DESIGN & DECORATION

Bedrooms often get overlooked when it comes to designing a home. Unlike the public rooms in a house – the living space and kitchen – they are less likely to be scrutinized by others, and can consequently fall to the bottom of the 'to do' list.

Yet we all love the treat of staying in a boutique hotel, or harbour nostalgic memories of being snuggled under a floral eiderdown in grandma's cosy spare room, so it's worth taking time over the bedroom, to maximize its potential for comfort and sensuality.

Each of us spends a great deal of time in the bedroom, but for most of it we are asleep; by the age of 50 we will have spent more than 16 years asleep. However, our bedroom is still the first and last thing we see each day, and a well-designed space can do much to ease us pleasantly into the day and soothe us gently to sleep each night. When carefully thought out, it can also be much more than a place to sleep and store clothes, becoming a relaxed haven, somewhere to read, potter, work or just gaze out of the window.

The private nature of bedrooms also offers great decorating opportunities. This is the one room of the house that can be really personal, giving you a chance to experiment. Why not try that dramatic wallpaper or deep-pile carpet, or play with materials, textures and colours that would not work as well in any other room?

It's easy to assume that a bedroom requires less planning than a kitchen or bathroom. But careful consideration of how it will be used and a creative approach to storage can turn a basic sleep space into a brilliantly functioning, beautiful room.

PLANNING

Begin by thinking about all the ways you will want to use the space and incorporate these activities into your plan. Increasingly, we use our bedrooms not just for sleeping and clothes storage, but also for reading, watching TV, maybe even working. Sketch out some plans for the room, thinking carefully about use of space and the best position for your furniture. Would custom-built fitted storage make better use of the room's dimensions than freestanding pieces? Could you position the bed in the centre of the space and build clothes storage behind it? Do you need to store clothes in here, or is there space in another room? Do your homework at this point, and you are less likely to make costly mistakes.

Think about which style you are drawn to. Sometimes, the room itself will point you in the right direction. A low-ceilinged bedroom in a country cottage demands a warm and relaxed look, whereas an anonymous, square room in a new-build home can take a more modern, chic style. Consider your budget, too. You may need funds for major work like joinery, electrics, flooring and plumbing. You will also need to allow money for paint, wallpaper, fabrics and carpet, for fixtures and fittings like lighting, and for finishing touches like rugs, bedding, mirrors and artwork.

RIGHT **Built-in cupboards provide maximum storage capacity while keeping the look sleek and uncluttered. Custom-made to fit the space in question, you'll be able to tailor their style to suit perfectly too, whether you opt for a classic installation, such as this one, or a contemporary flat-panel sliding door.**

ABOVE RIGHT **You might think that you should avoid placing a bed in front of a window, but in actual fact it can work very well – and can give you a lot more layout options, especially if your bedroom isn't particularly large. Here a white-painted metal bedstead ensures that the headboard doesn't block out too much natural light.**

OPPOSITE **Some bedrooms, particularly those in chalet-style properties, loft conversions or attic rooms, have restricted head space in some areas. Make sure you take this into account when you're planning the layout – the eaves can be the ideal place for storage, with through-routes and access to the bed requiring maximum headroom.**

OPPOSITE ABOVE LEFT **A neutral scheme doesn't have to be restricted to shades of grey, white or brown. Here a sludgy khaki adds warmth, with slightly fresher green tones picked out in the room's accessories.**

OPPOSITE ABOVE RIGHT **In a small bedroom, don't assume that you have to opt for a pale colour scheme to maximize the feeling of space. A cocoon-like ambience can be created with darker shades, and this approach might actually be better for rooms which don't benefit from much natural light.**

OPPOSITE BELOW LEFT **If you're looking to evoke a soothing and calming atmosphere, then select complementary shades that tone together harmoniously. Use different textures to create contrast, such as the combination of natural linen and smooth ceramic shown here.**

OPPOSITE BELOW RIGHT **For brighter mornings, even in a room which features a north-facing window, you can't beat some sunny soft furnishings. Here an attention-grabbing print in vibrant blue and yellow steals the show, while softer shades (and luxe textures) feature on the cushions and bedspread.**

ABOVE RIGHT **Think pink. It can create a warm, restful feel, and if you use it carefully you can avoid any hint of 'little girl's bedroom'. Eschew candy shades in favour of more delicate hues (including shell, cameo, blush and buff), and combine with neutrals and natural tones, for a more sophisticated take on the classic feminine boudoir.**

RIGHT **Pastels can be just the ticket for combining with the easy-going white-painted backdrop of beach house architecture – just make sure that the shades are knocked-back and delicate, rather than sweet and saccharine. Here plain pink bedlinen pretties up a room decorated in whites, greys and blues.**

It's traditional to opt for calming colours when you're decorating a bedroom, but that doesn't mean the room must be awash with neutrals, or that you should completely rule out using splashes of bright colour.

BEDROOM PALETTES

Colour is very subjective. A shade that appears refreshing to one person is garish to another; one person's warm is another's gloomy. There are no rules, therefore, about how to paint a bedroom, but it makes sense to steer clear of stimulating shades, or you may struggle to switch off at bedtime.

Remember, too, that whatever colour you choose will be seen mostly in strong morning light and by artificial light at night, so find a shade that can cope with both extremes. If you stick to neutrals, work in lots of texture – rugs, throws, quilts or textured wallpaper – to add visual interest. Dark colours can be warming and sensuous and will help a large or high-ceilinged room feel cosier; olive green, teal and chocolate work well. Bright colours can be stimulating, and they also 'advance', which can make a room feel small, so if your heart is set on a loud shade, try using it as an accent on bedlinen or curtains, or paint it behind the bedhead. This will create focus and give the room personality, but won't distract you at bedtime.

FURNITURE

From a simple bed to a room kitted out with wardrobes/armoires, dressing tables, bedside tables and more, the bedroom can be as cramped or as clutter-free as you choose.

One thing is certain: you will need a bed. A good mattress is a must and the choice of what to put it on is huge. Divans/box springs often offer storage underneath and look elegant topped with floor-skimming sheets or finished with a dramatic headboard. For some vintage character, scour antique shops and markets for old iron bedsteads or French carved wooden frames, or try the high street for a modern take on the elegant sleigh bed or four-poster.

The bed need not be the focal point of the room. You may wish to incorporate a big antique wardrobe/armoire or tall chest of drawers. For further storage, consider blanket boxes, wooden chests and baskets. A whole range of pieces can operate as a bedside table/nightstand: a stool, antique washstand, hatbox or chair. Floating shelves are a slick alternative. The foot of the bed is a good place for a more unusual piece, but think beyond the blanket box that traditionally stood here. A sofa, an ottoman, even a desk can all tuck against the end and function as a footboard.

If your room is large enough, consider incorporating some seating. An armchair or chaise longue will tempt you in during the day to read, relax or just daydream.

FAR LEFT **Bedside tables/nightstands can be made from any object of the right height (roughly the same as the mattress), provided it has a flat surface. Here a section of tree trunk adds a rustic touch to a simply-furnished bedroom, its rough texture contrasting beautifully with the floaty curtains and crisp bedlinen.**

LEFT **If you have the space, a comfy seat is a lovely addition to a bedroom, making the ideal spot to curl up with a book. This 19th-century nursing chair has been given an update with plain white upholstery, which accentuates its curvaceous shape and sumptuous buttoned detailing.**

BELOW LEFT **A butler's tray table is particularly useful for small bedrooms, since when it's not required it can be folded up and leant in a corner – while the tray can also be utilized for bringing breakfast in bed! You'll find a good choice of original antiques and reproduction options available.**

OPPOSITE **An original antique bed is an investment – they don't tend to depreciate provided you look after them, and usually will increase in value as time goes on. However, you may find you need to have a mattress custom made, as the bed's dimensions may differ from the standard sizes that came in with mass production.**

* When you're buying a mattress, don't be influenced by the term 'orthopaedic'. It simply means that the bed is a firmer specification from that manufacturer, not that it is designed especially for those with back pain.

* 100% down duvets are super-soft as, unlike feathers, down is pliable and does not contain a 'spine'. Geese that live in cold climes produce the fluffiest down, so expect to pay more for a Siberian goose-down quilt.

* Airing is essential for natural down duvets and pillows. Give them a regular shake and plump, to circulate air and stop the filling compacting.

* When buying cotton sheets, look out for the thread count – the number of threads per square inch of fabric. Basic cottons will be around 150, good-quality sheets start at around 180, and anything above 200 is a luxury cotton.

* Synthetic duvets are ideal for allergy sufferers, as they can be machine washed at 60 degrees, which kills dust mites.

* If you like to use a blanket with your duvet, spread it underneath the duvet and over a sheet, to prevent the air that traps the warmth inside the duvet being squashed out.

OPPOSITE If an occasional bed is to be used as seating, it's wise to pile it high with pillows and cushions for comfort, and push it right up against the wall so that there's some support behind. Here a simple palette of blue and white helps to create a relaxed, low-key ambience.

LEFT Choosing a very low bed – perhaps a futon or just-off-the-floor platform – can make a room seem larger. However, it's not wise to place a mattress directly on the floor long-term (especially if it's the foam type, or the environment is quite humid), since air circulation is important for avoiding mould growth.

ABOVE RIGHT Cushions and throws are great for dressing a bed – particularly if you've opted for classic white bedlinen and want to inject a little colour into the proceedings – but don't forget they'll need to go somewhere at night. A blanket chest at the foot of the bed can work well to conceal them neatly.

In a room that's designated for sleep, the bed needs both to look great and feel wonderful, so that means mixing beautiful bedding with a quality mattress.

BEDDING & MATTRESSES

If you have a comfortable bed you are, on average, likely to sleep for 42 minutes more each night than if your bed is not comfortable. So it's a good idea to invest in the best quality mattress you can afford. Before buying, spend plenty of time lying on a new mattress in a variety of positions and, if you buy your base separately, remember to make sure the dimensions are exactly compatible.

Duvets come in a wide range, so decide on your budget first. Choose between natural feather fillings and synthetic fibres. Natural materials feel luxurious, are breathable and draw moisture away from the body. They generally last longer than synthetics, too. The most basic natural filling is duck feather and down, which gives a cocooned feel, while pure down is lighter. A synthetic duvet is practical, because you can throw it in your washing machine, but feels less cosy than a feather filling.

Duvets are very popular, but traditional blankets and quilts are a great way to add colour and texture. Try a mixture; blankets make a low-tog duvet warm enough for winter and give that tucked-in feeling.

The bedroom is the place for romantic, indulgent window treatments. Just remember practicality – they need to block out morning light and offer privacy, too.

WINDOW TREATMENTS

When choosing material for blinds/shades or curtains, soft, light-absorbing fabrics give a warm feel, while shiny, reflective surfaces create a cooler, more glamorous atmosphere. If you want an opulent look, allow extra fabric for curtains so that they pool on the floor. Remember that strong sunlight will bleach coloured material, so if your bedroom is sunny, go for a pale or neutral option.

Roman or roller blinds/shades work well on smaller windows, but can be cumbersome on wide windows, and if more than one is fitted across a single pane light will inevitably seep in. Layering works well at a bedroom window. Fit a practical roller blind/shade close to the glass, to block out the morning light and provide privacy, then hang floaty curtains, lace panels or lavish drapes from a rail fitted in front.

If your bedroom faces east, you will need window treatments that block out the early morning sun in summer. You could have an existing pair of curtains lined with blackout fabric, or hang a blackout liner that fits behind your curtains, either on the same rail or clipped onto the curtain.

LEFT **Statement windows might be best left without any dressing at all – especially if the opening mechanism is unconventional, such as with this pivoting pane. There are options such as opaque or reflective window film if you need to ensure privacy, or you might be able to use a row of potted plants or climbers on a trellis outside to help screen against prying eyes.**

ABOVE RIGHT **In a room with plenty of pattern – such as this vintage-style rose wallpaper and pretty duvet set – a simple Roman blind is the best choice (as it is when a room boasts awkward proportions, which is also the case here). The classic striped fabric provides a geometric foil to the romantic floral pattern.**

OPPOSITE **Plantation shutters are a superb choice for small rooms with a pared-down aesthetic, since they don't extend beyond the window area and can be painted to tone in with the rest of the interior woodwork. They also provide some privacy when open, so are great for rooms that are overlooked.**

✳ *As well as blocking out unwanted light, quality blackout fabric is often thermal-lined, so it reflects heat and can help regulate the bedroom temperature during the summer.*

✳ *Shutters are a stylish alternative to fabric window treatments. Typically made of wood, their slats can be moved up and down to let light in or provide complete privacy.*

✳ *Vertical blinds/shades are versatile and inexpensive, but can recall the office. Opt for Venetian blinds/shades in coloured metal or warm wood instead. They can filter light, cut it out totally or pull up to let maximum light in.*

✳ *If your bedroom is overlooked, consider fitting frosted film to some or all of the windowpanes. Available in a range of perforated designs, it allows light in, but provides complete privacy.*

✳ *Modern, top-of-the-range blinds/shades offer solar protection, to prevent flooring or furniture becoming faded in the sun, and also block out heat.*

✳ *Bottom-up roller blinds/shades are ideal for providing privacy for dressing while still letting light in through the top half of the window.*

Lighting can dictate the atmosphere of a room. Take time getting it right in your bedroom to suit morning dressing, late-night reading and everything in between.

LIGHTING

A bedroom is used mostly at each end of the day. While it is a room to relax and prepare for sleep in – demanding soft light – it's also where we dress and put on make-up, which needs strong light. A mix of general, task and mood lighting is therefore essential. Flexibility is key, so ensure lights work independently of each other. Fit dimmer switches for fixed lighting and add freestanding lamps.

Most bedrooms are fitted with a single central pendant, but this provides a flat light that deadens texture, so supplement it with uplighters to create a soothing glow without glare. Downlighters provide an even background light, but are not good fitted above the bed, where the light will shine directly into your eyes. For bedtime reading, a table lamp works well, or go for task lighting in the form of a directable Anglepoise light. Wall-mounted reading lights are a great idea, and free up space on your bedside table.

* *Consider fitting a light inside your wardrobe or closet so that you can find clothes easily.*

* *Wall lights fitted either side of the bed are a stylish way to provide reading light, but be sure that you will always want to keep your bed in the same position before you install them.*

* *Matching bedside lamps either side of a double bed give a stylish, symmetrical look to a bedroom, especially when sited on co-ordinating units.*

* *The central pendant light often gets little use in a bedroom, but dress it up in a twinkling chandelier or oversized shade and it will look good even if it's rarely used.*

* *Rope lights, made of hundreds of LED lights inside a see-through cable, produce a warm glow – perfect in a bedroom. Try trailing them over a headboard or across a mantelpiece or shelf.*

* *Candlelight is seductive and relaxing, ideal at bedtime. Light scented candles for subtle perfume as well as ambient light, but remember to blow them out before you drift off to sleep.*

OPPOSITE ABOVE LEFT **Low-hanging pendants can take the place of lamps, with the benefit of keeping the look streamlined and maintaining the maximum amount of free side table space (and floor space, if a standard lamp might be the other option). It's just a case of choosing the design carefully, so the effect isn't literally dazzling.**

OPPOSITE ABOVE RIGHT **An adjustable, directional standard lamp can provide flexible lighting that's just as useful for reading in bed as it is for creating a cosy ambience – simply angle the shade up or down as appropriate. This design channels industrial chic, reminiscent of early 20th-century desk lamps.**

OPPOSITE BELOW **A pair of matching lamps helps to play up the symmetry in this vintage-chic bedroom. If you want to use lamps of this type for bedtime reading, make sure the bottom of the shade is slightly lower than eye level, so that the light is cast onto your lap rather than into your eyes.**

ABOVE RIGHT **Bedroom lighting should be flexible – sometimes you'll need good light, perhaps if you're getting ready to go out, whereas other times you'll need task lighting, or lower light levels to set a relaxed mood. Using lamps as well as fixtures, and opting for dimmable designs, will help ensure the right ambience at all times.**

RIGHT **Candles can help supplement the lighting scheme when it comes to creating a restful or romantic atmosphere, but always use proper holders and keep them away from flammable materials and draughts (making sure all candles are fully extinguished before you go to sleep). Alternatively, you can buy very realistic LED votives for a similar effect.**

FLOORING

In many rooms of the house, flooring is all about practicality, but in the bedroom you can afford to be more indulgent and choose something that feels as good as it looks.

Bedroom floors experience little traffic and are seldom walked on by outdoor shoes, so a pale or deep-pile carpet can be enjoyed here. Beware of deep pile, however, if you suffer allergies, as they can harbour mites. Similarly, if you have a penchant for breakfast in bed, bear in mind that vacuuming toast crumbs from the shag-pile carpet is hard work.

Natural fibres like coir, seagrass and sisal are hardwearing and look great, but can feel rather hard and prickly underfoot. A good alternative is coir-effect carpet, which has the look and texture of natural fibres, but is made from wool, so it's softer. Wooden boards are a great bedroom option. Wood is warm, stylish and practical. Go for either newly laid boards that are sleek, knot-free and seamless, or just strip and treat the original floorboards for a more relaxed look.

Rugs are a versatile asset to a bedroom, adding softness, colour, warmth and pattern. Choose a sensual sheepskin – next to the bed so it's the first thing your toes sink into in the morning – fluffy flokati or woven mats that add a shot of colour and can be machine-washed.

ABOVE LEFT **Original floorboards are the obvious choice for the vintage chic style** – but it's particularly important in a bedroom to ensure that draughts are minimized. You might be able to fill small gaps with strips of wood, but it might be more effective (and aesthetically pleasing) to re-lay the boards more closely.

ABOVE **This dark, brooding colour scheme of charcoal and mid grey is enlivened with the addition of a Beni Ourain carpet** – which is given even greater prominence within the scheme through its reflection in the huge gilt-framed mirror leaning against the wall.

OPPOSITE ABOVE **Hard floors** – whether wood, stone or ceramic – can really benefit from a textured rug or two, both aesthetically and from a comfort perspective. Placing one right by the bed, so it's the first thing your toes feel when you swing your legs out of bed in the morning, is a particularly savvy choice.

OPPOSITE BELOW **Plant fibre flooring comes in an array of beautiful choices.** Jute is the softest fibre, and so is better for bedroom spaces – you can find it in a variety of textures, from fine weaves to bouclé, and shades of beige from greyish tints to golden tones.

❋ Carpets come in a range of constructions: loop, velvet, twist, pile or pattern. Those made with densely packed pile are the most hardwearing, while plush, velvet-pile and shag-pile carpets are super-soft and luxurious options.

❋ The colour of your flooring can play visual tricks in your bedroom. Light colours recede walls and suit a small space, while dark tones make walls seem nearer, creating a cosy feel in a big room.

❋ Carpet retailers often sell end-of-roll lengths at knock-down prices, so as long as your bedroom is on the smaller side, you could get a much better quality carpet for your budget than you might think.

❋ Good underlay will prolong a carpet's life, so don't cut corners on quality here, and make sure your new carpet is laid by a professional carpet-fitter.

❋ Painting floorboards is a cheap and easy way to hide discoloured wood and ugly knots. Floor paints are available in a huge range of colours, too.

❋ If you have a big budget and want a really individual look, bespoke rugs can be commissioned at many major rug specialists.

❋ Take along colour swatches of the fabrics in your bedroom or a paint chart showing the wall colour when choosing rugs, carpet or floor paint, as it is very hard to remember colours accurately.

* Invest in good-quality wooden or padded clothes hangers for your clothes. Wire versions can stretch garments out of shape.

* If you are having wardrobes/ closets built in, consider having them fitted with small spotlights, which can be fixed to the tops of shelves and over the rails to help you find clothes easily.

* Pine furniture has fallen out of fashion lately, but the wood responds well to a coat of paint. Sand it down first, then prime it, before applying eggshell in the colour of your choice.

* Free up storage space in your wardrobe/armoire by keeping out-of-season garments in zip-up or vacuum-closure plastic clothes bags on a high shelf.

* Clear out your bedroom storage every so often and edit your clothes collection. If you haven't worn the item in the last year, give it to charity.

OPPOSITE **Open shelves offer easy access, which is great when you're getting ready in a rush. Casual clothes are fine kept in neatly folded piles, though some lighter and dressier garments will benefit from being hung – and be particularly careful of fading, if there's no cupboard door or curtain to shield things from direct sunlight.**

LEFT **In period homes, the alcoves either side of a chimney breast are the ideal location for large cupboards, since these pieces will then impose less on the usable floor space of the room. Here a very traditional freestanding wardrobe/armoire has been given a contemporary twist with a coat of grey paint and a flash of fuchsia.**

RIGHT **A much more economical option than sliding doors, a simple curtain can screen off an alcove or nook and transform it into a built-in storage solution. Here the curtain and clothes rails match, for a coherent, polished look.**

BELOW RIGHT **This minimalist bedroom boasts storage furniture that seems to meld into the room's walls, thanks to a clever use of matching colour. A floor-to-ceiling unit echoes the white-painted wall beside it, while a teal sideboard almost disappears into the background too.**

Bedrooms should be relaxing sanctuaries, places to potter around, dress, read and, of course, sleep. So it's vital to work in plenty of storage, because nothing spoils the atmosphere of what should be a peaceful haven faster than clothes strewn everywhere and a floor scattered with shoes.

CLOTHES STORAGE

The principal piece of storage in any bedroom will be the wardrobe/closet, but do you go for custom built or freestanding? Custom-made wardrobes are not necessarily much more expensive than freestanding or flat-pack, and they make the most efficient use of space – vital in a small or awkwardly shaped room. You can also tailor the storage to your own requirements: extra-high hanging rails if you have a lot of dresses, for example, or plenty of shelves if you have clothes that need to be stored folded.

Freestanding wardrobes/armoires, on the other hand, are versatile – you can change their position in the room – and you can take them with you if you move. If you like retro or vintage style, you can pick up old wardrobes on eBay or in second-hand markets for very little money. Whichever you choose, allow for more rail space than you currently have. You are bound to need more in the future, so factor in an extra 20%. A generous rail will also allow clothes to hang properly and makes it easier to find each item when you're dressing.

FINISHING TOUCHES

Whether you love the boutique hotel look or want the cluttered
country vibe, finishing touches bring a bedroom to life.

Mirrors are an essential ingredient in all but the most spartan bedrooms and a floor-
length design is vital for checking your appearance. Fit one inside a wardrobe/closet
door if you want to keep the space clean, or simply prop one against a wall. Take
care to check what the mirror is reflecting, though. It won't look as dramatic if it's
showing everyone all the boxes and bric-a-brac you store under your bed. Mirrors
are easy to pick up second-hand, cropping up in antique shops and flea markets
regularly, so keep your eye out for something with a fabulous frame or pretty
mottled glass, a handsome sign of its age.

Pictures and photos will add personality to your room, but as less is often more
in the bedroom, stick to simple images or small-scale prints, to add interest without
dominating. Remember, too, that the eye feels most comfortable viewing rows of
odd numbers, so it has a central image to alight on. A row of three pictures hanging
above a bed works very nicely.

As the bedroom is a personal space, it's a good place to display treasured photos
or precious ornaments. As few people enter this room, delicate or special pieces are
less likely to be damaged, too.

OPPOSITE ABOVE **Kill two birds with one stone** by hanging jewellery and accessories on wall-mounted hooks. Not only will you keep necklaces and bracelets in a way that prevents them getting tangled, and also ensure they're easily to hand, but you'll create a decorative display, too.

OPPOSITE BELOW **Symmetry can be a wonderful tool,** but make sure the look doesn't become overly regimented. Here a bed has been dressed with two identical sets of cushions, and there are matching nooks and lamps either side – but an off-centre display of three pictures (of different sizes, subjects and styles) avoids monotony.

RIGHT **Because the fireplace is so often the focal point of a room,** the mantelpiece is an ideal prominent spot for a carefully curated collection of favourite decorative items. Here the diverse pieces share a common colour palette of creams and warm metallic tones for a harmonious effect.

BELOW RIGHT **Just one strongly patterned item can lift a scheme** and give it a bit of character – without this geometric cushion, which picks up both the colours of the bedlinen and the wooden headboard, the aesthetic would be much more pedestrian.

BELOW FAR RIGHT **An oversized statement mirror is not only a practical choice** – large looking glasses being much more useful, as well as flattering – but it's a wonderful way to introduce a touch of grandeur, as well as bounce natural light around the room.

* We so often keep them for the living room, but fresh flowers are an easy and inexpensive way to add colour and beauty to a bedroom. Stick to simple bunches of the same bloom, rather than fussy mixed bouquets, for a pretty but tranquil feel.

* A folding screen makes an elegant addition to a bedroom and can be used to partially obscure the window for privacy.

* Instead of hiding jewellery away in boxes, display it. Decorative hooks can hold necklaces, or you could drape them from the frame of a picture or mirror.

* Hang your favourite dresses or shirts from your wardrobe/closet door, so you can enjoy their patterns and colours every day.

* Seek out attractive old pieces that may not have been intended for life in a bedroom. Crystal cake stands, pretty teacups and vases can be used to hold jewellery. Old wooden boxes, tins and suitcases can double as storage and bring character to a simply styled room.

* A welcoming and familiar scent is a key finishing touch for any bedroom. Light scented candles or sprinkle eau de cologne over freshly laundered bedding for subtle perfume.

OPPOSITE **Vintage and reclaimed pieces are often a key part of a contemporary take on country style – and industrial influences can work well. In this bedroom three factory-style light fittings provide flexible and atmospheric lighting, while their metallic patina brings an accent of lustre to a largely neutral scheme.**

RIGHT **Country style doesn't always have to be about rough, rustic finishes. Here crisp white bedlinen echoes the whitewashed brick walls and painted timber ceiling, while a turned wooden bedstead has been polished to bring out the beauty of the natural material, and a faux fur throw ups the comfort factor.**

FAR RIGHT **In this gardener's-hideaway-inspired bedroom, a headboard fashioned from natural branches simultaneously contrasts with the corrugated steel wall and looks completely at home with it. The bedlinen and the cosy knitted throw add a softer touch, but one that is in keeping with the natural aesthetic.**

When well done, a modern makeover of the comfortable cottagey look combines its easy-going rusticity with a contemporary freshness.

MODERN COUNTRY

Modern country style takes the best ingredients from the classic country look and blends them with contemporary touches. Natural materials are vital to anchor the look, so think cotton sheets, woollen blankets, flatwoven rugs and lots of wood. A classic country-style bedroom feels that it has evolved over time, with furniture casually positioned and displays added to and moved around. This relaxed, organic feel is at the heart of modern country style, too, which never looks overstyled or self-conscious and is flexible and welcoming. Colours are predominantly neutral or muted, with plainly painted walls, but fresh modern colours are used as accents – a bright cushion, a patterned rug, floral wallpaper on one wall.

Fabrics and textures that would not belong in a traditional country bedroom can look great in this modern version, so consider mixing in some light-reflecting silk, lush velvet or ethnic weaves. On cushions and throws, sequins or glass beads add sparkle (useful in a dark room), while decadently fluffy sheepskin rugs dyed a strong shade soften wooden floorboards and inject some colour.

Traditional country bedrooms would have a striking bedstead, often in iron or perhaps carved wood, but modern country opts for less obtrusive styles. A plain divan/box spring or four-poster will keep the look light and uncomplicated. Forget piling on blankets, eiderdowns and quilts and instead choose simple bedlinen in white or cream that can be draped with a blanket or throw in a warm shade. It's just one of the ways that the look feels cleaner and less cluttered than the original.

Hunt around in second-hand shops or markets for pieces that have seen a bit of life, for that casual, warm country feel. In addition to units, chests of drawers, old pictures and mirrors are easy to find and will inject personality into your space. Then throw in the odd piece of modern design – a dramatic floor lamp, designer chair or contemporary rug that will strike a modern contrast with any old pieces and original timbers or boards in the room, to bring the space stylishly up to date.

* *Ditch the symmetrical look that's found in so many bedrooms for a looser, more informal arrangement. Choose bedside units/nightstands of different sizes and styles, introduce lamps with varying shades and bases, or position the bed in a corner.*

* *Keep bedroom walls simply painted to fit the modern aesthetic.*

* *Stick to unfussy window treatments like roller or Roman blinds/shades in a fabric that tones with the wall colour.*

* *A woollen blanket or throw draped over the bed adds extra warmth and a subtle note of country style. Choose a plaid or stripe in a soft shade.*

* *Keep the room uncluttered and let a few carefully chosen pieces of much-loved furniture take centre stage. Texture, warm wood and a little pattern or colour will prevent the room feeling sterile.*

* *Floral fabrics are traditionally a stalwart of any country scheme, but a modern take also relies upon contemporary patterns, toile de Jouy textured plains, embroidery, ticking stripes or checks.*

Calming and uncomplicated, white is a great colour for a bedroom. Far from being cold, it can hit just the right note of serenity, perfect where relaxation is key.

WHITE NIGHTS

There are lots of myths about all-white schemes. They feel chilly or sterile, they are not practical, they don't suit some rooms. None is true. In fact, with the right mix of ingredients, using white throughout a space is actually incredibly easy, stylish and versatile. Just follow a few simple tips.

Avoid using pure brilliant white paint, which has optical brighteners in it to give it a really stark effect. This can look too bright and clinical, especially in a bedroom. Instead, choose a basic white emulsion with a more chalky finish, or pick one of the hundreds of off-whites available on the market. Test them as you would a coloured paint, as you may be surprised how 'coloured' they can appear. What looks white in the can may seem purplish, peachy or grey once on the wall.

For a totally white room, paint floorboards white or lay pale carpet, but remember that they will take more looking after as both show up dirt and fluff. If you want a little softness and warmth without spoiling the aesthetic, keep the floorboards in their natural state – the glow of wood fits in well with an all-white room and adds a touch of warmth. Or consider using Danish lye, a traditional treatment that bleaches boards and stops them yellowing.

When it comes to furniture, an easy and inexpensive way to kit out a white bedroom is by picking up old pieces – chests of drawers, tables, chairs, cabinets – at antiques markets or car boot/yard sales. If need be, paint them with some white eggshell. It will hide old marks and ugly knots in the wood and transform even the most battered piece.

To prevent an all-white bedroom looking boring or unwelcoming, mix in plenty of texture. On the bed, layer up blankets, embroidered bedspreads or traditional quilts. Scatter tactile cushions over or dot the floor with toe-tickling rugs in sheepskin or fluffy flokati. Work in some light-reflecting surfaces, too, for subtle sparkle and shine. Prop old mirrors against the wall or on a tabletop, choose photo frames made from glass, shell or glossy painted wood and hang a twinkling chandelier. This will all add personality and richness to a one-shade scheme.

RIGHT **There's no danger of a white-on-white bedroom appearing cold if you combine subtly different shades of white. Here a slightly putty-coloured bed and table sit in front of a brighter white wall, while an almost-cream lamp, wicker basket, and natural timber floor add warmth.**

LEFT **Crisp white bedlinen – perhaps plain, perhaps with a small self-coloured embroidered detail – is an absolute classic. Combined with a white bedstead, white walls, and floaty curtains, it can take on an almost ethereal quality (which is grounded here by the use of rustic and vintage elements, too).**

OPPOSITE **Texture will prevent an all-white scheme from appearing unremarkable and flat just as effectively as introducing a variation in shades of white. Here the distressed paint finish on the bedside chair and the decorative white bedspread help create interest as much as the touches of cream and metallic accents in evidence.**

❋ *Every paint manufacturer makes inexpensive standard white. Keep a pot to hand to paint over marks easily.*

❋ *Shop around for old white furniture with a few knocks. It will fit in with the all-white look, but without looking too pristine and edgy.*

❋ *Don't be too 'strict' about your white bedroom scheme. You might include grey or palest cream – use them on floors or old furniture – to introduce variety and interest.*

❋ *Use baby wipes to clean marks and smudges off white paintwork.*

❋ *Keep pattern subtle and restricted. A single wall of wallpaper, for example, or a delicately embroidered bedspread will add interest without spoiling the calm, balanced feel.*

❋ *Bring in natural colour with plants and flowers. Put a few sprigs in a selection of old jars or glasses, or include the odd pot of an easy-to-grow plant like ivy or mind-your-own-business.*

* Mix feminine, curvy furniture, such as a French carved bed, with pieces that have a more masculine feel; a battered leather armchair or dark wooden chest of drawers, for example.

* Play with scale. Curtains adorned with oversized blooms will look great next to wallpaper with a small-scale pattern of tiny sprigs on a pale background.

* Beware of the bedroom becoming too pink. Soft plums, mauves, sage green and watery blue are good colours to incorporate, and should be balanced by creams and antique white.

* Old china can be bought cheaply at markets or junk shops and adds a shot of floral romance, on a small scale.

* An old iron bedstead is the perfect partner for traditonal floral bedding. Many new versions of classic bedstead designs are available, or scour antique fairs and markets for an original.

When we think of florals we often picture a cottage pattern with big blossomy roses in pinks and reds, but there are numerous variations on this flowery theme.

ROMANTIC FLORALS

From the 1950s-style florals revived by Cath Kidston to modern, abstract versions, from tiny sprigs across an all-white background to oversized blooms amid a sea of colour, there is a floral to suit most tastes.

While florals add a touch of romance to any bedroom, they need not look ultra-feminine or twee. Choose muted or earthy shades rather than pink tones, or pick a pattern of trailing stems with only the occasional flower, to suggest a floral style without splashing blooms all over.

The walls are the biggest surface area in any room, and a floral bedroom often incorporates wallpaper, which transforms a plain room to a flowery oasis in a few rolls. Use it on just one wall as an accent or take your bedroom to floral heaven by papering it on walls and ceiling for a cosy, but tongue-in-cheek look. Modern wallpaper designers usually have their own take on the classic floral, so check them out, or plunder the archives for old prints that still look fresh today.

Textiles with floral patterns are widely available. For the bed, pick a pretty duvet cover or have fun layering quilts, sheets and bedspreads for a more ad hoc look. Shop on the high street, or track down antique florals in specialist shops or on the internet. The window is another part of the room that can benefit from the romantic floral look. Pretty curtains peppered with sprigs or a Roman blind/shade in a bold floral pattern that can still be glimpsed when rolled up suit this scheme. You might even have a plain headboard upholstered in a floral fabric. Remember to keep an eye on the balance. Too many florals, in too many different designs, will look busy and chaotic, so stick to florals that tone in together and use them in just one or two places in the room.

For small hits of floral prettiness, look out for lampshades or cushions or beautifully painted screens that will contribute to the look without making it claustrophobic. And don't forget fresh flowers, too – the original and still the best romantic floral.

OPPOSITE **In a more traditional-style treatment, dramatic and impactful florals are often reserved for smaller items such as cushions, while smaller-scale designs are often chosen for bigger items, such as this quilt. Picking colours from the prints, to reflect in the room's accessories, also helps draw the scheme together.**

ABOVE **Checks and gingham can be great partners for a vintage-style floral, especially if you're looking to create a casual, feminine look. In this shabby chic bedroom, a distressed, rusty bedstead provides a foil to the sherbet colours and pretty patterns of the quilt and cushion.**

RIGHT **Although this wallpaper and bedlinen don't match, they are strikingly similar. It can be difficult to combine almost-identical patterns, although selecting two designs with the same scale and colour palette will go a long way to ensuring success. Other decorative elements have been kept to a minimum to allow the busy florals maximum impact.**

LEFT **A glamorous boudoir doesn't need to eschew fresh white bedlinen – just make sure that your sheets and bedspreads have got a high thread-count and elegant detailing, and are ironed to perfection. Here the effect of the very dark walls, with pale lamp, curtains and bed reversed out against them, is very intense and refined.**

RIGHT **With such opulent interior architecture – namely the fabulous moulded cornice – there wasn't really any other style quite so befitting for this space as grown-up glamour. Shades of cream, blush and shell pink create a relaxed, feminine feel, while black accents add drama to the scheme.**

GROWN-UP GLAMOUR

Any bedroom can be transformed from basic to glamorous. For pure grown-up glamour, just add plenty of luxurious touches, tactile fabrics and subtle colours.

Think about colours first. Grown-up glamour rejects whites and neutrals in favour of colours that are muted, but not sludgy. Watery blues, dusky pinks, greys, purples and mossy greens all suit a glamorous scene – nothing too bright, nothing too earthy. Deft touches of silver and gold can work, too, but keep them to a minimum to prevent the look becoming too glitzy. Use colour on walls, bedding and accessories, but keep your flooring simple to help balance the look.

Furniture should blend beauty with practicality. A dressing table is a key piece. The perfect place to preen, it also looks pretty and elegant when not in use. Triple mirrors were typically fitted to dressing tables, so you can see your face from any angle, but they also help bounce light around the room and catch interesting reflections. A beautiful bed with a striking or unusual headboard is another essential ingredient. Team a tall, padded headboard with a plain divan/box spring for that boutique hotel feel, or hunt for an old French carved wooden bed, complete with part-padded head- and footboards, or an unusual metal frame. The bed must make a glamorous statement, even when dressed in plain linen.

Glossy and reflective surfaces are central to the grown-up glamour look. Freestanding mirrors propped against a wall and draped with sparkling jewellery look stunning, or look out for a mirrored console table, bedside table/nightstand or dressing table. Choose wallpapers with a slight sheen and perhaps throw in a satin bedspread, to add a subtle glimmer to the bed.

An armchair is a great addition if you have space. Choose something elegant, like an ornate French piece, or tactile, like a thick-armed, low chair in velvet. It all adds to the impression that in this bedroom one can linger, relax and daydream.

Mix in a few splashes of luxury, too, that are wonderful to gaze at or touch: lush fabrics like velvet and silk; thick pillows and soft cushions, heaped on the bed; a chandelier or ornate lamp; silk curtains, pooling on the floor or tied back into deep sweeps. Anything pleasing to the eye and the skin is vital for a glamorous feel.

* *Panels of vintage lace hung at a window look glamorous and help filter light and provide privacy.*

* *A large, statement piece of furniture suits this kind of bedroom. If it isn't the bed, make it an oversized chest of drawers, elegant side table on which you can arrange favourite accessories or an ornate French armoire that will hold all your clothes.*

* *Curtains look more glamorous than blinds/shades, which are too neat and minimal for this style. Fit curtains to the floor for a luxurious feel.*

* *Pay attention to details. Install pretty light switches, door handles, drawer knobs and sockets – you touch and use them every day and they can really lift the appearance of a room.*

* *Grown-up glamour is all about quality, but not necessarily brand-new materials, so shop in both antique stores and on the high street when putting together this look.*

THIS PAGE **Crisp linens, sculptural furniture, beautifully framed art and the clever use of accent colours (a touch of gilt here, some black trim there) leave us in no doubt that this is the bedroom of a connoisseur — a connoisseur of glamorous living.**

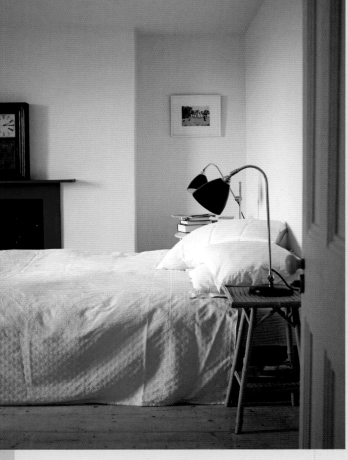

ABOVE LEFT **When taking a Spartan approach to furnishing and using a neutral palette for the décor, make sure to include some sumptuous textural touches, to avoid the ambience from seeming too frugal to be relaxing and welcoming. Here a deeply buttoned, oversized headboard adds a touch of luxury to a very pared-down space.**

LEFT **White bedlinen is a classic that will never date. Whether plain or with self-coloured patterning – perhaps a stripe, check or floral – it's a great investment, so do buy the best that you can afford. Egyptian cotton is considered superior, and a high thread count can be a good marker of quality too.**

ABOVE **A pared-down look doesn't have to be neutral – here a number of pretty pastel shades have been used to create a relaxed, feminine air. With mint green panelled walls, a pale blue fabric-covered headboard and a white side-table, there's a definite vintage vibe, while blowsy peonies and some favourite garments add a decorative accent.**

SIMPLE RETREATS

Pared-down and unfussy – but never lacking in comfort – the simple approach to bedroom décor is not only an easy option, but one that creates the perfect relaxing ambience.

The first thing to remember when you're creating a simple retreat is to embrace blank space rather than feel the urge to fill it with an unnecessary piece of furniture or artwork. This is not a style which calls for slowly-pieced-together collections of flea-market glassware, or the perfect combination of vintage prints – by all means take your time to build the look, but because the pared-down aesthetic calls for relatively few elements, you'll find it fairly hassle-free.

Because of the lack of decorative detailing, this is an aesthetic that often suits paler, warmer colour schemes. Darker and cooler shades can be unforgivingly stark without the option to soften the effect with some carefully chosen accessories or a wall full of pictures, plus the sort of design influences you might want to consider – Scandi style, minimalism, hotel luxe, vintage chic – tend to lean towards such a palette. That said, a shot or two of bright colour might be just the ticket for enlivening the space (just don't get too carried away).

Furnishings should be modest. A plain divan/box spring (perhaps either without a headboard, or at least with a very simple, neutral design) or a utilitarian metal bedstead will look the part, while bedside tables/nightstands should be small and simple (or use a stool or chair instead). Fitted cupboards/closets that don't draw the eye are the ideal choice, though an unpretentious, clean-lined wardrobe/armoire or chest of drawers are very suitable too.

Pattern should be used sparingly – perhaps just one or two small elements – though creating contrast with texture is a thoroughly viable alternative. Team crisp linens with a touchy-feely throw, sleek enamel wall lamps with chalky matt walls, and sumptuous upholstery with rustic surfaces.

* *While the odd luxe touch can elevate this sort of scheme into something special, don't overdo the fine finishes. The idea is to keep the look unpretentious and relaxed.*

* *If you decide to use pattern, don't opt for a design that's too busy. Small-scale florals or sprig designs can be a good choice for a more feminine take on the look, while contemporary simple retreats might be better suited by a geometric.*

* *Wooden floors (with an oiled or varnished finish) are a particularly suitable choice for this type of pared-down style, because they bring a significant amount of warmth and texture into the space without dominating it too much.*

* *Make sure you've thought very carefully about where you're going to keep all your clothes, linens and other belongings, as this sort of look cannot tolerate clutter of any kind. A storage bed is a wise choice – especially the ottoman style – since it can offer a huge storage capacity.*

BATHROOMS

THIS PAGE **In a room with high ceilings and period detailing a classic roll-top bath really looks the part, while a table-style vanity unit also plays up the historic feel – and its marble top adds a luxurious touch, contrasting beautifully with the shabby chic elements of the room.**

RIGHT **As well as being practical for a small bathroom, making the most of the floor area, and facilitating easy cleaning, fitted furniture can also create a sleek aesthetic that gives the impression of more space. Keeping the look coordinated (such as here, where the mirror matches the cabinetry) will also help.**

FAR RIGHT **In a bathroom with an understated appeal, a statement mirror will shift the look up a gear from 'satisfactory' to 'splendid'.**

Here an unusual design, crafted from a slice of a gnarled tree trunk, adds a distinctive air while at once being thoroughly in tune with the neutral aesthetic.

BELOW RIGHT **White on white is a timeless scheme. Here a built-in tub has been given prominence through its central placement (in line with the window) and an additional aesthetic lift with the use of a warm-toned timber surface to contrast with the room's painted panelling.**

Creating a new bathroom or updating an existing one is something you can't afford to do too often, but get it right and it will add value to your home in more ways than one. It is all about practicality plus wellbeing.

DESIGN & DECORATION

Today's bathroom must be functional, of course, but it should also be a sensual and sybaritic space, a private oasis where you can unwind. Getting this twofold formula right takes thought and careful planning, so before you start choosing hardware, consider exactly what you want.

Browse through magazines and websites for inspiration. Many bathroom manufacturers now provide room sets (both in-store and online) to show you how a finished design will look. Consider the shape and size of your bathroom and think what arrangement would work best in the space. If you have a tiny cubicle, perhaps a wet room is the answer? Can you squeeze in a big, sculptural bath? Would a separate toilet be the solution to early-morning congestion? By analysing your needs at the outset, you'll save yourself time and money later on.

Once you have a favoured layout, think about what look you would like to achieve. Do you want a traditional bathroom or something streamlined and modern? A simple white scheme or strong colour or dynamic pattern? Today, there are so many different options for sanitary ware and surfaces; you may find a particular design or material will set the tone for the whole room.

Designing a new bathroom can be a rewarding creative experience, but don't forget that – above all – the space has to be functional and safe. It is essential to plan the project very carefully and to obtain advice about structural, plumbing and electrical issues before you start.

PLANNING

Just how much professional guidance you require depends on the size of the job, but if you are planning any major changes, it is generally worth calling in the experts. Architects, designers and even many bathroom suppliers can help you decide exactly which fixtures and fittings are right for the space and answer tricky technical questions. Is the water pressure sufficient for that power shower? Can the floor be raised to accommodate a sunken tub? Can the position of the toilet be changed?

You might be eager to start picking tiles and choosing paint colours, but it is vital to sort out the nitty gritty of the room right at the start. Think about heating. Is there enough space for an underfloor solution, and could you afford it? Take into account the position of drainage pipes and consider how to conceal them (the professionals will be able to help here). And don't forget about including custom-built fitted storage; the more you have, the easier it will be to keep the bathroom free of clutter.

One last, crucial, task is to consider the cost of a new bathroom. Shop around for good deals and be prepared to spend as much on advice and installation as you do on fixtures and fittings. Set yourself a budget and stick to it.

ABOVE RIGHT **In a cloakroom or small bathroom, eschew large basins and have a look at the many compact designs available. This one features a handy surface to the right hand side, allowing space for soap (and a few decorative accessories, if you like), which means the design can be shallower in depth and still practical.**

ABOVE FAR RIGHT **In a large room, consider ways of avoiding the fixtures all being placed around the edge, which can create a large empty space in the middle. Here a mid-height partition wall allows the bathtub to be positioned at right angles to the wall, and separates it from the WC on the other side.**

RIGHT **When you've got a sizeable space and a real showstopper of a freestanding tub, placing it centrally is the only way to go. Such a project will involve some significant under-floor works, to ensure drainage and water supply are in the right place – in which case why not add a wet-room-style shower, too?**

OPPOSITE **Bespoke shower enclosures work with the room's interior architecture, not only delivering the largest showering space possible, but also the sort of considered aesthetic that shows any space off to best advantage. This example features a tiled floor (which will have been tanked) rather than a bespoke shower tray.**

OPPOSITE **Family-friendly bathrooms will necessarily be less 'minimalist retreat' and more 'busy bathing zone', but storage can help you keep a handle on the potential chaos. A receptacle for bathtime toys, a basket for discarded dirty laundry and a wall-mounted cabinet (to safely lock away medicines) are all essential elements.**

ABOVE RIGHT **Avoid delicate surfaces in a family bathroom – they won't stay pristine for long. Tiled walls will help to ensure that the inevitable splashes won't leave marks or cause damp issues, while using a bathroom-suitable paint formula (water-resistant, and preferably scrubbable) will provide protection for plaster or wood surfaces.**

BELOW RIGHT **It's the little things that can make all the difference. A towel that's hung at the right height, and a step to enable them to use the WC and basin unaided, will help young children learn to be more independent when it comes to some essential life skills.**

If you don't have the luxury of multiple bathrooms, it is important to make sure the one you have caters to the needs of the whole family. Think about how and when the space is used and try to include family-friendly elements in its design so that it functions effectively at all times.

FITTING IN THE FAMILY

If you and your partner are always jostling for space in the morning, consider installing two washbasins instead of one, or even side-by-side baths if you have the space, the money and the inclination. The bathroom can be a sociable as well as a functional room, so take this into account when you are planning the layout and leave room – if you can – for a comfortable chair or cushioned bench.

If you have small children, try to make the design work as well for them as it does for you. Opt for baths and basins with rounded edges rather than sharp corners and make sure that the floor is nonslip, even when wet. Safety is a key issue in the bathroom, and with a little careful planning you can take practical steps to reduce unnecessary accidents. Underfloor heating gets rid of the need for radiators or heated towel rails/bars with their exposed hot pipes, for example; a twin-ended bathtub (one with the taps/faucets in the middle rather than at the end) creates safe and comfortable space for a child at each end.

To reduce the risk of scalding, go for a mixer tap/faucet rather than individual hot and cold spouts or, to eliminate the problem altogether, opt for a thermostatic version with built-in temperature control. It is also sensible to include a pull-out shower handset in the bath surround, even if you have a separate shower, for easy hair-washing.

We all want our bathroom to be clean and clutter-free, so encourage your children to keep it tidy. Fit hooks at child height so they can hang up towels and face cloths easily (plastic suction hooks work well on the side of the bath) and include easy-access storage space for bath toys, soaps and toothbrushes.

BATHTUBS & BASINS

The layout of your bathroom may dictate the size of your sanitary ware, but what about the material and the design? Choosing from the array of styles can be a daunting task.

Selecting the bathtub should be first on the list because, as the biggest feature, it will dictate the look of the rest of the room. Consider which shape would suit the space best. A freestanding, central tub can look dynamic in a big room; a corner model could be the perfect solution in a smaller one. Don't be afraid to try before you buy. You are going to be lying in there, after all, so comfort is key.

Most bathtubs these days are made of acrylic, which is warmer than steel and less likely to chip, but if your budget will stretch to it do consider the alternatives. Natural materials, such as stone or wood, work brilliantly in the bathroom; or opt for a design in a cutting-edge material, such as lightweight resin or recycled plastic. These should offer you a wide choice of colour, too.

Choose a basin that complements the bathtub in shape and colour, even if it is not part of a ready-made 'suite', and consider carefully the design of the basin unit/vanity. Modern wall-hung versions look neat and streamlined, but make sure your walls are strong enough to bear the weight. Splashes are hard to avoid here, so ensure the basin and its surround can drain effectively, and invest in quality taps/faucets that work aesthetically with the room.

The neatest toilets sit flush to the wall so the plumbing is concealed, but make sure that you can still access the cistern and pipework. And do your bit for the planet by installing a dual flush system that will limit water wastage.

ABOVE LEFT **Original cast iron bathtubs can be very heavy – so do check the strength and stability of the floor structure before choosing one. That said, there are reproduction designs available which offer the same classic look, but are made in modern composite materials, which are much lighter.**

ABOVE **Hewn from a piece of natural rock, this basin sits on an appropriately rustic-style wooden vanity, while a minimalist tap/faucet offers a contrast to the organic materials. Granite, marble, onyx and travertine are among the available stone basin choices, or for an opulent look you could choose a semi-precious example in agate or amethyst (if your budget will stretch).**

OPPOSITE ABOVE LEFT **A classic roll-top tub can either stand in the middle of the room, with standpipe-mounted taps, or close to a wall, in which case there's the option to have the brassware wall-mounted for a sleeker – and therefore easier to clean – take on the look.**

OPPOSITE ABOVE RIGHT **A simple ceramic basin can suit a farmhouse-style bathroom, or it can be the ideal neutral choice in a space that's got a more exotic appeal. Here the use of Zellige tiles and an iridescent mirror adds a more glamorous edge to the grey palette, humble basin and old-fashioned cupboard doors.**

OPPOSITE BELOW LEFT **A table-style vanity unit is a great choice if you're looking to keep the look light – but make sure you choose a trap and waste that stands being on show (chrome or stainless steel are the usual options, though copper and brass are available).**

OPPOSITE BELOW RIGHT **This large bathroom features a centrally-placed bath, which effectively separates the space into two zones. The bath is encased in marble, for a luxurious look, and to provide a welcome variation from the white, minimalist treatment of the rest of the room.**

OPPOSITE **Wet rooms are often thought of as stark, minimalist spaces – but there's no need to subscribe to that aesthetic when creating one. Here a shower space includes a curved wall, while a richly coloured shimmering mosaic ensures that the ambience is warm and welcoming.**

RIGHT **Tanking and well-planned drainage have enabled a relatively small space to be transformed into a bathroom which feels luxurious in its spaciousness, despite the industrial-style wall and floor surfaces. The sculptural form of the freestanding bath is able to take centre stage without being visually impeded by a shower enclosure.**

BELOW RIGHT **In a smaller wet room you might like to control the splashes from a shower rather than leave the whole space open, in which case it's best to opt for a frameless glass partition. This one is supported by chrome rods, allowing access on both sides, keeping the look light.**

Showering in an open space, unhampered by steamy cubicle walls or damp shower curtains, is a luxurious experience. To make it work takes preparation.

WET ROOMS

Whether you want a self-contained wet room or an open shower within a bathroom, you need to make the room absolutely watertight before you start. The best approach is to get the area sealed by a professional, who will cover the floor and walls with an impermeable membrane. This can then be topped with your choice of covering; bear in mind that stone and tiles should also be sealed if porous.

The existing floor may need to be strengthened and should be sloped slightly so water can easily drain into the waste outlet. The outlet can be central or, better still, tucked neatly against the wall if you opt for a modern linear design. If there is space, consider installing underfloor heating.

Sealing a bathroom is an expensive business. To get the look for less, fit a shower tray so that it sits flush with the floor. Unless it is made bespoke, however, you will be restricted to standard sizes.

A wet room is just the place for a power shower, so hunt around for suitably extravagant water features. Consider installing a pump to guarantee a good jet. As for fixtures and fittings, wall-mounted models are best, allowing you to keep the floor clear. Include a small shelf or alcove for stashing shampoos and soaps.

SMALL BATHROOMS & SHOWER ROOMS

With some careful planning and a few decorative tricks, even the smallest bathing area can be turned into a sybaritic sanctuary. Make sure the layout of the room is as efficient as possible, and use every available bit of space.

Think first about stealing space from elsewhere. If your shower room is cramped, can you raise the ceiling or drop the floor? Is it possible to extend your mini bathroom into an adjacent bedroom, or to create an en-suite with a screen or sliding door, which needs less room than a hinged one?

If this can't be done, then build as much hidden storage into a bathroom as you can, creating a cupboard in the area above the door, for example, or inside a panelled bath. Wall-mount fixtures and fittings and invest in space-saving kit – a corner bath or a fold-down towel rail/rod.

A shower room requires less space, particularly if you opt for a ready-made cubicle. Choose the biggest and most comfortable you can, with as many built-in features as possible. Some now come with integral seats, lighting and even steam or sauna options (though these will demand good ventilation).

When it comes to decoration, choose surfaces that are light and reflective and use mirrors to expand the room visually. A mirror can double the space; opt for acrylic over glass if the walls can't bear the weight.

ABOVE **In a small or awkwardly shaped room, consider whether installing a sliding pocket door might allow you to design a better layout – without the door swinging inwards, you can gain a surprising amount of useable floor area. Alternatively, hang the door so it opens outwards.**

ABOVE RIGHT **A vibrant colour palette doesn't need to be avoided in a small space, but do make sure that you keep the treatment bold, with a simple, pared-down aesthetic. Here the minimalist chrome brassware has been deliberately chosen to let the glossy blues tiles do all the talking.**

OPPOSITE **Just because a room is compact doesn't mean you have to avoid freestanding-style furniture – just make sure you choose pieces with more modest dimensions, and always measure up carefully before making a scale drawing, so that you can be sure there's comfortable room between the elements.**

OPPOSITE **Naturals are easy to combine, especially against a backdrop of soft, chalky white. Here pale-, mid- and dark-toned timbers have been used with a beautiful piece of natural stone in a mottled warm grey, while metallic accents provide a touch of contrasting glamour.**

RIGHT **In a period-style bathroom a strong shade can create an opulent, traditional look – this deep plum hue offers a dramatic foil to the pretty, old-fashioned hand basin and high-level WC, as well as a collection of old prints and oval antique mirror.**

FAR RIGHT **This particular shade of green – almost reminiscent of the verdigris on copper – is very much appropriate for an Art Deco palette, and therefore works beautifully with sanitary ware which evokes the era, such as this sink with its angular detailing and upstand.**

BELOW RIGHT **Whether you buy a new or reclaimed example, cast iron bathtubs can be painted almost any shade – coordinating with the paint on the bathroom walls can be a wise choice, as it creates instant coherence. Some manufacturers even offer colour-matching services.**

BATHROOM PALETTES

White is often the first choice for the bathroom. Bright and pure, it can make the tiniest space seem clean and airy. But strong colour and pattern can work, too, if you're brave enough to experiment.

Consider first what kind of look you are after: a bold, modern statement or a pretty, subtle scheme? And flick through books and magazines to discover which colours and finishes inspire you. Buy tester pots of paint and get samples of materials you like – tiles, stone, wallpaper – so that you can see how they will work in your space.

A simple and effective option is to go for the monotone room, where one colour is used for walls, floors and surfaces. This wraparound effect creates a cohesive feel and works well when offset with white baths and basins. Or why not get your sanitary ware to co-ordinate? Contemporary bathroom kit comes in all kind of colours, and an old bath can be repainted or repanelled to fit in.

A neutral scheme is also successful, particularly when teamed with natural materials. By keeping the backdrop subtle, the textures and patina of stone, slate or cork, for example, will shine through. Conversely, a bold, high-gloss look also works brilliantly, as well as being practical.

If you are after more dramatic decoration, consider creating a feature wall or floor. With countless options out there, from photo-wallpaper to intricately patterned mosaic panels, getting creative has never been so easy.

LEFT **For the ultimate relaxing ambience while having a soak in the tub, you can't beat the warm glow of candlelight. Antique candelabras or sconces are great accessories for the period-style or vintage-inspired bathroom, while huge pillar candles and votives offer a sleeker look that more befits a contemporary space.**

BELOW **It's wise to check the specific regulations in your area before settling upon your lighting scheme – many will dictate that fixtures must meet certain safety standards if they are to be installed in a bathroom. This lovely exposed bulb fitting is hung far enough away from the basin to be safe and compliant.**

OPPOSITE **A grand period room cries out for a chandelier – though you'll need to add some task lighting too, since this type of fitting will only provide atmospheric ambient light (and a design with candle-style exposed bulbs will need to be fitted with fairly low wattage examples, to avoid discomfort when looking at it).**

Today's bathroom is a sensual space. It needs good bright task lighting, of course, but also its antithesis – a soft glow to bathe by. The solution is in the mix.

LIGHTING

Safety has to be the first consideration when you are planning a lighting scheme for the bathroom. Water and electricity can be a dangerous combination and, thus, there are tight regulations governing what lights you can have in 'wet' areas and where you can put them. Before buying anything, check out the guidelines. However, the rules need not be restrictive. There is a wealth of interesting and innovative fixtures and fittings out there and, if you look beyond the standard bathroom kit, it is still possible to create an individual scheme that is right for you.

Whether you are revamping an existing bathroom or creating one from scratch, it's worth identifying first exactly how much light you need and where you need it. Rather than opting for the classic overhead solution, it is better to think in terms of layers of light or a scheme that mixes a variety of different options. You may want strong task lighting when you are shaving or putting on make-up, for example, but a much softer wash of light for an evening soak in the tub.

✳ *Safety is a key issue when it comes to bathroom lighting, so make sure to consult a qualified electrician before you start planning your scheme.*

✳ *There are regulations about what lights can be used in a bathroom and where; for example, you may need to enclose bulbs. Read up on the rules before you go shopping.*

✳ *Don't limit yourself to one light source; your lighting needs will change at different times of the day. Combine bright task lighting with a more moody ambient option to give yourself flexibility.*

✳ *To save on energy, maximize daylight wherever you can. Light colours, glossy surfaces and mirrors will all make the most of the available natural light.*

✳ *Think carefully about the position of your lights. While you might want a brightly lit mirror, remember that an overhead light can cause unflattering shadows.*

✳ *You don't have to stick to standard fixtures and fittings; consider the alternatives. There are so many innovative solutions available, from submersible bath lights to colourful fibre optics.*

ABOVE LEFT Concrete flooring matches a built-in basin plinth exactly, creating a coherent look, and enhancing the feeling of space. The scheme is prevented from embracing full-on minimalism by the addition of an elegant chandelier, matching wall sconce and ornate gilt mirror.

LEFT Original floorboards make a charming – and inexpensive – flooring option, but you must seal them (varnish, wax polish or oil), and keep on top of regular re-finishing to maintain water resistance. It's also wise to use a good bath mat and mop up splashes speedily.

ABOVE Ceramic tiles are practical, low-maintenance and inexpensive – but watch out because certain types can be slippery when wet, so a non-slip mat is advisable. These tiles are also very suitable for laying over underfloor heating, and come in a variety of colour and design options.

THIS PAGE **Here stone flags provide a lovely neutral mid-grey, with a slight variation of shade, to add a natural texture to a sleek white-painted room. They work beautifully with the natural timber accents, and provide a foil to the flat white of the composite bath.**

Rubber, concrete, vinyl, mosaic – options for the bathroom floor have never been greater. Make sure whichever material you choose will give you a floor that's comfortable underfoot and easy to clean, durable, functional and good-looking.

FLOORING

A new floor needs an under-surface that is solid and even – whether it's a concrete foundation or existing floorboards. And, if you are planning to top it with a heavy material like stone, it should be strong enough to support its weight. It's advisable to get advice from a professional before you begin.

At this point, too, think about underfloor heating. It can work brilliantly in the bathroom, where it can warm up cold materials like marble or ceramic tiles and get rid of the need for radiators in what is often a small room. However, it is a luxury option and should be fitted by an expert.

Safety underfoot is paramount in the bathroom, so choose a material that won't be slippery when wet – natural slate, perhaps, or textured mosaic. If you must have a smooth stone surface, keep it away from the shower area and add a large mat to prevent accidents. Don't forget, too, that stone is porous and needs to be properly sealed to prevent staining.

Alternatively, opt for eco-friendly cork or bamboo – both perfect for damp areas and sustainable. Lino and vinyl are ideal, too; easy to lay, they can also camouflage uneven floors and come in countless colours.

* *New flooring can sometimes be laid on top of old if the existing surface is dry, flat and stable. It's a good idea to get advice from the experts before you rip up what is already there.*

* *In a shower area or wet room, it's crucial that the floor is not slippery when wet. Choose rougher, textured materials here to give good grip.*

* *The bathroom floor is often the smallest in the house, so it's just the place to splash out on a luxury material without breaking the budget.*

* *If you opt for coloured mosaic or ceramic tiles, use a grout to match, giving a seamless modern finish. And make sure the grout is mould-resistant and waterproof in a wet room or beneath a shower.*

* *Intricately patterned mosaic will make an impact on the floor, but it is expensive. To lower the cost, opt for a few 'feature' panels in an otherwise plain floor.*

* *Wood looks good on a bathroom floor, but use engineered boards to avoid warping.*

STORAGE

Damp towels, wet soap, half-empty shampoo bottles – the bathroom is a prime spot for mess. But with plenty of well-planned storage solutions, you can conquer the clutter and keep your bathing space calm, clean and tidy.

If you are creating a new bathroom from scratch, build as much storage as possible into the fabric of the room itself. Carve alcoves into a shower wall for stashing shampoos (if the wall is thick enough) or squeeze a cupboard into an awkward space at the end of the tub. In a large room you could create a run of cupboards along one wall. Decorated to match the room, these will 'disappear' when the doors are closed.

Alternatively, build around your sanitary ware. A vanity cupboard beneath the basin can house boxes and bottles without taking up too much space. Or why not raise the bath slightly so that you can fit a couple of drawers for towels underneath? And invest in some ready-made 'secret' storage solutions: a mirrored cabinet, for example, or a hollow seat-cum-chest.

If your bathroom is tiny, maximize the potential of whatever you have. Hang hooks underneath a shelf so you can make use of the top and the bottom, for example, or buy a shower curtain with useful pockets.

You don't have to hide everything away, but keep what is on show neat and tidy, and choose containers that can cope with a moist environment.

ABOVE LEFT **Baskets can keep all manner of clutter under control, and can be hung from the ceiling, attached to the wall or simply lined up on a surface or shelf. Just make sure your chosen design can cope with the high humidity without rusting or growing mould. Why not dedicate one to each member of the family?**

ABOVE **Large cupboards can be useful, but in a bathroom – where many of the things you need to store are likely to be small – a bank of drawers may be better. Not only is the useable storage capacity increased, but things will be easier to find when you need them, too.**

LEFT **Behind the glazed doors of this antique cabinet a row of baskets hides away clutter, and adds another texture to the decorative display. The pale wicker has been carefully chosen to tone with the shells and sea urchins, creating a harmonious and elegant effect.**

* Opt for wall-hung storage where possible. Anything that keeps the floor clear will help you achieve an uncluttered look.

* Before you assess how much storage you need, have a clear-out. You might find that you can reduce your bathroom bits and pieces dramatically.

* Use the back of the door for storage. A piece of wooden peg rail, for example, can be just the thing for hanging damp towels and can be painted to match your colour scheme.

* If you have bath products on show, make a feature of them: decant lotions and potions into attractive glass bottles, for example, and line them up on a shelf.

* If your bath has no integral surround, make sure you have somewhere to stash the soap. A built-in mini niche can work well, or a suction-style soap dish.

THIS PAGE **You don't need to remodel to sort out better storage provision, just think about where you can make small changes and additions. Here just a few hooks and a couple of capacious woven baskets provide a practical solution to storing towels and bath products.**

OPPOSITE **Plants can be a wonderful addition to the bathroom – in fact it's the best possible environment for species that prefer warmth and humidity, such as orchids, ferns and ivy. Plants are not only pleasing to the eye, many of them also help to purify the air, for a healthier atmosphere.**

ABOVE LEFT **Fabric bags can be hung on hooks and used to conceal all sorts of bits and bobs, from bath products to pumice stones and**

loofahs. It's wise to check and wash them regularly, however, since the humidity could perhaps make them a little musty.**

ABOVE CENTRE **Practical things can be decorative, too, especially gorgeous products such as soaps and bath salts, or perfume and lotions in beautiful packaging. Here a stash of mini soaps has been displayed in a pressed-glass bowl, rather than being left in their wrappers and hidden away in a cabinet.**

RIGHT **Wallpaper is usually best avoided in bathrooms, because of the humidity, but in a small cloakroom an unusual wallpaper creates a quirky look – or you could even use documents or prints pasted onto the wall. Here a sheet of clear glass has been used as a splashback, to protect the papered walls.**

Given a personal touch and some special details, the bathroom should become a space you can't wait to spend time in.

FINISHING TOUCHES

In a large bathroom, consider adding elements that aren't usually associated with utility spaces – an armchair, perhaps, or a shaggy sheepskin rug. Pieces like this will give even the most functional bathroom a comfortable touch (soft furnishings used in a damp or humid environment need to be aired regularly to prevent mould).

If you don't have underfloor heating, consider installing a feature towel rail/bar. Bathroom radiators now come in all kinds of innovative designs and colours. Alternatively, you could hunt down unusual storage items – an old-fashioned wall-mounted soap dispenser, for example, or a cutting-edge toothbrush rack.

The window is another great spot for self-expression. If you want a cottagey look, opt for curtains (these will need regular washing); or invest in a statement blind, printed with a graphic image or even a photograph. For the ultimate sleek minimal look, do without a covering altogether in favour of frosted glass.

Finally, introduce a few decorative details. Whether it's a row of old glass bottles or a bowl of shells, little extras can make all the difference.

❉ *If you don't want your windows to be permanently frosted, cover them with vinyl frosting instead. Window stickers now come in countless finishes and patterns, can be made to measure and peeled off when no longer required.*

❉ *Get creative with the side of a bath. Cover plain wood panels with a giant laminated photograph, perhaps, or cut a piece of coloured Perspex/Plexiglass to fit, and light it from within so that it glows in the dark. (Remember to get advice about the safety of any light fittings in the bathroom.)*

❉ *Bring in a vase of fresh flowers. Though any arrangement has to be changed regularly, a floral display will transform the room – even if it is only a bunch of daffodils. Some houseplants are happy in bathrooms, too.*

❉ *The bathroom is the most sensual space in the house, so make it smell nice. Avoid chemical air fresheners; opt instead for scented candles or natural perfumes. A few hyacinths or a bundle of dried lavender, for example, will do wonders.*

❋ Stick to natural materials for floors and surfaces – stripped wood, stone or ceramic tiles. Stainless steel and vinyl are not what you want here.

❋ Add a homely touch with floral fabrics or wallpaper, but make sure you buy a wipe-down version, specifically designed for moist and humid environments.

❋ If your old bath is chipped, get it re-enamelled. You can buy DIY kits, but to get a really good result it is best to employ an expert.

❋ A copper bath will give you old-style looks in an instant and will naturally retain the heat. Hunt down an antique or buy a reproduction or new design.

❋ The traditional bathroom should not be a minimal space. To make it feel lived in, bring in collections of old glassware, mirrors or pictures (but make sure the latter are well sealed, to protect them from damp).

❋ Include fabric washbasin 'skirts' and shower curtains (but be sure to fit a plastic liner).

OPPOSITE **A classic roll-top tub occupies pride of place in this light, bright take on country bathroom style. Essential ingredients for success include natural timber, wicker and painted surfaces in muted, knocked-back shades and soft whites – plus a little glimmer from metallic and mirrored accents.**

ABOVE LEFT **Wooden panelling is a good choice for a traditional bathroom, especially one with 18th-century influences. Here the use of the same shade of paint on the moulded panelling and walls (as well as the freestanding step stool) brings the look a bit more up to date.**

ABOVE RIGHT **Older homes might feature bathrooms with restricted head space due to sloping ceilings or supporting beams – this, along with the provision of drainage and water (without damaging the original fabric of the building), will need to be taken into account when designing your bathroom layout.**

LEFT **Because the fully-plumbed-in bathroom only became widespread at the time of the Industrial Revolution, there's no 'authentic' contemporary period design for homes from the 18th century or earlier. Pieces with 19th-century influences might offer the best stylistic fit.**

An old-fashioned bathroom has to function like a new one: recondition antique fixtures or buy reproductions to give you a classic look with all the mod cons.

TRADITIONAL STYLE

There is something very homely about an old-style bathroom. Think curvy roll-top baths with twisty copper taps/faucets; wicker laundry baskets; simple scrubbed floors in stone or wood. It's an honest, unpretentious room, which can work well in a contemporary setting as well as being just the thing for a period town house or country cottage.

Traditional fixtures and fittings, from a old butler's sink to an Art Deco shower mixer, can be tracked down at salvage yards or on the internet. If it is in good condition, don't expect such bathroom kit to come cheap; if it isn't, take into account the cost of getting it reconditioned. Alternatively, opt for reproduction pieces, which combine classic looks with the advantages of modern technology.

A traditional bathroom should be familiar and comforting. Choose classic colours for walls and woodwork and avoid garish tones. Use wallpaper, if you like, and add the odd soft furnishing – curtains, perhaps, or a pile of cushions on an armchair (these will need regular airing).

Accessorize with old-fashioned pieces – a vintage bath rack, traditional soap, pretty glass storage bottles. Just don't be tempted to bring out the tin bath.

✱ If you opt for an all-white bathroom, think about adding pattern in unexpected ways. Slatted shutters at the window will cast fantastic linear shadows on the floor, for example; set against a plain background, a curvy basin will become a sculptural focus.

✱ Don't opt for cold, blue-whites; instead choose warmer tones or creamy whites, which will glow in the sunlight. Think laundry rather than clinic.

✱ The all-white bathroom demands a bit of maintenance. Wipe down surfaces and furnishings regularly to keep it looking fresh and clean.

✱ Don't be afraid to add an accent of bold colour. A brilliant cushion, vivid towels or even some coloured lights will lift the decorative scheme and add visual interest.

✱ Texture is key in any all-white space, so introduce plenty of contrasts, whether rough and smooth or glossy and matt.

Bright, fresh and light-enhancing, an all-white scheme is perfect for the bathroom, but remember to add some texture to soften the look.

CLASSIC WHITE

White brings with it associations of purity and cleanliness, and thus is often an automatic choice for the bathroom. Bright and light-enhancing, it can freshen up dark or dingy spaces and blur the boundaries of a tiny room to make it seem larger. What's more, a white scheme is supremely versatile, catering to all tastes from minimal to smart Scandinavian to vintage washroom style.

For a wraparound white look, choose a tone that has an element of warmth in it to prevent the room looking too cold or clinical. And – for the same reason – opt for bathtubs and basins with a bit of a curve to soften the effect. Wooden floors can be whitewashed or limed for a subtler finish; walls could be painted in chalky distempers or shiny gloss – whatever your preference.

To add visual interest in an all-white room, turn up the emphasis on texture. Invest in some curly candlesticks; hang a diaphanous shower curtain; or add waffle towels. A white bathroom can be high maintenance, so opt for practical hardware and surfaces to make cleaning easy.

OPPOSITE LEFT **This all-white bathroom boasts a few small colourful touches, including blue coolie lamps, green vintage scales and a warm-toned checked towel. Additionally, the wood grain on the floor, seen through the limed finish, adds texture.**

OPPOSITE RIGHT **When a space is all-white and features flat surfaces and sleek lines, it's easy for the ambience to seem a little clinical. However, when the shade is soft, and subject to the variation of a distressed finish, the effect is charming and rustic.**

THIS PAGE **You'll never manage to colour match all the white elements of a room, so don't even try – besides, a slight difference will prevent the look from seeming flat and contrived. In this room, a small geometric floor tile provides the interest of a pattern, thanks to grey grout, without introducing any colour.**

OPPOSITE ABOVE LEFT **Natural materials don't need much in order to show them off to best effect – in fact, it's best to keep all the other elements understated. Here rough, rustic stone tiles benefit from the simplicity of a white ceramic basin, plain enamel bath and a wooden-framed mirror.**

OPPOSITE ABOVE RIGHT **In a room with old exposed beams, the beauty of the natural wood takes centre stage thanks to the simple treatment of the space. A white-painted floor, white walls and a sleek white tub offer a minimalist foil to the rough texture and honey tones of the timber.**

OPPOSITE BELOW LEFT **With a wall of natural granite setting a luxurious tone, it's only fitting that the sleek timber bath surround has been crafted in an equally glamorous tropical hardwood – it's also a practical choice, since timbers such as teak boast superior water resistance.**

OPPOSITE BELOW CENTRE **In this white-decorated space, which also features cool metallic accents, a wooden table and a wicker hamper add contrasting warmth and texture. If old timber furniture is to be repurposed for use in the bathroom, particularly as a vanity, it must be sealed properly to avoid mould growth and rot.**

OPPOSITE BELOW RIGHT **Original and reclaimed natural materials come to the fore in this bathroom. The exposed brick creates interest in terms of texture and colour (with a varied palette of earth tones), while a black stone surround adds an appropriately faded sense of luxury to the tub.**

RIGHT **Natural materials offer plenty of scope for decorative display – driftwood, pebbles and shells can all offer ornamental value in their natural state, while carved bowls or statues made from timber or stone can be a more refined, elegant option.**

Capture the sense of calm you feel when you're at one with nature, by choosing organic materials and free-flowing shapes.

NATURAL BATHROOMS

Whether they're used in a rustic scheme, or a room that's more sleek and contemporary in its style influences (think Japanese zen, spa-like spaces), there's something familiar and honest about organic materials – so it's no surprise that a bathroom featuring the natural textures of stone, wood and metal can evoke a feeling of calm like no other.

For maximum soothing effect, stick to a neutral colour palette for the décor, and let the organic elements do all the talking. In nature, even contrast is harmonious. Try teaming a smooth polished-wood cabinet with a rough-textured slate tile, a rock-hewn basin with a minimalist tap/faucet, or a pebble floor with a stone tub with a honed finish. Accessorize with woven grass baskets, cotton or linen towels, seashells, river pebbles and – of course – living plants (selecting only those which thrive in a humid atmosphere).

One key to using natural materials well (and so they look good for years to come) is to ensure you're choosing the right finishes. Timber can become watermarked or even turn black with mould (and begin to rot) if it's not protected with a suitable finish – though certain woods do have greater moisture resistance than others, such as the tropical hardwoods – while natural stone is porous, so will need sealing to avoid staining (as will engineered surfaces made from marble or quartz). Additionally, organic fibres such as cotton and grasses can start to develop mould if they remain in a damp atmosphere, so good ventilation is a must. Invest in a powerful extractor fan, and open windows regularly to let the fresh air in.

* *A rainwater shower head will bring the power of nature to your bathroom in a way that goes beyond aesthetics – look for multiple settings, and remember bigger is better when it comes to the size.*

* *Position your tub so that you can enjoy the view from the window – provided it's bucolic, and not overlooked, of course. Or if you live in warmer climes, why not create an outdoor shower area, or an al fresco bathing zone in a private courtyard or balcony space?*

* *Wall- and ceiling-hung planters and green walls offer a more contemporary look than traditional pots, especially if you choose plants such as mosses, succulents and ferns.*

* *Not every element has to be made from natural materials, just a single eye-catching feature can be enough. For example, utilizing the same rough stone tile for floor and walls can provide a beautifully contrasting backdrop for a curvaceous freestanding bathtub in a pure white composite material.*

LEFT **A twin basin adds a sense of luxury to a bathroom, while the overall ambience of this space – balancing period style with minimalist design, a pale palette with ornate and traditional detailing – would be entirely befitting of a classy historic hotel.**

RIGHT **White marble simply exudes luxury. This floor-to-ceiling treatment, with matching floor, sink and counter, is at once very simple and ostentatiously lavish. Fittings, such as the tap/faucet and mirror, have been kept sleek and understated so as to allow the beauty of the natural stone to shine unhindered.**

OPPOSITE **Hotel bathrooms don't just inspire in terms of luxury style, they often feature savvy design elements too. For example, sleek wall-hung vanities are commonplace, since they not only allow easier cleaning, but they make the room appear more spacious, too.**

HOTEL GLAMOUR

A designer bathroom may be beyond your budget, but by stealing ideas from hotel suites you can bring a bit of five-star luxury to your own bathing space.

Contemporary hotel bathrooms are luxurious and indulgent. Beautifully designed and free of domestic clutter, they offer a vision of the ultimate bathing experience. Recreating such an extravagant space at home is beyond most budgets, of course, but you can steal inspiring designer elements or ideas.

A statement bathtub will instantly give five-star glamour, whether it is in hand-carved stone or sparkling mosaic. Set it in the middle of the room for maximum impact, but make sure first that your plumbing can cope with central drainage. Alternatively, splash out on a sunken tub. This can't be undertaken lightly – you will need to raise the floor and create steps up to the bathroom – but can be very effective. The infinity bathtub, created as a tub within a tub so that water can brim to the top of the inner shell and pour over the sides, is also a luxurious option, particularly when filled from the ceiling with a waterfall-like jet.

In a bathroom like this, you want a shower that cascades, so hunt around for extravagant water features; giant showerheads or rain panels that drench rather than dribble. Prices aren't necessarily prohibitive, but check that your water pressure can cope or fit a new pump.

Glamour can come as much from your bathroom surfaces as the fixtures and fittings, so flick through magazines to see what appeals. Quality counts, so buy the best material you can afford – whether it's smooth natural stone, patterned mosaic panels or rich dark wood – and use it wherever your budget will allow. Just a strip of golden tiles, for example, will lift an otherwise plain bathroom to a new level.

And don't forget to tap into modern technology. It is constantly evolving, so keep up to date and consider what could transform your space. A shower with MP3 connection, perhaps; a tub you can fill remotely at the touch of a button; a chromatherapy feature to flood the water with coloured light? Finally, add a little luxury in the details with top-quality towels and cleansing products.

❋ Before you splash out on designer fixtures and fittings, make sure that they will function effectively in your bathroom. You may need to get your water pressure checked, for example, or install a new pump for a power shower. It's wise to seek advice from the experts before you begin.

❋ Choose fashionable toning shades for the walls, floors and surfaces. A one-colour room will always look chic.

❋ Half the appeal of a sleek hotel bathroom is that it is calm and uncluttered. Achieve the same effect by building clever storage into your space (see page 142-143) and keeping mess to an absolute minimum.

❋ In a plain bathroom, make light a decorative element. Invest in a chromatherapy shower, create your own illuminated bath panel or simply install some recessed floor spots.

CHILDREN'S ROOMS

OPPOSITE ABOVE LEFT **A favourite theme will always delight a child – but it's best to make sure that you choose to express it in an impermanent fashion, so it can be updated easily and inexpensively as the child grows up. Wall stickers are a cheap, quick way of adding mural-style decoration, without the permanence.**

OPPOSITE ABOVE RIGHT **With a very neutral base scheme – here a mid-toned wooden floor, white walls and white furniture – the accessories can be easily switched out to match the child's changing tastes as they mature. Here an easy update of the toys, cushions, rug and wall decoration would give a new look quickly and cheaply.**

OPPOSITE BELOW LEFT **Even if the rest of your home is relatively refined in terms of colour, often when decorating a child's room you'll gravitate towards a more colourful palette. Here flashes of chartreuse, lime and coral lift a space that's mainly decorated in an elegant pale grey.**

OPPOSITE BELOW RIGHT **Here jade green, orange and coral pop out against a white-on-white backdrop, but some more natural shades have also been included to add some contrast and texture. The wicker chair, natural wood boxes and retro lamp all help to ground the scheme.**

ABOVE RIGHT **Toys and books have a dual purpose, as they can be used as decorative accessories too – they bring colour and character to a space. Display your child's large picture books facing forward; picture ledges are an easy and inexpensive option for achieving this look.**

DESIGN & DECORATION

When designing and decorating a child's room, flexibility is key. Children's rooms need to change and evolve as fast as the child does. From a calming nursery to a high-tech teenage hangout, the room must be adaptable, well-planned and creative.

A child's room should reflect his or her personality and preferences, while also remaining similar in style to the rest of your home, so it fits in. Involve your child in decision-making; young children can feel very upset when their room is transformed and familiar pieces in it changed, so let them make some choices to reduce the risk of their feeling unsettled.

That said, your input is essential. Do not trust a four-year-old to pick a scheme that he or she will still love in six months' time, so avoid Spiderman wallpaper on every wall, as your son may prefer Batman in a few

weeks, but do leave a wall free where he can hang posters or pictures, which can be swapped easily.

Pick furniture that can be adapted, to accommodate a child's ever-changing interests without compromising your own sense of style too greatly; wooden furniture that can be painted, a dressing-up box that can double as seating, a shelving unit that can be wall-mounted once the child is taller. Then have fun with inexpensive accessories like lights, wall stickers, rugs and bedding, to create a space that is both stylish and child-friendly.

RIGHT **School-age children will need somewhere they can do their homework (though a desk is equally useful for hobbies and creative activities), including space for a computer and possibly a printer – so you'll need to bear in mind the position of the room's power sockets when planning what goes where.**

BELOW RIGHT **The room's layout should take into account the child's activity preferences, just in the way that you'd plan an adult's space based on their usage of it. Here the dressing table and a deep cushioned bench are positioned right by the window, to ensure as much natural light as possible for getting ready and dressing up and for reading.**

OPPOSITE **In a shared bedroom it's often a good idea to provide some kind of screen or divider to enable each child to have their own private area – this might be as simple as a curtain, or as permanent as a partition wall. In this panelled room, a matching tongue-and-groove divider is the ideal solution.**

PLANNING

Children's rooms demand as much planning as the more public rooms in your home. Your child's tastes and interests should be reflected, there should be easy-to-access storage and it must be able to switch from play area to sleep space in moments.

If you are starting from scratch, choose flooring that marries practicality with comfort. Children spend a lot of time on the floor and need a comfortable surface to play or generally roll around on. On walls, go for neutral tones and liven them up with textiles and accessories. Funky bedlinen and rugs add colour cheaply, so you may be happy to let your child choose.

If you want to use bright paint or wallpaper, try limiting it to one feature wall, so it's less time-consuming and expensive to change. Children do love bright colours, but they can make a room feel small and have a stimulating effect, which might prevent a child sleeping well.

Although adults often love clutter-free living, children enjoy having all their things around them and should be able to access them easily. So, rather than custom-built drawers and cupboards, opt for a mix of closed storage and open shelving, baskets and crates, so the room can be tidied quickly – by your child – but toys are still easy to get at.

Kids and teenagers like to have posters and their own artwork on their walls, but instead of using tape try pinning them to large corkboards or buy magnetic paint. Blackboard paint means children can chalk up their own designs when feeling creative.

THIS PAGE **Babies' rooms can be simple, since their needs are fairly straightforward – a place to sleep, storage for clothes and toys, and a changing area are really all that's needed. A calming ambience and careful attention to safety are important, while life with a tiny person is made easier with practical choices such as an easy-clean floor and washable paintwork.**

BABIES' ROOMS

A baby's room must tick certain boxes if it is to be a good environment for the first year of life. It needs to keep a constant temperature, fulfil specific lighting requirements and be comfortable and calming. Little furniture is needed, but the right atmosphere is key.

Research suggests that pastel shades comfort babies, so choose delicate, chalky colours and avoid anything too bright. Pay careful attention to lighting. Strong natural light is the enemy of good sleep, so make sure you have adequate window treatments fitted for daytime naps and to prevent early waking. A blackout roller blind/shade with curtains hung in front will block out most light, as will shutters. Dimmer switches mean you can keep light soft for bedtime and night feeds, brighter for dressing and play.

Choose a soft carpet or rug so baby can lie down and crawl. Fit a thermostat to the radiator so you can regulate the room's temperature – overheating has been linked to SIDS (Sudden Infant Death Syndrome). Make sure all sockets/power points are covered and electrical leads hidden behind furniture or clipped to the wall. Avoid putting the cot/crib anywhere near a radiator, as baby could burn his or her fingers or overheat, or near a window, which can be draughty.

ABOVE LEFT **Small clothes are often best stored folded rather than hung, and open storage allows the easiest access (which is very handy if you're running on very little sleep, and likely to be changing outfits more than once a day, as babies may require).**

ABOVE **You could change your baby on a mat on the floor, but to save your back it's worth investing in a purpose-made solution. Whatever your preferred aesthetic, there are all sorts of changing stations available, from cot-top options to freestanding and wall-hung designs.**

RIGHT **For the best possible value, invest in a cot /crib that can be converted into a toddler bed as your child grows older. Look for designs which boast a number of mattress heights, teething rails and possibly even the ability to be converted into a day bed when completely outgrown.**

ABOVE **By the changing table you'll need to consider practicality as well as aesthetics – it can be a good idea to keep some supplies out, easily to hand for speedy grabbing, while the majority of your stock of nappies/diapers, cream and nappy/diaper sacks can be neatly hidden away in boxes.**

NURSERY FURNITURE & STORAGE

Comfortable, good-looking furniture and versatile storage are just as essential in the nursery as they are in the kitchen or living room. Look for furniture that will last, suiting your child from a few months old to several years.

You won't need a wardrobe/closet at this stage in your child's life – tiny baby and toddler clothes and other necessities can be stored flat – but a chest of drawers is essential. Try to include a bookcase, too, and easy-access storage for toys and stuffed animals. Baskets, crates and buckets work well and allow a child to see what's inside. Store the baskets on high shelves to return the room to calmness at bedtime.

A standard cot/crib will last a child around two and a half years, while a cot bed, which is slightly larger, lasts five years. If you buy a second-hand one, always buy a new mattress, for health and hygiene reasons.

Include an easy chair in the room if you have space, so you can sit comfortably when feeding baby at night or bedtime. Chairs designed especially for breastfeeding are available, but they tend to be expensive, so simply choose a comfy armchair that you can both snuggle into for bedtime stories once your child reaches toddlerdom.

A changing table is always a good investment, particularly if you suffer from back pain, as bending to change nappies/diapers on the floor creates strain. Otherwise, buy a changing board that fits over the cot/crib – an inexpensive alternative.

ABOVE **A sizeable chest of drawers will provide all the clothes storage you need, plus room for linens and nappies/diapers too. Opt for a design which has drawers that close easily, without being shoved, to help reduce the risk of small fingers being injured if they're accidentally trapped.**

OPPOSITE **There are some lovely ranges of children's furniture available, but actually for value and longevity it can be better to choose adult-sized pieces, as they can be adapted decoratively over time. This built-in wardrobe/closet can be repainted, and the armchair's cushions can be recovered, as the child's tastes change.**

GIRLS' ROOMS

Girls often take a great interest in how their room is decorated, so have fun choosing pretty shades, stylish furniture and colourful accessories together.

It's a generalization, but some girls tend to be more tidy and organized than boys and enjoy arranging their belongings attractively. Provide plenty of open shelves, box shelves or other surfaces for them to arrange favourite things on.

Girls also tend to favour pink, but beware – the love affair with this shade can dwindle and die by the time they are six or seven, so use it with restraint. Instead of Barbie pink, introduce your daughter to brighter shades of fuchsia, magenta or salmon. Use on one wall to make an impact without dominating, or keep the walls neutral and work in some colour on curtains, bedding and rugs.

Then have fun personalizing and prettying up the space. Strings of bunting or mini lights add colour, tacked to a wall or hanging from shelves, while a simple canopy made from inexpensive coloured muslin, draped around the bed, will make her feel like a princess. Colourful cushions on the bed or used on the floor are welcome. Keep stuffed animals on the bed during the day, but at night limit your daughter to one or two and store the rest in a basket by the bed – they can harbour dust and trigger allergies.

OPPOSITE **This little girl's current penchant for pink is obvious – but of course that is likely to alter as she grows up. The turquoise and grey colour scheme (teamed with white furniture) allows for the chimneybreast and mantelpiece displays to be reinvented without having to redecorate.**

ABOVE LEFT **Children love to display their favourite belongings in their rooms. Pretty accessories – such as jewellery, scarves and bags – can be hung up as decoration, so provide hooks or clips that are easy to use (which will enable your child to re-curate their selection whenever the fancy takes them).**

ABOVE RIGHT **Keeping the walls white and furniture simple will help ensure that a child-chosen selection of soft furnishings doesn't look too busy and chaotic. Here a mixture of patterns, colours and textures creates a fun, relaxed feel.**

RIGHT **This little girl's room is actually largely monochrome, with large expanses of white, grey and black providing an almost minimalist backdrop – throwing emphasis onto the jumble of colourful plain and print soft furnishings. There's plenty of pink in the mix, though a little blue and eau de nil is thrown in for good measure, to add balance.**

LEFT **Many young boys like to collect lots of small toys** – whether mini figures, cars, model dinosaurs or any number of other things – and will be delighted if these cherished possessions can take pride of place in their bedroom. Look for trinket shelves in cute shapes, or use picture ledges, to display their favourites.

BELOW **Lots of easy-access toy storage** – such as these under-bed drawers on casters – will hopefully aid in keeping the bedroom floor relatively clear (and encourage good habits), as they make it quick and easy to tidy up once playtime is over.

OPPOSITE **This fabulous castle-style built-in** not only comprises a bed, and a platform for make-believe play, but storage, too – there are drawers in the steps. The higher level might also be used as a reading nook (with the addition of a cushion or two), while at night-time its owner can snuggle up in a cocoon-like space.

BOYS' ROOMS

It's easy to assume that little boys are oblivious to their environment, but that's not true – they can take a great interest in how their space is organized, what colours are used and where pieces are positioned, so involve them at each stage.

Boys often love bright colours and might want them on their walls, but strong shades can make a space feel claustrophobic. Try using them just on furniture or woodwork, a chimneybreast or curtains, or let your son choose a zingy duvet cover or rug.

Interesting second-hand furniture often appeals to boys. Old lockers, metal trunks, school desks with the traditional hinged lid or beaten-up suitcases may intrigue them and will add tons of character to the room. Or buy sturdy wooden pieces from second-hand shops and refresh them with a colourful coat of paint and some fun handles or knobs.

A bookcase is important. Those that store books with covers facing out make it easy for a child to find the book he's after. Then make the most of fun, inexpensive decorative products. Wall stickers that can be repositioned again and again allow him to personalize his walls, or buy a stencil and paint footprints, grass or a train track onto floorboards.

Many children love the security and sociability of sharing a bedroom with a sibling. Organize the space well, so that each child has an area of his or her own.

SHARED BEDROOMS

Where you position the beds in a shared bedroom is crucial. Single beds ranged side by side look cute and symmetrical, but it's sometimes better to place them at different angles, so the children can't easily see and distract each other after bedtime. If the room is not a simple square or rectangle, exploit its odd angles by tucking beds into corners, creating a sense of privacy, important for older children.

Alternatively, opt for bunk beds. They are great space-savers and kids can use them to climb and play on, as well as for sleep. Make sure the ladder is sturdy and that the sides are sufficiently high to prevent the child on top falling out. Many bunk beds have the bonus of built-in storage underneath – another space-saver. Whether you choose bunks or singles, fit a wall light or table lamp by each bed, so one child can read without disturbing the other.

Low-level, freestanding shelving units make great room dividers and provide lots of storage, too. Choose one that can be accessed from either side, or a unit on casters so it can be moved to open out the space or create personal zones.

OPPOSITE **In a shared bedroom, privacy can be a particular flashpoint for disagreements – even the closest siblings need alone time once in a while. Here a den-like comfy space has been created, complete with curtains, cushions and a collection of cuddly toys, just perfect for when a little quiet solitude is needed.**

ABOVE **Even in a small room, it's possible to give each child their own portion of the space to express their creativity. Here the wall by each child's bunk has been turned into a mini gallery, where they can choose which drawings, postcards and trinkets to display.**

RIGHT **Bunk beds can be great space-savers for small rooms that have to be shared. The older child should always go on the higher level, and you should bear in mind their age when you choose the design – the younger they are, the lower the top bunk should be.**

TEEN BEDROOMS

Teenage bedrooms need to be more than just a place to sleep – they become a private place away from the family where the young person can relax, express their interests and entertain friends, too.

While children have a lot of toys, teenagers have a lot of equipment. Laptops, video games, TVs, stereos, hairdryers, guitars, skateboards, amps… it will all need incorporating into their space, so work in as much storage as possible. As well as all this kit, the usual bed, wardrobe/closet and chest of drawers must find a space, and make sure there is room for a desk for studying. It should be equipped with adequate task lighting for late-night revision sessions, too. If space is limited, a mezzanine-level bed with desk and storage beneath is a great choice, and cool, too. Find this type of bed in large furniture stores or have one built to your specifications.

Your teenager will also want to choose what goes in the room. If your budget doesn't stretch to the furniture of their choice, let them pick new bedding, rugs or window treatments, which can radically alter the look of a room without breaking the bank. Get them to paint the room, too. Finally, privacy is key for teenagers and should be respected. They may even want a lock on the door!

ABOVE **Freedom of expression is paramount in a teen's bedroom – but there's no reason why they shouldn't be encouraged to make compromises for reasons of cost or practicality. For example, they might want to paint their whole bedroom black, but actually a single black wall might achieve the right effect without making the space feel oppressive.**

OPPOSITE BELOW **Inexpensive furniture, whether from the charity/ thrift shop or a mass-market manufacturer, is ideal for a teen's room. Not just because it might have to put up with lots of wear and tear (expensive, delicate pieces are a no-no), but because it's often great for customizing easily and cheaply with paint, stickers or even permanent marker pens.**

RIGHT **With inexpensive white paint used to decorate the wall, there's no reason to worry about adhesives damaging the surface – so posters and flyers can be easily put up, taken down and switched around at will. Here a diverse collection of photographs, postcards, magazine clippings and print-outs adds colour and a very personal touch to the space.**

FAR RIGHT **For a more grown-up collection of artwork, frames are required. Teach your teen how to safely put up picture hooks (checking for wires and pipes first, before wielding the hammer) – it may also provide an opportunity to learn how to fill, sand and paint holes in plaster, depending on how their early attempts go!**

THIS PAGE **A string of lights fixed up across a wall, or draped over a bedhead, will create a twinkly, atmospheric effect after dark – and it's much safer than candles. There's a huge selection of designs available, from flowers to flamingos, and paper lanterns to chilli peppers.**

You will need different types of light for different ages, but a few basics should last from baby's first year into teenage times.

LIGHTING

Toddlers often like a small amount of light in a room during the night. It helps them sleep better, as they feel more confident. Night lights that create a soft glow, either in table-lamp style or wall lights, are widely available.

Fairy lights or rope lights are great in kids' rooms. They can be strung across shelves, mantelpieces or curtain rails or just pinned on a wall to create an ambient glow that acts as a night light, too.

Dimmer switches are very practical, as they allow you to turn a wall or ceiling light down very low for night-time feeds, soothing bedtimes or checking a sleeping child. They can be left on low for a child who is afraid of the dark, then put on full when needed.

Directable spotlights are a good option, too, available as wall-mounted or clip-on spots, or in lamp form, like the classic Anglepoise. They can work as a reading lamp, be turned towards the ceiling or wall for a softer light and, when a child gets older, make good task lighting to do homework by.

RIGHT **Novelty lamps are great for kids' rooms** – not only are fun shapes thoroughly appropriate for the kind of carefree, joyful décor children love, but such designs often provide a soft, non-directional light that's ideal for creating a cosy atmosphere in the run-up to bedtime.

BELOW **Whether they need to do homework or are indulging in a creative hobby, a lamp is a vital element of any older child's bedroom** – whether it's the sort that sits on the desk, stands on the floor or clamps to either the desk top or a nearby shelf.

* *Night lights and wall lights that look decorative whether on or off come in many designs – choose them in the shape of a flower, moon, star or football.*

* *Illuminated globes create subtle light and make learning about the world appealing and accessible.*

* *Once children can read, incorporate a reading light next to their bed, fitted with a low-wattage bulb.*

* *A single central pendant light creates a very flat, unhelpful light, so always incorporate several light sources in your child's room to boost it. Some wall lights, task lights and soft, ambient light are necessary, and dimmer switches will give even greater control over brightness levels.*

* *Make sure hot light bulbs are never within reach of curious fingers. Choose a lampshade that conceals the bulb, or fit lights high on walls, out of reach.*

* *Coloured bulbs create atmospheric light that children often find appealing, but are not useful for reading, working or playing, so don't rely on them as the sole light source in the room.*

Children spend a great deal of time on the floor. When you choose flooring for a child's room, comfort is a key consideration.

FLOORING

Let's start with what you don't want. Although hardwearing, natural fibres like sisal and seagrass are too rough for children's delicate skin. Deep-pile carpets, while beautifully soft, can trap dirt and crumbs (not practical for children) and also harbour the dust mites that can irritate children with allergies and eczema – conditions very common in childhood. So if you'd like a wall-to-wall floor covering, choose a short-weave carpet that has been treated with protective Scotchgard, so it's stain-resistant and easy to vacuum.

Wooden floorboards are also a practical choice. Easy to clean, durable and good-looking, they can be softened with rugs and mats, making them kind to floor-dwelling kids. In a dark room, go for painted floorboards in a pale shade that will make the room seem brighter and larger.

Vinyl and rubber flooring are other appealing options, combining practicality with good looks. Rubber comes in a huge range of colours, is slip-resistant – ideal for kids who like to run around in their socks – and makes it easy to wipe up spills.

ABOVE LEFT **Painted wooden boards are a very practical choice for a child's room, since they are very hardwearing – and easily re-finished once the wear and tear becomes more 'shabby' than it is 'shabby chic'. Make sure you choose a hardwearing and non-slip formula made specifically for wooden floors.**

ABOVE **Stripped boards are a classic look. You'll need to make sure they're well-sanded, and that all the nails have been punched below the surface, before you apply your chosen finish. Oil will have a softer matte effect, and is easier to patch repair, while varnish is hardwearing and easy to clean.**

LEFT **Carpet for a child's room should above all be chosen with practicality in mind – a cut pile can make it easier to clean up the inevitable spills, as can choosing a product that boasts a stain-resistant finish. It's also possible to have such protection applied after the carpet has been laid.**

THIS PAGE Carpet is soft underfoot, and helps to avoid draughts – but it's best not to choose one with a deep pile. Not just because it takes more work to keep it looking its best (particularly when dealing with spills), but because toys won't roll so easily across it, and train tracks won't always stay together properly.

✳ Make sure any gaps in old wooden floorboards are filled – small children love to 'post' things through them. Sand down any rough sections and check for protruding nails or splinters, too.

✳ Use a mix of flooring to zone your child's space. Choose a cosy rug for by the bed, where he or she can sit quietly to read or draw, and a practical, wipe-clean surface in activity areas.

✳ Soften and brighten wooden floorboards with cotton mats or rugs that can be machine-washed.

✳ Shaggy rugs can hold mites and mess, and they do not provide the smooth surface kids need to put jigsaws together, stand play figures on or push toy cars over, so use them sparingly or not at all.

✳ Rugs can be educational and fun too. Many children's stores sell rugs with a world map or streetscape designs.

✳ Choose a hardwearing fitted carpet in an oatmeal shade or with a flecked pattern – both are good at disguising marks and crumbs. Stripes will make any room seem longer or wider and also provide 'tracks' for children to drive toy cars along.

ABOVE **Storage featuring pull-out bins is just the ticket for robust toys – and solid-coloured plastic examples will hide away all the clutter for a more streamlined look. Low-level units are best to allow children to access their belongings without help, and the top surface is perfect for displaying sizeable favourites.**

✳ *Children often have a great many toys but only become attached to a small selection at any time, so try rotating them, storing some on high shelves or in cupboards for a few months, then swapping them. It gives the child a sense of having 'new' things; they can focus on them clearly and enjoy them more.*

✳ *Choose baskets and buckets with lids. Toys can be casually tossed into them at bedtime and, once the lid is on, the space looks tidy and uncluttered.*

✳ *Choose units with solid bases, rather than legs, so that toys can't get lost underneath. If you don't mind a busier look, clear plastic storage boxes will enable the child to find a particular toy more easily – and won't empty every single one looking for it.*

✳ *If your child is at reading age, labels on drawers and boxes help with easy identification and organizing.*

✳ *Hanging baskets and mesh cylinders that can be suspended from the ceiling or hung on the back of a door are great for storing and displaying soft toys.*

✳ *Avoid cupboards, trunks and chests with locks; a little one could get trapped inside.*

✳ *Boxes on casters that can be stored under a bed help keep mess under control and floor space free for playing.*

✳ *As well as closed storage, work in open shelving for displaying favourite things, artwork, certificates and family photos.*

Sturdy furniture that can take a little rough handling and easy-to-access storage will cater for all your child's needs, from infancy to the teenage years.

STORAGE

Choose a wardrobe/closet with a height-adjustable rail so it can fit bigger clothes as your child grows. Adjustable shelves on bookcases are also useful as large picture books are exchanged for paperbacks.

Second-hand furniture that looks better with the odd bump and chip is a safe bet and economical, too. Old armoires, shelving units, chests of drawers and boxes crop up at markets and can be revived with a coat of paint and some decorative knobs or handles.

To encourage your children to clear up, provide adequate, easy-to-access storage. Rather than stackable storage, choose big toy chests, baskets and buckets that make tidying easy. Different-sized boxes and small drawer units keep small toys and stationery under control, too. Position some storage at child level and consider building in high shelves or cupboards for those pieces you don't need so often, like bedding, out-of-season clothes or excess toys.

ABOVE **In a shared room, it's nice to be able to offer the same storage space to each child – though of course it's not always possible. Here a pair of sleek tallboys creates a very symmetrical look and adds a touch of elegance with their curved legs.**

RIGHT **Wall-hung storage is particularly good if space is tight – and hooks serve a myriad of purposes, from displaying treasured accessories to offering a place to hang the next day's outfit, which will aid a smooth and speedy morning routine.**

For a fun, contemporary look which is easy to create and maintain, paint the walls white and use accessories to add colour.

WHITE AND BRIGHT

You might think that white is the worst colour to use in a child's room – because they're not known for their tidy habits and meticulous handwashing – but thanks to the marvel of modern science it's actually a rather practical choice for décor. Hardwearing paint formulas which stand scrubbing, not just wiping, will help keep things looking fresh, and provided you make a note of the specific formula, shade of white (there are an incredible number!) and brand, then retouching will be easy and inexpensive.

With the ultimate neutral as a backdrop, vibrant shades really pop, and rooms appear brighter and larger thanks to the amount of natural light that's being bounced around. This effect is heightened if you use a white flooring (there's virtually no risk of the finished room being too clinical, it will have too much colour and pattern going on for that), but warm, natural tones are a good alternative, and will ground the look.

When combining brights, look for accessories which have the same intensity of colour – and for maximum impact choose shades from the opposing side of the colour wheel. You might combine a dazzling turquoise with a fuchsia pink, a lime green with a pillar-box red, or a vibrant teal with a blazing orange. It's a good idea to balance their placement throughout the room, and if you still find the look too intense, temper it with some natural shades and textures; maybe a piece of wooden furniture or a wicker basket.

Select patterns which are bold and graphic; this is a strong look, and subtle colouring or small-scale prints don't really cut the mustard. Especially if your child is younger, you may not need to add much in the way of colourful furnishings or decorative accessories. Many pre-school toys and books are bright and bold in their design, so will add all the interest that's required.

Keep the shapes simple wherever you use brights. Roller blinds/shades, plain picture frames, streamlined storage boxes and furniture with minimalist or mid-century influences all work well.

Lastly, if you're confident with colour, try painting a feature wall (or even just an alcove) in a zingy shade, then position a colourful piece of furniture in front of it – for the most dramatic effect make sure the two shades have as much contrast as possible.

✳ *Use some vibrant wallpaper as a feature on one wall. There are plenty of funky florals, lively patterns and cool abstracts around, and a single roll won't break the bank.*

✳ *Choose colourful furniture that can stand against a colourful wall – painted wooden pieces or brightly upholstered chairs and beanbags look great.*

✳ *Hang a bright roller blind/shade at the window. The strong tone will make an impact, but the unfussy roller design will keep this injection of bright colour looking crisp and controlled.*

✳ *Bring the brightness down to floor level – a surface that sees a lot of action in a child's room – and leave the walls white. The eye will be drawn downwards, which is also a useful effect in a high-ceilinged room.*

✳ *Create a feature wall behind the bed or cot, so the child isn't directly facing it while lying down and will not be distracted by the bright shade.*

OPPOSITE ABOVE **In this room most of the colour actually comes from the toys and storage boxes – décor-wise, there's just a bold red and white duvet set, and some rainbow-coloured hanging decorations in addition. A wooden parquet floor, in a herringbone pattern, also provides a touch of visual warmth.**

OPPOSITE BELOW **A couple of old-style bentwood school chairs and a small mid-century cabinet have been given character and coherence with a bold painted facelift – the straight lines are easily achieved with masking tape and careful brushwork, while an acrylic topcoat will add durability (and maybe shine, too).**

ABOVE RIGHT **With white walls, and key items such as curtains and bedlinen in plain colours or graphic patterns, a room can be easily and inexpensively updated as a child grows up. Here the side table and wall decorations fit in with the woodland theme – but the space would look equally stylish with a quick change of accessories.**

ABOVE RIGHT **Not confident using strong colour? Keep most of the elements neutral and choose vibrant patterned bedlinen and cushions to create a punchy layered look. Once that's been put together, you can build the look further, perhaps starting with painting a bright feature wall.**

RIGHT **Don't feel you have to keep all walls and woodwork white. Here a strong shade of orange contrasts dramatically with the green doll's cot/crib and whale mobile, as well as accentuating the shape of the white vintage-style cot/crib.**

Whereas once every little girl would want a pink bedroom, and every little boy's space would be blue, times have changed…

GENDER NEUTRAL BEDROOMS

Of course, gendered décor is always going to be there – pink schemes with a fairy or floral theme will always appeal to some girls, and some boys will always gravitate towards primary colours and traditional 'male' motifs such as cars or trains… But in recent years there's definitely been an increase in parents and children making gender-neutral decorating choices.

Avoiding the pink-for-girls and blue-for-boys look is easier than you might think. A good starting point is to find either a theme or a colourful piece (maybe a picture, a duvet cover or even a favourite toy) to act as a catalyst for the scheme. Animals, numbers, musical instruments and nature would all be thoroughly suitable – or you could simply create a style that's quite grown-up and complementary to the other spaces in your home, with toys and books being the only clue that the room belongs to a child. This would be a great way to approach a baby's nursery, and as they grow older, they would be able to put more and more of their own stamp on the space.

In terms of colours, a neutral scheme – whether white-on-white minimalism, or a restful combination of natural shades – will always be a stylish choice, and can be easily given a fresh look periodically as your child gets older, while blues, greens and yellows can all work beautifully too. You might want to avoid pictorial prints deliberately aimed at youngsters (they're often gendered), and stick to checks, spots and stripes, or other geometrics.

OPPOSITE Graphic patterns are a great way to add interest to any child's bedroom – checks, stripes, chevrons and ethnic designs are all ideal, and can be combined with textured plains (perhaps knitted or quilted accessories) for a layered look. Here some animal-shaped cushions also add a quirky, fun touch.

ABOVE RIGHT Understated schemes not only easily bridge the decorative gender divide, but have a better chance of being timeless, too. Here shades of white and cream are accented by a couple of simple patterns, while scraps of fabric make up a string of bunting that's not too girly.

RIGHT If you're preparing a nursery for a new baby, but don't yet know the gender, neutral shades are a good choice – green and yellow are also popular options. Here a combination of whites and pale wood are accented with soft green and a knocked-back yellow, creating a restful ambience.

* Grey doesn't have to be boring – in fact, it's a great neutral choice for a child's room. Vibrant colours sing out in contrast, wood tones complement it easily, while used with white (especially in geometric patterns) it can offer quite a sophisticated, fresh look.

* Use plenty of texture, particularly if you've opted for a more neutral palette. This will add interest, and is likely to up the comfort levels too.

* Track down picture frames that allow children's artwork to be displayed and switched out easily. An ever-changing gallery of their masterpieces should encourage the creativity of even the most reluctant artist, and a room that's as personalized as it comes.

* Murals can be a good gender-neutral option, but to get a good result you either have to be an accomplished artist or have deep enough pockets to pay one. A lower-budget alternative might be a photographic or illustrative wallpaper, or wall decals.

Few children don't see the appeal of their very own little space, where they can be alone or with a small and select group of friends.

DENS AND HIDEAWAYS

As the perennial popularity of cushion forts, blanket tents and garden dens might suggest, children love to build their own hideaways during play – and there's also a significant market in ready-made examples, including play houses and tents, which certainly nods at the universal nature of the desire to call a space their very own. Kids love being kings of their (usually cardboard) castles, so do provide them with the means to have their own private, secret spot, whether that's in their own bedroom or another part of the house.

If your home is on the small side, a tent would always be the wisest choice, since it's easily collapsible and doesn't take up much space when stored. There are all sorts of designs available to buy at a variety of price points, from camper vans to big tops, toadstool houses to rocket ships, A-frame tents to tepees. Or, if you're feeling crafty, why not track down a pattern and make your own? Alternatively, a temporary version can be fashioned using a sheet and a couple of chairs.

If floor area is not an issue – or you have a child who really values their own space, particularly if siblings share a room – a more permanent solution might be a good idea. Built-ins with doors and shutters, or a corner of the room sectioned off with curtains, will give a sense of privacy and provides a quiet spot for reading or simply gathering thoughts.

RIGHT **When a bed is transformed into a den using a bespoke built-in, do try to squeeze out every useful inch of space by designing in some under-bed storage. This example boasts a couple of drawers, painted the same colour as the structure for a sleek look.**

OPPOSITE ABOVE **A tepee is a popular choice as a play tent, but it's worth bearing in mind that its shape often means the amount of space inside isn't really very much when** **you consider the size of the footprint. Make sure you check dimensions carefully when buying ready-made, or using a sewing pattern.**

OPPOSITE BELOW **By enclosing the bed in what is effectively a built-in cupboard, this bedroom features the comfiest hideaway – and the cocoon-like experience is ideal for encouraging a peaceful night's sleep… or maybe some illicit comic reading by torchlight/flashlight!**

❊ To get the most out of a den, comfort is a must – so take your child shopping, to help choose some suitable floor cushions.

❊ Buy a number of suitable cushions (large box-shaped floor designs work really well) and a few throws or blankets, then on a rainy day when the kids are stuck inside, challenge them to build a cushion fort.

❊ An under-stairs cupboard can have great hideaway potential, provided there are no utility meters in the way. Your child could help you decorate it, and furnish it with cushions or maybe small-scale furniture, depending on the size of the space.

❊ More permanent dens would benefit from storage – particularly bookshelves, and a surface on which to play games or put snacks and drinks. If you really want to play up the secret hideaway element, you could also include a 'treasure chest'.

From pretty pictorials to bold stripes, graphic motifs to joyous multi-coloured designs, children's rooms are the ideal place to have fun with pattern.

PRINT AND PATTERN

Some people shy away from using pattern, because it can be tricky to combine colour, scale, shape and texture while still ensuring a sense of coherence – but it's an important skill to master, since without this kind of layering a space can seem a bit impersonal and unwelcoming.

Start small. Create a neutral background scheme, and choose a patterned duvet set – or maybe plain bedlinen gussied up with a few patterned cushions and a throw. A simple strategy for combining involves choosing one main pattern, and then seeking out others which complement it, adding plains as accents.

Mix up different scales of print, making sure that you stick to only one large design (or the combination might be overwhelming), and limit the number of small-scale designs (too many of these can make the look seem fussy). Colours from the same family tone well together, but it's also worth trying shades from the opposite side of the colour wheel, for a contrasting effect.

It's a good idea to make a mood board – or the digital alternative – using images found on the websites of online retailers, blogs and media platforms. This way you'll see for sure which colours and patterns work well together, and which miss the mark, before making any purchases.

---

* *Try pairing florals with checks or gingham, chevrons with stripes, ikat with Paisley, or animal prints with textural patterns.*

* *The simplest approach – ideal for those nervous about using pattern – is to opt for a colour scheme of white and one other colour. Create a white-on-white background scheme, then choose accessories in two-tone patterns including stripes, zig-zags, checks and graphic motifs.*

* *An easy way to achieve success with the layered look is to pick one statement pattern, one which features a couple of the same colours but is half the scale, and one which is either small-scale or just textured, in a complementary colour.*

* *Always stick to the same colour intensity, for instant coherence. Don't, for example, mix jewel-like shades with pastels, or primary colours with muted hues.*

OPPOSITE **One of the simplest ways to use pattern is to select a single attention-grabbing design and use it prominently, keeping the other elements plain. Here a very busy wallpaper sits behind furniture painted in shades picked out from the pattern (red and pink), as well as from the opposite side of the colour wheel (blue and green).**

ABOVE **You might think that a striking or unusual wallpaper is difficult to use in a child's bedroom, where there's likely to be a proliferation of different colours and patterns, but it can work beautifully. This birch forest design is eye-catching yet doesn't dominate, thanks to its monochrome colouring.**

RIGHT **In this feminine bedroom vintage florals have been combined to create a pretty, cosy room with plenty of old-fashioned charm. The patchwork bedspread's use of large- and smaller-scale florals, with brighter shades contrasting with paler ones, provides plenty of visual interest in a room that's actually quite neutral in its décor.**

Young children need a table or desk for all kinds of activities. Practising their writing, drawing and painting, sticking and making, jigsaw puzzles – they all demand a wide, wipe-clean surface that is the right height for a child to sit up at. Children's tables can be rather small, so position two together to make a longer run, or buy a second-hand kitchen table and cut the legs down to make it lower.

ACTION STATIONS

Storage for pens, glue, art materials and paper needs to be positioned close to hand. A simple row of shelves alongside the table or just above (but not out of reach), topped with boxes and trays that can neatly hold paper and colouring books is a good idea, while an array of old glass jars, jugs or mugs can keep pens and pencils tidily on the desktop.

A desk remains key for older children and teenagers, too. It is somewhere to study, draw, paint, sew or arrange favourite objects. In later years, it will become home to the ubiquitous laptop or, when topped with a mirror, can double as a dressing table. As the child grows taller, so too can the height of shelves arranged above, there to hold not just books, but study materials, souvenirs and pictures.

The need to personalize one's space becomes greater the older one gets, so as your child becomes a teenager, work in flexible pieces that they can leave their mark on – furniture that can be painted the colour they choose, an unusual chair, shelves that can become crammed with significant pieces.

Add corkboards or magnetic boards to an older child's room so they can pin up photos, postcards and certificates. Their bedroom is so much more than a place to sleep; it is the one space in the house that is uniquely theirs, a place to rest, but also entertain, study, listen to music, surf the internet, practise an instrument or just read. Flexible furniture, plenty of storage and space-saving ideas will help their room work hard and meet all their growing needs.

ABOVE RIGHT **A broad shelf, affixed firmly at the right height, can play the part of a desk – this very long example is ideal for larger families, where more than one person might need to use it at the same time, or for kids who like painting or modelling with clay (there's plenty of drying room).**

RIGHT **Noticeboards are an essential element of a working or arts and crafts zone. You can pin important reminders there, but kids can also curate their own little collection of clippings and pictures, to inspire creativity or simply express their decorative preferences.**

* If your young child's bedroom is also his or her chief activity area, consider laying practical flooring such as rubber or vinyl over some of the floor, so it's easy to clean up spills and scuffs.

* For an older child, try to find a desk large enough to fit their computer on one side, so there is still a decent-sized work surface for writing, painting or sketching, to encourage all facets of your child's creativity.

* Good lighting is essential in a room that multi-tasks. Work in general light with ceiling and wall lights, then add directable task lighting for close work and soft, ambient lighting for relaxing.

* Try to zone the space so there is a calm area, too. Perhaps position the bed facing away from the main activity area, so your child isn't distracted when trying to get off to sleep.

* A chair on castors allows an older child to whizz quickly between desk, drawers and shelving without getting up.

ABOVE RIGHT If a child has a selection of craft supplies to be kept to hand – such as this collection of washi tape – then it's worth placing a few small-scale shelf units on the desk top to help with organization. They're also a good choice for displaying trinkets and small toys.

RIGHT In a small room, keep the look light with a slim-legged desk design that doesn't feature low-level shelves or drawers. The fact that this desk and chair set matches also helps ensure a simple aesthetic, which will always suit a more compact space.

FAR RIGHT When choosing wallcoverings for behind a desk area, pictorial wallpaper or a decal might be a good choice – anything that a child wouldn't want to sully with crayon or pen. It's probably best to avoid illustrative black and white designs, or geometric patterns, since the colouring-in temptation might be too great to resist!

HOME OFFICES

OPPOSITE **If you're creating a work space in another part of your home – say, in a hallway, perhaps on a landing, or maybe in a living room – then you'll need to choose your desk to fit in with the existing décor. Here a sleek white design is appropriately contemporary, and understated enough not to draw the eye too much.**

RIGHT **A home office can easily be combined with a hobby or crafting space. Both tend to need a sizeable table or desk, and both will benefit from good natural light levels – whether you're working, carrying out household admin or indulging in a little leisure time.**

FAR RIGHT **A custom-built desk space will ensure that your office suits your needs perfectly, and also makes the most of the room and its layout. This configuration, for example, works around a long, low radiator and therefore utilizes a part of the space that might otherwise have been tricky to furnish.**

BELOW RIGHT **By placing the desk at right-angles to the wall, this home office provides a nicer environment to work in – it can seem a bit claustrophobic to always be sitting facing the wall. As the back of the computer will be seen, it's always better to choose a sleek design-led model, if possible.**

Whether you work from home full-time or just need somewhere quiet to tap away at the computer, creating a home office is a necessity these days. But if you haven't got a room to spare, where can you put your work zone and how best can you integrate it with the rest of your living space?

DESIGN & DECORATION

If you don't have a study, there may be somewhere else that you could house an office. Can you convert a junk room, perhaps, or fit a workstation into the attic or on the landing? If you are short of space, could you section off part of a large living room or create a mezzanine level in a high-ceilinged bedroom? Consider what you can afford and get advice from an architect if you want to make structural changes.

A cheaper solution is to double the function of a room so that it can play the office role part-time. A spare room could be work space by day and guest bedroom by night, for example. The key is to keep the décor neutral and to be organized, so one function doesn't intrude on the other.

The bonus of creating an office in your own home is that it needn't look corporate or dull. You will have to accommodate all the technology, but you can make the room as comfortable and colourful as you wish. Keep in mind that certain colours can affect your mood and try to keep clutter to a minimum to help concentration.

Today's home office can be a fixed space or something altogether more fluid – a laptop at the kitchen table, for example, or just a tablet and a mobile phone. Decide what's right for you then plan the space down to the last detail to make sure it meets your needs.

PLANNING

In any office, technology is a top priority. Consider just how much equipment your work space will need to accommodate and devise a layout to suit. The last thing you want is for your office to become a hotch-potch of ugly plastic machines, so think how to arrange them neatly and discreetly so they won't dominate. Could you house a printer or a scanner in a shelving unit, for example? Could the router be stashed away beneath your desk?

Despite the prevalence of wireless technology, many machines still need plugging in. Avoid trailing cables by positioning related equipment together and install extra electrical sockets/power points wherever needed. If you have a fitted desktop, cut a hole at the back so that wires and cables can be channelled away from the working area, and use cable tidies to keep mess off the floor.

If your home office is located within another room, think of ways to separate it off. After all, you don't want to be thinking about work when you are relaxing in the living room, for example. If a permanent partition is not an option, consider positioning office space behind a screen or a large piece of furniture. A tiny workstation can even be hidden away inside a large cupboard when not in use.

Good and copious storage is a necessity, so make sure you have enough. If you are constructing an office from scratch, get as much built in as you can; if not, opt for freestanding solutions, making sure that whatever you choose can accommodate your equipment. An organized office not only looks better, it is far easier to work in, too.

Flat-pack and fold-away elements always work well in a home office – particularly if it is in a shared space. Consider putting a flap-down desk against a wall or within a cupboard. Flexible features like this can easily be tucked out of sight when not in use.

ABOVE RIGHT **This mezzanine space offers the ideal characteristics of a home office – it's tucked away from the hustle of communal areas, but benefits from lots of natural light and a feeling of openness. Its selection of vintage furniture harmonizes with the monochrome scheme downstairs.**

RIGHT **This bespoke desk has been built in along a short length of wall, and made to seem part of the interior architecture by echoing some of the period detailing in the room's original woodwork. Painting the desk in the same colour as the walls brings the look bang up to date.**

THIS PAGE **A showstopper of a desk deserves to take centre stage. This sort of approach only works in large rooms – partly because the design should be table-style, rather than a bulkier example with lots of drawers, so plenty of other storage space will be required.**

OPPOSITE **Some hobbies will need considerable space when it comes to worksurface. Whether you're a painter or calligrapher, quilter or jewellery maker, try to work out how to incorporate the biggest table possible into your scheme. Remember to include enough shelves to store equipment and finished work.**

RIGHT **If all you're looking to do is surf the web, and perform a little light household administration (such as paying bills and writing letters), then a small desk will do just fine – especially if you use a laptop rather than a desktop computer.**

FAR RIGHT **If there's more than one member of the household looking to use the space at the same time, try placing two desks of the same height together. Here contrasting designs add an eclectic element that suits the quirky, crafty vibe of the room.**

BELOW RIGHT **The edgy industrial look of this X-legged desk adds a contrast to the classical interior architecture, which features plaster mouldings and a graceful alcove. The desk's distressed finish adds much-needed texture in a monochrome room where the other dark elements have a fairly even colouring.**

WORKSTATIONS

Today's home office needs to be ultra-efficient and equipped with the latest technology, but that doesn't mean it has to have its own dedicated room. A compact workstation can include all the elements of a larger office but can be slotted against a wall or tucked into the corner of another space.

So where should your workstation go? Ideally, the location should be well-lit (natural light is best), quiet and set apart from the hurly-burly of daily life, so you won't be constantly interrupted. A workstation won't take up too much room, so consider setting it in an in-between space, such as a half-landing or the end of a hallway, if it doesn't get too much traffic. Have a look at your home and work with what you have.

Apart from computer kit, a workstation requires three basic ingredients: a desk, a chair and storage. You can buy modular units ready-made, so investigate these first and consider if any combinations would be right for you. Alternatively, take the DIY route and design your own (an architect or designer can help here). It might cost more, but a custom-built workstation will fit its allotted space perfectly and give you exactly what you want.

Make sure your desktop is fitted at exactly the right height and don't be tempted to skimp on your office chair. Look for an ergonomic model that is comfortable, supportive and adjustable to avoid bad posture and back pain.

CORNER OFFICES

A laptop on the kitchen worktop; a bureau in the bedroom; a desk in the living room – the home office is often squeezed into borrowed space, but that doesn't mean compromising on function or style.

In a dual-purpose room, the key to success is to create defined areas for each function, so that one doesn't intrude on the other. One way of doing this is to partition the space physically, perhaps with sliding doors, a fabric curtain or a simple screen to divide your work area from the rest of the room. This will give you the advantage of a distinct office space as and when you need it.

If you opt, instead, to keep things open, make the office element as unobtrusive as possible. Rather than buying in standard utilitarian furniture, choose pieces that will fit in with the look of the rest of the room. An old wooden desk, for example, could be just the thing for your computer as long as it is the right height and big enough to work at. If you don't have anything suitable at home, hunt around for old office fixtures and fittings that will slot neatly into your decorative scheme.

Ideally, choose pieces that come with integral storage space, so you can contain your office paraphernalia or shut it away when not in use. Planned carefully, a corner office shouldn't dominate the rest of the room.

OPPOSITE ABOVE LEFT **If you need to put your home office space within another room, it can be a wise idea to find a way to screen it off when you're not in work mode. This understairs desk has been given folding doors for that very reason.**

OPPOSITE ABOVE RIGHT **If your office space is within a built-in storage unit in a living or dining area, then you'll minimize the visual effect of the room's additional function. It also might be possible to design in a shutter or sliding panel that can be drawn across to hide work paraphernalia and paperwork.**

OPPOSITE BELOW **Creative types who live and breathe their occupation have no need to play down the presence of their work area. This living room features a long worksurface across one end, with plenty of space for arts and crafts as well as a computer.**

THIS PAGE **This alcove by the fireplace has proven the perfect place for a home office corner. A compact desk, wheeled filing cabinet and a shelf come together to create an inexpensive workstation, which also features metallic accents to lift the monochrome scheme.**

THIS PAGE **Whether you need lots of storage for books and magazines, files full of papers or boxes of craft or artists' materials, floor-to-ceiling built-in shelves will always offer the greatest capacity for any space. Include an ornament or two, as well, to make the look a bit more homely.**

OPPOSITE LEFT **Keep things you will use often in an accessible place by using open storage. Your essentials should always be within arm's reach, without you having to rise from your chair. Less critical items can be stored at height or in drawers or cupboards.**

OPPOSITE RIGHT **For a streamlined look that offers plenty of capacity, opt for large cupboards painted in the same shade as the walls. You might need to consider keeping a stool or small step-ladder handy for reaching items stored on the upper shelves.**

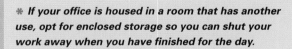

* If your office is housed in a room that has another use, opt for enclosed storage so you can shut your work away when you have finished for the day.

* For the ultimate 'now-you-see-it-now-you-don't' office, create a mini-workstation inside a cupboard. Remember that you will need to fit internal plug sockets here for computer equipment and the phone.

* Invest in a desk with integral storage. Multi-level models with overlapping tiers, for example, will allow you to stack monitor and keyboard on top of each other – a practical and space-saving option.

* Freestanding storage solutions won't fit your space exactly but will give you more flexibility, allowing you to move things around if you need to. Put heavy items – such as filing cabinets – on casters, if possible, to make them moveable.

* Clear out your office regularly: old files and paperwork can be stored in a loft or cellar, leaving you more space for your current bits and pieces.

LARGE STORAGE

You can't have too much storage in your home office. Whether you opt for a built-in solution or freestanding furniture, include more than you think you need and make sure it is suitable for the task.

In a small office, integral storage always works best. A wall-to-wall system of shelves and cupboards, for example, will provide you with copious places to put things but it won't intrude on the room. Similarly, if you fill an alcove or disused chimneybreast with shelves, you will create a practical storage solution without compromising the central space.

A mixture of open and closed storage works well because it allows you to display certain elements and hide others, but remember that open storage boxes or shelves will attract dust. One solution is to shut up your storage behind see-through doors (in glass or Perspex/Plexiglass, perhaps). Solid cupboards are the answer in a dual-purpose space, however, so that your office equipment is invisible when not in use.

Build flexibility into your work space, too, so that you can easily accommodate new office kit (adjustable shelves are a good option) and put large freestanding storage on casters to make it mobile.

* Reduce your paperwork by scanning important documents or articles and storing them digitally – but remember to back up your files regularly.

* In a small home office, make the most of every available bit of space. Suspend a fabric shoe tidy in an awkward corner and use it for storing folders and files, or invest in a hanging filing system which can be hooked onto the back of a door.

* Turn the wall above your desk into a giant noticeboard. Not only will it keep your worktop clutter-free; it is just the place to pin up inspirational bits and pieces.

* Bring in some unconventional containers to add a quirky and personal look to your work space: use an old cigar box as an in-tray; recycled tin cans for pens and pencils; a toast rack for cards and invitations.

* To make your desktop neat and tidy, choose uniform storage containers. A row of stainless-steel pots, for example, or a series of wooden boxes will look smart and organized. If you do opt for a disparate collection of containers, stick to one colour to unify them.

BELOW LEFT There's no need to invest in purpose-made desk accessories – in fact, creative alternatives can look much better. Vintage boxes or tins will keep all manner of correspondence and small items from becoming clutter, while a jar or mug serves perfectly well as a pencil pot.

BELOW Just because it's an area for work, doesn't mean everything has to be serious! This colourful pencil tree has been made simply by drilling suitably-sized holes in a cut section of a branch.

RIGHT Wall-hung small storage above a desk keeps surfaces clear and clutter free, while ensuring bits and bobs are close to hand. This design classic is the Uten.Silo, created by Dorothee Becker in 1969. Made in plastic, it boasts a variety of different containers, as well as metal hooks and clips.

OPPOSITE Sometimes storage for little things can come in a pretty sizeable package. This industrial drawer unit is ideal for keeping a variety of small pieces of equipment safe, or providing a well-organized home for stashes of craft supplies or artist's materials.

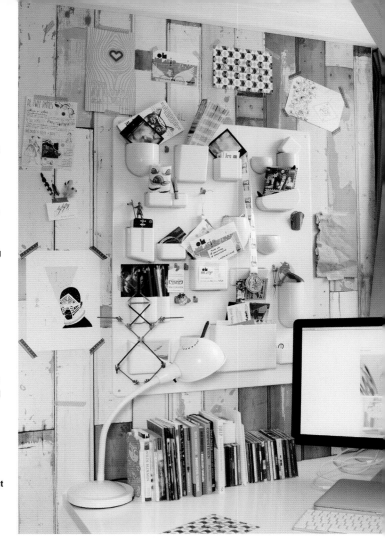

It is easy for a home office to become overtaken with clutter. Keep your work paraphernalia under control by bringing in some useful storage containers.

SMALL STORAGE

There is a huge variety of office accessories on the market, from the classic tubular plastic desk tidy to smart letter trays in leather, wood or stainless steel. If you are buying new, choose a style you like and stick to it. A uniform set of storage containers will do much to make your worktop look organized. Similarly, opt for a row of identikit magazine files in one or two colours, or buy plain ones and cover them to match your office décor. Lined up in a row, they will bring instant order to your bookshelves.

Don't feel you have to buy in a quota of standard office kit, however. You may have just what you need already to hand. A collection of vintage tins or some old wooden boxes, for example, can make great organizers, or you could even recycle tin cans or shoeboxes to make unconventional storage containers. Not only will these add a quirky edge to your home office, they are eco-friendly options to boot.

OPPOSITE **Whether you're hanging pendant lights or positioning spots, over-desk lighting needs to be in just the right place to illuminate your working area. If it's over your head, or slightly behind you, you'll end up trying to work in your own shadow.**

ABOVE LEFT **A centrally-placed desk will benefit from a low-hanging pendant to illuminate the working area – just make sure that it's not so low that it impedes the use of the desktop surface, or risks dazzling those trying to concentrate.**

ABOVE **Sometimes all you need to be productive is a desk, a chair and a laptop – and some decent light. This minimalist office corner features industrial metal furnishings in tones of distressed white, while the lamp is appropriately utilitarian in its styling.**

LIGHTING

In a home office, more than anywhere in the house, it is crucial to get the lighting right. A badly lit work space can lead to headaches and even eyestrain.

Daylight is the easiest to work by, so if you are creating an office from scratch try to site it in a naturally well-lit location. If you can't, consider other ways of bringing in the light: could you install a skylight, a solar tube or an internal window, perhaps? Failing that, bring in bulbs that simulate daylight.

Supplement sunlight with a mix of ambient and task lighting so you can create the level of light you require. A central pendant or ceiling spots will give you good general cover, but you will also need targeted lights to illuminate your desktop effectively. In-built solutions can work well if they are strategically placed (under an eye-level unit, perhaps); freestanding lamps will give you greater flexibility. Opt for jointed models – such as the classic Anglepoise – so that you can easily change the direction of the light.

If more than one person works in the office, make sure there's sufficient task lighting for everyone, and always turn off lights when not in use.

* *In summer you will need to screen out brilliant sunlight to prevent computer glare and excess heat, so make sure your windows can be covered without losing the light. Diaphanous curtains or vinyl frosting applied to the lower panes are good solutions.*

* *Effective task lighting is particularly important if you will be using the office at night. Bright overhead illumination is not what you want here.*

* *Build adaptability into your lighting scheme so that you can create just the amount of cover you need. Take advice from an electrician and install adjustable solutions, such as dimmer switches, to give you maximum flexibility.*

* *If your office is stuck in a gloomy space, consider using full-spectrum bulbs, which simulate daylight more effectively than ordinary light bulbs. Some can also help alleviate symptoms of SAD.*

* *Electric lighting consumes copious amounts of energy, so keep the environment in mind when you are kitting out your home office. Switch to low-energy light bulbs (daylight versions are available) and always turn off the lights at the end of the day.*

FINISHING TOUCHES

Although functionality is the key ingredient in the home office, don't forget to decorate it. Adding colour, pictures and personal details will make it a far nicer place to be.

Just because this is a working space doesn't mean you need to temper your taste. What works for you in the rest of the house should work for you here, so put up floral wallpaper or photos if they inspire you. Think what colours would work best with the light; what flooring is appropriate; what window treatments you'd like.

A shared space, however, demands a different approach. Here, your workstation needs to slot into the general scheme, so consider the other role the room has to play and decorate accordingly. Though you might paint the walls all one colour, using different or raised flooring for the work space can be a subtle way of defining it without making it too obtrusive. A colourful rug would also be effective. Though you want your home office to be efficient and uncluttered, don't leave it bare. It is a home office, after all, and calls out for a bit of comfort and character.

❋ *Your desktop needn't be dull. Give it a curvy edge or top it with an interesting material (vinyl or rubber tiles, perhaps) to achieve a distinctive look.*

❋ *Create an eye-catching feature wall with something that inspires you, whether it's wallpaper, a blown-up map or a giant black-and-white photograph.*

❋ *Display fresh flowers. Not only will they bring a bit of life to your work space; they should make it smell nice to boot. Just remember to replace them once they are past their best.*

❋ *As well as books, files and folders, think of displaying more unusual things in your office space. Overscaled items can work well, such as giant wooden letters, a station clock or an outsized calendar.*

❋ *Colour-code your folders and files to make an easy and good-looking filing system. Don't over-complicate it; just two or three tones should do the trick.*

ABOVE LEFT **Surrounding yourself with favourite trinkets and inspirational pictures can set just the right ambience for creating your best work. Here a beautiful mish-mash of decorative pieces, framed pictures and adhesive-tacked photos makes for a dramatic display against a smoke-grey wall.**

ABOVE **This very refined desk area hits just the right balance between harmony and interest, thanks to a mainly monochrome palette which features shots of warm wood, woven raffia, chrome and gilt. The carefully curated selection of pictures looks coherent, without being too closely matched.**

OPPOSITE **Fixing a shelf just a few inches above your desk surface will give you plenty of room for decorative objects as well as office essentials. Picture ledges also come in handy, as they provide slimline shelf space which doesn't intrude too far over the desk area.**

Whether shop-bought or custom-made, a fitted office system makes good use of space. With adaptable elements, it can be both functional and flexible.

PURPOSE-BUILT OFFICES

There are countless ready-made office systems on the market, so if you want to buy off the peg, trawl the high street and internet to find out what is available. To save time and effort, it's wise to have an idea of what you want before you start. What size workstation do you need? Which finish would suit your space? How much do you want to spend? Prices depend on material and quality, so set a budget (and remember you usually get what you pay for).

Any fitted system will offer office components in fixed sizes, whether shelves, desktops or drawers, and many suppliers will allow you to mix and match different elements to create something that will work in your space. Try to include as many adaptable features as you can to give yourself maximum flexibility. Opt for adjustable shelving, fold-down desks or light fixtures that can be moved to different positions, for example.

Always include more storage than you think you need (you will fill it). Closed cupboards give a neat, streamlined look; open storage boxes offer you easy access to your bits and pieces and also provide you with a useful display space. A combination of the two is often the best solution.

The one-wall home office makes the most economical use of space, particularly when a desktop is incorporated into the design. This linear system is streamlined and good-looking but it is not necessarily the most ergonomic solution. A corner office, by contrast, will create a self-contained 'work triangle',

allowing you to move with ease between the prime working spots – the computer screen, the desk top and the filing cabinet, for example – possibly without even leaving your chair.

If you can't find a suitable ready-made solution, consider a bespoke office. Get quotes from architects or designers and give a very detailed brief. Discuss what size the shelves should be to accommodate your box files; how many drawers you need; at what angle you would like the desktop. Getting something custom-made is the ultimate indulgence, but you will end up with a working space that is perfect for you.

OPPOSITE **Custom-built office furniture can help to provide maximum functionality within any sized space, and even if you're on a modest budget you don't necessarily need to stick to one of the off-the-peg systems. Investigate the cost and capabilities of local carpenters, too, as you might be surprised.**

LEFT **Purpose-made office furniture doesn't need to be expensive, and it doesn't have to create an office-y feel either. This white desk and matching fitted wall cabinets offer the perfect understated solution to a modern home office within a period house.**

BELOW **Fitting a desk across one end of a room, and filling the space above it with wall-mounted shelves, is a great option to maximize functionality and storage capacity in a smaller room. This chic example features two workstations, and room for a sizeable collection of books too.**

* *Don't forget that any open storage system will only be as tidy as you make it. If clutter is problem, closed cupboards may be a better bet for you.*

* *Planning from scratch means you can create good task lighting and hide trailing wires and cables.*

* *Even an off-the-peg office system can include custom-made elements. Combine shop-bought pieces with bespoke to create just what you need.*

* *If you haven't much space, choose smaller purpose-built pieces of furniture, such as the hard-working old bureau or writing desk, which gives you a whole office in miniature.*

* *Note down the exact position of your electrical sockets/power points and, if you need any extras, get them fitted before you start.*

* *Ask suppliers if they offer a fitting service for their off-the-peg office systems. If not, measure up and make a floor plan yourself so you know exactly how much space you have to play with.*

* *To avoid a home office looking too corporate, make sure you include the means to display few decorative pieces within your scheme.*

Unstructured and adaptable, the freeform office should give you the space to be creative. Just remember not to let the clutter get out of control.

FREEFORM OFFICES

The best thing about creating a working space at home is that it need not look like a corporate office. You can do away with the formula of functional grey furniture, uniform filing units and flickering strip lighting and create an individual and expressive space that is just right for you.

You will still need the key office ingredients, of course – a desk, a chair and sufficient storage – but these don't need to be purpose-built. For a less structured effect, gather together an ad hoc collection of furniture, but make sure that whatever you choose is practical and comfortable. Think what you need in your office and look around the house to see if you can use something you already have, or hunt for interesting second-hand or vintage pieces.

A freeform office should be a fluid and adaptable place, so opt for freestanding furniture that you can move around at whim, and don't let your display space stagnate. Show off different bits and pieces week by week, or even day by day, to keep your work area alive. While a streamlined, ordered office is not what you are after here, do try to keep clutter at bay. Even in a freeform office, you need a bit of space to be creative.

* **Make sure the essentials are in good working order – the phone, the electrics, the wireless router. Even a freeform office needs to be functional.**

* **Mix and match different pieces of furniture for an idiosyncratic look. Make sure to find a comfortable chair and storage that is fit for purpose.**

* **Turn your working area into a display space. You don't need collections of art or recherché artefacts to make it look good. Pinned with a collection of interesting bits and pieces, even a noticeboard can make a visual impact.**

* **Rather than a dull filing cabinet, choose more unconventional storage options. Hang bags or baskets from hooks on the wall to accommodate your office kit, for example.**

* **Surround yourself with things you love. Whether it's a family painting, an antique desk lamp or a knitted cushion, old favourites will inspire you and make you feel at home.**

ABOVE **If you're only planning to use your office space for things like shopping online and paying bills, then you won't need to worry about ergonomics quite so much as if you were a full-time homeworker. This upholstered stool and low-level table offer a relaxed, elegant look at one end of the living room.**

RIGHT **Console tables can work as occasional office spaces, especially if you use a laptop. This design features a handy internal shelf for storing essentials, though its height means that high stools are a more comfortable choice than chairs.**

OPPOSITE **Sleek mid-century designs and retro classics will add a Mad Men vibe, recalling the glamorous golden age of the modern office. Here a few other elements bring the look into the contemporary realm, such as the graphic artwork, the exposed brick wall and the distressed-finish wooden floor.**

OPEN-PLAN LIVING

OPPOSITE **If you don't want to go the whole hog and start knocking down walls – or your home's architecture dictates that you can't – there is an alternative. Simply removing some internal doors, or switching to the sliding variety (preferably those which disappear into a wall cavity), will help to achieve something of the same feel.**

RIGHT **Conversions of chapels, halls and warehouses often feature an open-plan layout, because carving up the space with walls and solid partitions destroys the original room volumes, and impacts negatively on the original charm of the interior architecture. A mezzanine level is often used to add first-floor rooms.**

BELOW RIGHT **In this high-ceilinged building an open-plan layout was really the only way to go, since dividing the space into separate rooms with full-height walls would have created some odd and unappealing proportions. Low partition walls can help to add flexibility to a layout, especially if you're siting kitchen cabinets or appliances.**

BELOW FAR RIGHT **Shelf-style room dividers – whether built-in or freestanding – perform the dual purposes of providing storage (and display) capacity, while breaking up a large living area into cosier zones, without compromising on the feeling of a generous space.**

WHY OPEN-PLAN?

Whether you want to knock two small rooms into one or crave an expansive living area, an open-plan space has become the latest must-have. Free-flowing and flexible, they seem perfect for modern life, but why have they become so popular?

The domestic interior used to be a very fixed and formal affair. There was the kitchen for cooking; the dining room for eating; the study for working. A hundred years ago this formula made sense, but today it seems outmoded and the separate rooms inappropriate for modern life. People like to chat with their friends as they cook; rustle up supper at the kitchen table; surf the net while the kettle boils. An open-plan layout offers just this flexibility.

It will also, of course, maximize the sense of space and light. Freed of dividing walls, even a small home can seem spacious. Think of combining a tiny bathroom and small bedroom to create one large sleeping and bathing space, or making the downstairs one multi-purpose area.

In new houses and loft-style apartments the open-plan layout has become standard, particularly downstairs, but in an older house some restructuring will be in order. Plan what you want to do, get advice from a structural engineer or an architect and cost the project carefully. Knocking down walls is a job for a professional, particularly if the walls are load-bearing.

An open-plan interior will give you space, light and freedom of movement, but before you start knocking down walls, it's prudent to think about the drawbacks, too.

PROS & CONS

One large, transformable space, rather than a series of rooms, allows you to organize the layout just as you like – and reconfigure it at whim. If you spend little time cooking, for example, minimize the kitchen area and leave more room for eating or lounging. If you sometimes work from home, create an ad hoc office wherever you like. And open-plan is perfect for entertaining – from six to sixty people – as long as you have the right furniture to make it work.

Without dividing walls, it can be tricky to know how to partition a space. In a do-it-all downstairs, for example, how can you separate each zone? How do you give a multi-purpose space a cohesive visual identity? Could you cope with a boundary-less area and keep it tidy?

Then there is the noise factor. Every sound, from the television to screaming children, will carry right through an open-plan interior. You won't have to worry about slamming doors, of course, but will you manage without a spot of quiet, private space? Cooking smells, too, may permeate and, while you may have acres of space, an open-plan area is always harder to heat than the average room.

ABOVE **Open-plan is usually associated with living areas, but private zones such as bedrooms can receive the same treatment. Where a sleeping area is open-plan to an en-suite, some kind of screen is usually employed, whether it's freestanding or built-in (a sheet of flip glass, which turns opaque as the touch of a button, is a more contemporary alternative).**

RIGHT **An open-plan space generally benefits from a single, coherent colour scheme. In this kitchen-diner there's just the right amount of colour-matching going on, but the off-white space is enlivened by the red range cooker, grey-blue lights and natural wood accents.**

OPPOSITE **Open-plan can be cosy, it's just a case of thinking carefully about your use of space, and using complementary colours to tie the whole look together. This quirky interior boasts a combination of warm oranges and rusty browns, along with a bit of a monochrome to add definition.**

Opening up the kitchen, dining room and living room to create one do-it-all downstairs space can prove very liberating, but how do you start?

COOKING, LIVING & EATING

First consider your needs and priorities. Are you a great cook who needs a big kitchen? Do you want a large dining table to accommodate friends? Would you rather give most of the space to a giant modular sofa? Think what would work for you and plan the layout on paper.

For practical reasons (extractor fans, water supply and so on), it is generally best to position the kitchen against a wall. This will allow you to incorporate lots of storage – a must in any open-plan space – but remember that it should also connect to the surrounding space. Installing an island unit with an integral hob/stovetop is a good solution, as it allows you to face the living area as you cook and it will also partially screen the kitchen and any dirty dishes.

Remember that in an open-plan space furniture will be viewed from all sides, so choose pieces carefully, and opt for multi-purpose or adaptable models – an extendable dining table, perhaps, or a bookshelf-cum-screen.

OPPOSITE **In an open-plan room, the placement of furniture helps to designate the different zones, and facilitates easy movement between them. Here a sofa placed across the space creates a living area in front of it, while still leaving plenty of room behind for kitchen-diner access.**

ABOVE **With a concrete staircase almost floating in the air – allowing the most open ground-floor space imaginable – this very large room benefits from clever zoning. A centrally placed coffee table is surrounded by comfortable seating, while the kitchen area is given definition by the use of an island unit.**

RIGHT **One of the best ways to maximize storage and preparation space, and demarcate the living space from the kitchen's working area, is to opt for either a well-placed island or peninsula unit – the latter is useful if space is tight, or if a greater amount of storage space is required.**

THIS PAGE **The trend for luxury hotels to install a bath in the bedroom, rather than in a separate en-suite, has trickled through into the domestic domain. It's deliciously convenient – just soak, dry and nap – but attention should be paid to the practicalities (a good bath mat, over a water-resistant hard floor, and an effective extractor fan are all must-haves).**

SLEEPING, DRESSING & BATHING

Your bedroom and bathroom should be peaceful, personal spaces, so how can you incorporate them into an open-plan scheme? The trick is to use ingenious partitions to give you privacy without doors.

If you are creating an open-plan apartment from scratch, position your bedroom at the margins of the spaces so you can transform it into a private cocoon. If you are working with an existing interior, incorporate flexible partitions into the architecture so that you can shut off your sleeping space when you need to. During the day you might be happy for your bedroom to be on show, but at night a secluded sanctuary is what you should be after.

Whether you opt for an en-suite or decide to create a larger open-plan bathing, dressing and sleeping space, incorporate convertible elements into the design. Sliding doors or panels, track-hung curtains or screens – all will allow you to enclose space one minute and keep it open the next, giving you maximum flexibility. Alternatively, use the existing architecture. Retain part of a bedroom wall to create a giant bedhead, for example, which can conceal a dressing area or bathroom on the other side.

Combining bedroom and bathroom is a luxurious option, but some form of screening may be necessary. You could conceal the bath behind a half-wall, perhaps, or use a glass screen to define the bathing area without blocking out light. Make sure the space is well ventilated, air bedlinen to prevent mould and – if you are overlooked – don't forget curtains.

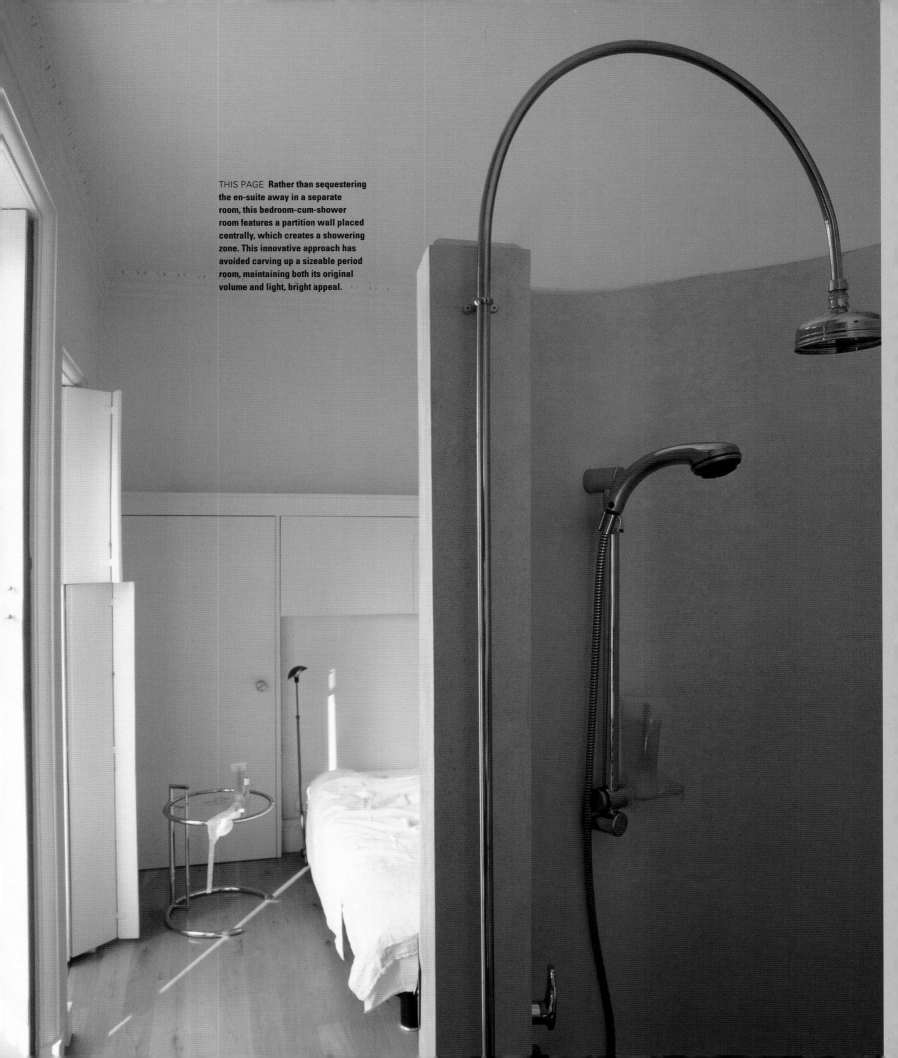

THIS PAGE **Rather than sequestering the en-suite away in a separate room, this bedroom-cum-shower room features a partition wall placed centrally, which creates a showering zone. This innovative approach has avoided carving up a sizeable period room, maintaining both its original volume and light, bright appeal.**

LEFT **Sometimes a very big space can be more of a challenge than a compact home – zoning becomes even more important, so that the feel remains homely. In this beautiful barn, the original timber framing has been taken into consideration when planning the layout, which means the placement of the kitchen looks deliberate and harmonious.**

An individual or idiosyncratic look can be the making of an interior, but in an open-plan space you'll need to keep those hoarding instincts under control. An open-plan interior gives you a good dose of creative freedom. Not only can you decide how to configure the space itself, you can also — if you want to — do away with traditional furnishing conventions. Why buy a dining-room table when you don't have a dining room? Why opt for a fitted kitchen when you have no room to fit it in? If you have a more freestyle approach to decorating, an open-plan space can be just the place to indulge it.

ECLECTIC

ABOVE **With its large room volumes, an open-plan space can work almost as a gallery might do, showing off the owner's collections of art and curiosities to best effect. In this sizeable living area, white-painted walls offer a neutral backdrop that is the perfect foil to a number of antiques and ethnic artwork.**

ABOVE RIGHT **If you're creating a busier look with diverse influences, it pays to use the same colour for the walls and floor, to ensure the end result isn't too visually confusing. Here the sofa and cushions are also in a similar soft shade of white to the floor and walls, which also helps.**

What's more, some conventional fixtures and fittings can look out of place in an open-plan arena. Rather than room-specific items, what you want here is more equivocal, go-anywhere furniture that will fit in with the flexibility of the surroundings. Choose pieces that work in the space, whether it's a convertible seating system or some old metal shelving, and don't be afraid to do your own thing.

A quirky collection of bits and pieces can look very effective if the end result expresses a strong personal style. Mix up vintage furniture with modern accessories; industrial elements with soft and comfortable furnishings; an antique sofa with brand-new cushions. Or just use the space to display a diverse collection of things you like.

One drawback of an open-plan interior with its combination of functions and furniture is that it can look disjointed and messy. If you opt for an eclectic scheme, the chances of this happening are all the greater, so it is important to keep control of the space. Try to unify a disparate group of bits and pieces by keeping the background of the space uniform. Stick to plain walls, perhaps, or use the same flooring throughout. And keep your hoarding instincts in check. It is better to put some of your possessions into storage if necessary so that what is left on show has space to breathe.

* *Don't forget that your furniture will be viewed from all sides in an open-plan space. Invest in shapely pieces that look just as good from the back as from the front.*

* *To unify a diverse collection of furniture and furnishings, use a uniform finish for the walls and floor.*

* *Be as creative as you dare – a one-off personal look can create a big visual impact in an open-plan area.*

* *Use colour carefully. An idiosyncratic collection of bits and pieces can be brought together effectively if they are in harmonious or toning shades.*

* *Make sure that whatever pieces you choose work effectively in the space. There is no point including vintage furniture or light fittings if they don't function properly.*

* *Keep mess and clutter firmly under control. Remember: less is more.*

An open-plan living space can look chic, modern and sophisticated. Give yours an exclusive flavour with ingenious design, sleek materials and smart colours.

SLICK & STREAMLINED

The key advantage of an open-plan interior is that it is a structure-less entity but, if you like your home to look streamlined and organized, such freewheeling space can seem dauntingly undisciplined. The solution is to devise a layout for the area that will superimpose a bit of order without creating boundaries.

First, plan the arrangement of space very carefully, employing professional help if necessary. Expertise costs money, but an architect or interior designer can help you achieve a smart and slick result.

To give a streamlined feel to any open-plan interior, the layout should be as unambiguous as possible, so it is important that the role of each part of the space is clearly defined. Create individual zones – the dining area, sitting area, kitchen – and mark them out with distinctive furniture, flooring or lighting. You might even choose to include the odd half-wall or convertible partition to clarify things further.

For a clean-lined look, keep both the architecture and the furniture of the interior as rectilinear as possible. Geometrical designs – whether an angular dining table or a set of parallel kitchen units – will create an instant sense of order and work most efficiently within the space. Use simple, good-quality materials – stone, metal, glass, wood – and keep fussy furnishings to a minimum. This doesn't mean you have to compromise on comfort, however; a giant rug or a vast modular sofa would be absolutely in keeping here.

As much storage as possible should be built in to the carcase of the interior so that you can easily keep your clutter under control without the need for extraneous furniture. A seamless wall of kitchen units, for example, will give a much neater finish than a bulky dresser/hutch.

ABOVE RIGHT **Open-plan might be a modern invention, but that doesn't mean that only contemporary decorating styles are relevant, even when creating a streamlined look. Here a restricted colour palette and minimalist approach are balanced with a more classic aesthetic and vintage detailing.**

RIGHT **Custom-built storage is more streamlined than freestanding designs, and so is particularly effective in open-plan spaces, where you have to be careful not to have too much going on visually. This example, with its different-sized compartments built into (and alongside) the stairs, lends coherence to a disparate set of objects.**

❋ *Keep your colour scheme toning and muted. A neutral palette will always look smart.*

❋ *You need clarity of layout for a clean-lined look, so give each part of the space a distinct identity and use half-walls or different flooring to define individual zones.*

❋ *Bring in the modernist materials – metal, concrete, glass – for a sleek finish and add the odd natural element to soften up the look.*

❋ *Remember that built-in elements – whether a fitted kitchen or a wall of storage units – will always give you a neater end result.*

❋ *Choose streamlined, unfussy furniture. If you can't find what you want on the high street (and if your budget is up to it), consider buying bespoke.*

❋ *Keep a rectilinear emphasis on the design. Geometrical shapes will create a smart overall look and will also make the most of the space.*

THIS PAGE **Running the same flooring throughout adjoining zones, and using the same colour on the walls, helps tie this scheme together. However, the grouping of greys in the living area, and warm-toned timbers in the dining space, helps to differentiate them.**

OUTDOOR LIVING

LEFT Wicker conservatory furniture can come out to play on dry days, bringing the comfort of indoors into the garden. With the addition of squishy cushions, these chairs provide the perfect spot for drinks with friends.

BELOW, FAR LEFT A simple hammock is just the job for solo relaxation with a cuppa and a book. If you don't have two sturdy trees at the right distance apart, you can get freestanding designs which hang from a frame.

BELOW LEFT On a veranda or covered terrace, a sumptuous sheepskin-draped daybed brings all the comfort and luxury of the lounge out into the open air.

Increasingly, we view our gardens not as a separate place, but as an extension of our homes, with the outside decoration complementing rather than contrasting with the inside.

TAKING YOUR LIVING SPACE OUTSIDE

By selecting key elements from your interior, you can create an outdoor space that can work as a dining room, sitting room, play area – even kitchen. A table and chairs are all you need in order to create an outside dining room, while a well-positioned barbecue can become your al fresco kitchen.

Plan carefully where you site everything. For instance, don't put a play area next to a dining space, or you may have footballs crashing into your lunch. Create the feel of an extra room by using the same materials inside and out. If a terrace leads directly off your home, lay the same flooring outside as in – ceramic tiles, sandstone and basalt, for example, or decking made of boards the same width as those inside and stained to match. Add splashes of the colours you have used inside, too, on cushions and tablecloths, to blur the divide between in and out. You don't need to buy pieces specifically for the garden, either. Just grab stools, chairs, cushions, candle holders and rugs, and transplant them to the garden when good weather arrives. Finally, even if it's just candles or solar lights on stakes, lighting will let you stay out after dark.

BELOW LEFT **Sliding or bi-fold doors that open right up will blur the boundaries between indoors and out. This contemporary home features décor that accentuates this unified feel, with natural materials and organic shapes – most notably the dining table and benches.**

BELOW **In hot climates, a shaded seating area is a must. Ideal for lounging in comfort on even the warmest days, this space features a built-in bench adorned with decorative tiles, a generous pile of cushions and a roof made of peeled canes.**

GARDEN ROOMS & CONSERVATORIES

Conservatories have come a long way. Forget the uninspiring half-octagons plonked on the side of many suburban homes; nowadays conservatories are all about maximum glass, minimum fuss, and enjoying the outside year-round.

Masses of glass and, on the best examples, well-designed retractable doors create a super-light, flexible space, which brings you closer to the outdoors without leaving your home. With so much glass, regulating heat and glare is an issue. Roller blinds/shades will provide privacy and keep out bright sunshine and some of its heat, but, when pulled down, prevent you enjoying the views. A good alternative is a specialist film for the glass. It can reduce glare, help retain heat in winter and repel excessive heat in summer.

    There's a big market in furniture for conservatories, but it makes more sense to dress your space as you have the rest of your home; as it flows from the interior, it will be constantly in view, so needs to blend in well. To define the space as a garden room, grow plants here. They will thrive in the light and give an outdoorsy feel distinct from the rest of the house.

OUTDOOR DINING

Eating outdoors is one of life's great pleasures. Whether it's a light lunch in the sun or a leisurely dinner party lit by twinkling tea lights, even the smallest garden can spare the space for a table and chairs.

It's a good idea to have your dining space close to the house or flowing off it, in the form of a deck or patio. If space is limited, choose extending tables and stacking chairs that can be stored easily and, unless you can store your outside furniture under cover, invest in weatherproof pieces, like those made from sealed or painted wood.

A barbecue is a must-have for every garden. Position it facing the table, so the chef does not feel isolated, but not so close that smoke blows into diners' faces. If you have a large garden, consider building a barbecue from reclaimed bricks. You could even create an al fresco kitchen, with worktop, cupboards and a sink.

Shade is essential for outdoor dining. Put a table under a tree or ask a carpenter to build a wooden structure that you can train a vine or climber over for living shade. Alternatively, hang a shade sail, available from specialists, or a length of sheer fabric that will filter harsh sun without blocking out too much light – ideal in a small garden. Inexpensive silk georgette or dyed organza are ideal.

FURNITURE

From the classic stripy deckchair to the ultra-modern lounger, the choice of furniture for outside is almost as great as it is for inside – and just as beautiful.

Decide whether you want built-in furniture, freestanding pieces or a mixture of the two. Built-in garden seats can be super-simple and inexpensive, and make great use of your space. A wooden platform built along a house wall makes a casual bench, but you may decide to create something more solid, with storage beneath for furniture, toys or cushions.

Don't install fixed furniture until you have considered how the sun moves around the garden, and whether you want to sit facing it or away from it. When it comes to freestanding pieces, do you have space to store them, or must they stay outdoors? Classic wooden deckchairs, director's chairs and French café chairs all collapse and are easy to store. Other furniture can be kept outside, but may need help to look its best. Unpainted wooden pieces need feeding with oil annually to keep them watertight and prevent fading. Painted metal furniture may rust, but can be refreshed with wire wool and new paint. If you have a roof space, choose solid materials like wood or iron; lightweight plastic furniture might blow away.

Alternatively, wicker or Lloyd Loom furniture, wooden stools, floor cushions, footstools, rugs and kelims from inside can all feel at home outside.

ABOVE Natural wicker is the ideal choice for a courtyard featuring tropical planting, and many such pieces channel Southeast Asian influences – just think of the type of design that would look at home on the terrace at a boutique hotel in Singapore or Thailand. These high-backed chairs are known as 'peacock' chairs, and bring a slightly hippy, 1960s vibe to the space.

OPPOSITE ABOVE LEFT You can't go far wrong with a classic wooden bench. Even if you only have a small plot, with no room for a table and chairs, it's usually possible to place one of these somewhere, so you can sit peacefully and enjoy your not-quite-so-great outdoors.

OPPOSITE ABOVE RIGHT It's possible to buy durable rattan furniture sets which can live out in almost all weathers, so all you have to store inside are the fabric elements – look for designs which boast showerproof cushions that have removable, washable covers.

OPPOSITE BELOW LEFT A deck with a view is just crying out for some adjustable loungers. Here these natural hardwood designs have turned silvery-grey with weathering, which – along with the stone-coloured cushions and neutral shades of the house's exterior – tones in beautifully with the landscape beyond.

OPPOSITE BELOW RIGHT A metal bistro-style table and chairs will bring some French chic to a terrace or patio. Here a distressed paint finish lends a shabby, vintage air, although you will want to keep an eye on the level of deterioration, to avoid the pieces becoming unstable.

Have fun with accessories in the garden, just as you would inside, to introduce colour, texture and comfort.

ACCESSORIES

The simple cushion can soften the hardest wooden bench and bring colour to the plainest garden. Choose a robust fabric like thick cotton, which will suit the rougher surfaces of an outdoor space and can be washed easily. For maximum comfort, work in a range of sizes; large floor cushions for low-level lounging, long oblong cushions to soften benches or loungers and simple scatter cushions. At ground level, a hard surface can be improved by throwing down a rug, inexpensive mat or runner in tough woven cotton or natural fibres.

Think about incorporating some more unusual accessories: a lazy hammock, strung between trees or garden walls; a colourful parasol or awning; some pretty bunting to cheer up a drab wall. Mirrors are useful outside, too, creating distance in a small garden, reflecting sunlight into shady areas and making plants look doubly lush. Braziers and firepits create a fantastic focal point and warm up the chilliest of evenings, allowing you to stay outside longer. It's even possible to get outdoor wallpaper. Who says colour in a garden has to come from plants?

Finally, for twilight meals, light tapers pushed in among flowerbeds, dot candles on your table and add freshly cut flowers in jugs or vases.

OPPOSITE ABOVE LEFT **In a leafy green oasis the punchy impact of hot pink, turquoise, gold and a myriad of other strong shades, combined with vintage furniture, creates a bohemian feel. Overhead, a fabric panel lends some shade from the hot sun.**

OPPOSITE ABOVE RIGHT **Candles will help to create a romantic atmosphere as dusk falls... but do make sure you choose lanterns which protect the flame from any breeze, and keep them away from combustible materials. Alternatively, you could use LED nightlights or strings of battery-powered fairy lights to create a similarly twinkly effect.**

OPPOSITE BELOW RIGHT **In a wooded and wild part of the plot, an ecru hammock with crocheted trim and decorative fringing adds a contrastingly pretty touch – and a glorious place in which to while away a quiet afternoon.**

OPPOSITE BELOW LEFT **If you eat al fresco regularly, you might want to consider getting an outside power supply put in, and adding some pendant lighting over the table. This way your outside room will still function fully after dark, in the most convenient way.**

ABOVE RIGHT **Nothing dresses up an outside table like a tablecloth. Try layering a couple for a different look, or try other suitably-sized textiles such as sheets, shawls or even decorator's covers for the basis of a table setting with informal appeal.**

RIGHT **Augment your more permanent pieces of outside furniture with some usually-indoor additions on warm, dry days – folding and side tables, floor cushions and other seating can all be combined for an eclectic, relaxed look.**

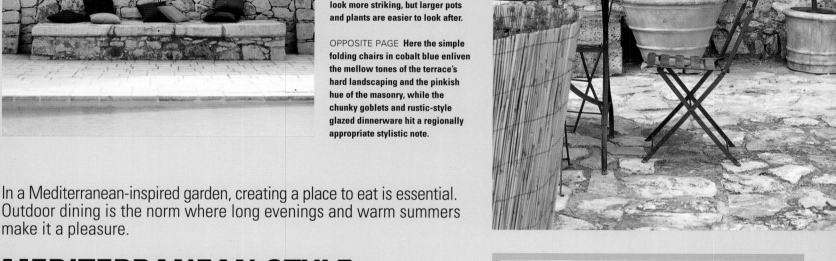

LEFT **The Mediterranean palette draws on the colours of nature, from the blue of the ocean to the green of the olive groves, and the neutral tones of earth and stone. Here a selection of cushions in shades of cobalt, azure and cerulean pick up the blue in the pool and sky.**

RIGHT **Terracotta pots give an authentic Mediterranean aesthetic, but they will dry out more quickly than metal or plastic containers, so you'll need to keep on top of the watering. When it comes to size, bigger is better – not only do they look more striking, but larger pots and plants are easier to look after.**

OPPOSITE PAGE **Here the simple folding chairs in cobalt blue enliven the mellow tones of the terrace's hard landscaping and the pinkish hue of the masonry, while the chunky goblets and rustic-style glazed dinnerware hit a regionally appropriate stylistic note.**

In a Mediterranean-inspired garden, creating a place to eat is essential. Outdoor dining is the norm where long evenings and warm summers make it a pleasure.

MEDITERRANEAN STYLE

Think about creating a decked area or, better still, a paved terrace. Warm terracotta tiles are ideal in a courtyard or terrace garden and create an attractive, rustic look. Natural sandstone paving can be teamed with coloured mosaics inlaid in circular or arcing patterns, reminiscent of ancient Roman floors. Or lay a few Moroccan encaustic tiles to brighten a paved patio.

To furnish your Mediterranean-style garden, choose unfussy folding chairs in wood or metal. The look is traditional and comfortable, so back away from contemporary designs or classic designer pieces in favour of more rustic furniture. Try scouring second-hand shops and fairs for old chairs, tables and loungers, and keep your eyes open for original French or Italian café chairs. Don't let a shabby appearance deter you, either. Both wooden and metal furniture can be sanded down and repainted to freshen it up. On furnishings, choose hot colours like bright oranges, pinks, blues and purples to add drama and a strong Mediterranean flavour. They also reduce the need to create colour in the planting. You can add further year-round colour and effectively warm up a chilly, shady corner by painting walls in bright Mediterranean shades like red, orange, blue and yellow. Exterior masonry paints now come in plenty of enticing colours.

Mediterranean gardens are generally fairly low-maintenance, with the focus on the terrace and dining space. Potted plants are a feature and are easy to look after. Many native plants will thrive in cooler or more humid climates, too. Small olive trees, agave, banana plants, eucalyptus and sculptural ferns all look authentic, while classics like geraniums and lavender bring colour. Find old terracotta pots, or invest in large new ones that can be arranged in rows for a symmetrical look.

* *Dress your table with chunky earthenware decorated with colourful patterns. Coloured glassware looks great, too, and will catch the light.*

* *Serve bread and salads from large rustic bowls, wooden platters and baskets lined with colourful napkins for an informal Mediterranean look.*

* *Think long term and have a simple wooden framework built over your dining area up which you can grow a grapevine or wisteria. Once the foliage has thickened, this will provide shade.*

* *Plant different-sized pots, so you always have a small pot of geranium or lavender to use as a table decoration and larger pots to define space.*

* *Make your own cushion covers using patterned fabric remnants or old curtains. Get foam cut to size to create soft seating for oddly shaped or large areas, like a long built-in bench.*

OPPOSITE LEFT **Contrasted against the verdant foliage of a tree fern, which creates a lush rainforest look, the neon shades of these four chairs are thoroughly in keeping with the tropical theme – while the mid-toned hardwood deck grounds the scheme.**

OPPOSITE RIGHT **Indoor-outdoor rugs will help to bring a sense of curated decoration to a balcony or deck space, as well as providing a more comfortable surface for bare feet. This geometric design adds interest (and a slightly retro edge) to a scheme mainly comprised of muted shades and plain surfaces.**

THIS PAGE **Against the blank canvas of a white-painted wall, a neutral monochrome scheme of pale fabric with dark timber and rattan is lifted by a delightful combination of floral cushions and real blooms. The choice of fabrics matches the colours of the flowers beautifully, resulting in a very pretty, coherent effect.**

Whether a modest platform at the back of an urban home or a terrace that wraps around the house, a wooden deck is a great place to enjoy the outdoors.

ON THE DECK

One of the most iconic examples of a deck is the American front porch. Covered by a roof and with a wooden floor, the porch has been incorporated into millions of American homes and is somewhere to sit, chat to passing neighbours and enjoy the fresh air. In Europe, terraces and decks at the back of the house are more common, but they share many traits with the American porch, many just big enough to house a couple of chairs, but not to dine on. Constructed from hardwood (expensive, but which comes in a range of lovely colours), specially treated softwood (which is easy to work with and cheaper) or modern resin composite, decks are good-looking and low-maintenance. They have a warm, easy-on-the-eye appearance and, unless painted with a stain, natural timber decking will fade gradually to a mellow grey.

Wood feels softer and warmer underfoot than paving, so it is ideal in a garden used by children. It can become slippery if not kept clean, but a regular brush with a stiff broom to remove any mildew or fine moss is all that's needed. The mellow wood of a deck or porch can host almost any kind of furniture. A striking designer chair or a chunky old bench will look equally good. If you prefer a rustic look, choose wooden furniture in a similar tone, topped with soft cushions in neutral colours. Lloyd Loom or wicker furniture looks good, too, or go contemporary with clean-lined modern loungers.

Decks and porches are often access routes to and from the house, so they need to be kept reasonably clutter-free. Potted plants will add some natural beauty without taking up too much space and can be moved easily. Plain terracotta pots or woven baskets maintain the laid-back, unfussy look. Fill them with geraniums or olive or bay trees for a classic look, or grasses or ferns for a tropical feel.

* *To provide privacy and protection from a prevailing wind, consider constructing a wooden screen around part of your deck, using the same wood.*

* *Grooved deck boards are often marketed as anti-slip, but perform no better or worse than plain, smooth decking that is kept clean.*

* *Many features can share a deck, from built-in storage to a submerged sandpit, pergolas to planters.*

* *When buying timber for a new deck, look for wood from a sustainable source.*

* *A corner or end of a deck can be fitted with an outside shower, for cooling off after a long day in the sun.*

* *Check whether planning or building regulation approval is required before you build a deck. Talk plans through with your neighbours, too. Neighbour objections are the most common reason for planning refusal or enforcement notices after completion.*

SOURCE LIST UK

LARGE RETAILERS

The Conran Shop
81 Fulham Road
London SW3 6RD
+44 (0)20 7589 7401
www.conranshop.co.uk
*One-stop shopping for
tasteful modern furniture and
accessories. Visit their website
for details of their other branch
in Marylebone plus overseas
stores in Paris and Japan.*

Habitat
196–199 Tottenham Court Road
London W1T 7PJ
and branches
+44 (0)344 499 1122
www.habitat.co.uk
*Accessible and affordable
contemporary furnishings.*

Heal's
196 Tottenham Court Road
London W1T 7LQ
+44 (0)20 7636 1666
www.heals.co.uk
*Stylish contemporary furniture.
Visit their website for details of
their other stores.*

IKEA
2 Drury Way
North Circular Road
London NW10 0TH
+44 (0)20 3645 0000
and branches nationwide
www.ikea.com
*Inexpensive furniture and
furnishings with a good selection
of kitchen designs.*

John Lewis
300 Oxford Street
London W1C 1DX
+44 (0)20 7629 7711
www.johnlewis.com
*Everything for the home, from
white goods to curtains to
bedlinen. Visit their website for
details of their other stores.*

Liberty
Regent Street
London W1B 5AH
+44 (0)20 7734 1234
www.liberty.co.uk
*Stylish modern furniture,
tableware and accessories plus
furnishing fabrics and wallpapers
in the iconic Liberty prints.*

Marks & Spencer
458 Oxford Street
London W1C 1AP
+44 (0)20 7935 7954
and branches
www.marksandspencer.com
*Traditional and contemporary
furniture, plus homewares for
every room.*

Selfridges
400 Oxford Street
London W1A 1AB
+44 (0)800 123400
www.selfridges.com
*Classic and cutting-edge design
for the home plus electrical
appliances and a large tech
department.*

FURNITURE AND FINISHING TOUCHES

Baileys Home
Whitecross Farm
Bridstow
Ross-on-Wye
Herefordshire HR9 6JU
+44 (0)1989 561931
www.baileyshome.com
*Sofas handmade to order,
1930s-style bathrooms and
everything recycled as well as
an eco-housekeeping range.*

Caravan Style
5 Ravenscroft Street
London E2 7SH
+44 (0)20 7033 3532
www.caravanstyle.com
*Ever-changing stock of individual
homewares and accessories; a
place to look at flea-market style.
Product viewing and collection
by appointment only.*

Classic Modern Vintage Design
www.classic-modern.co.uk
*Retro-style homewares, lighting
and accessories from the 1950s,
'60s and '70s.*

Graham & Green
4 Elgin Crescent
London W11 2HX
+44 (0)20 7243 8908
www.grahamandgreen.co.uk
*Glamorous glass, cushions,
tableware and a small range
of furniture including leather
pieces. Visit their website to
buy online or for details of their
other stores.*

Josephine Ryan Antiques
17 Langton Street
London SW10 0JL
+44 (0)7973 336149
www.josephineryanantiques.
co.uk
*Antiques dealer with an eye for
beautiful French pieces.*

LASSCO
41 Maltby Street
London SE1 3PA
+44 (0)20 7394 8061
www.lassco.co.uk
*Architectural salvage from
fireplaces to flooring, plus a
very authentic range of replicas.
Visit the website for details of
their other branches in Vauxhall
and Oxfordshire.*

Muji
6–17 Tottenham Court Road
London W1T 1BF
+44 (0)20 7436 1779
www.muji. eu
*Modern Japanese storage and
home accessories plus some
furniture. Visit their website for
details of their other stores.*

Pentreath & Hall
17 Rugby Street
London WC1N 3QT
+44 (0)20 7430 2526
www.pentreath-hall.com
*Beautiful and interesting
objects for the home, including
furniture, lighting, glassware and
decorative accessories.*

Petersham Nurseries
Church Lane
Off Petersham Road
Richmond
Surrey TW10 7AB
+44 (0)20 8940 5230
www.petershamnurseries.com
*Wide selection of plants and
antique garden furniture.*

Pimpernel & Partners
596 King's Road
London SW6 2DX
+44 (0)20 7731 2448
www.pimpernelandpartners.
co.uk
*French antique-style armchairs
and sofas in a select range of
styles upholstered in simple
white calico and ready to be
re-covered in any chosen fabric.*

Portobello Road Market
London W10 5TA
Friday and Saturday, 7am to 7pm
www.portobelloroad.co.uk
*Particularly good for antique
furniture and larger accessories
such as mirrors.*

SCP
135–139 Curtain Road
London EC2A 3BX
+44 (0)20 7739 1869
www.scp.co.uk
*Contemporary furniture, lighting
and accessories.*

Skandium
86 Marylebone High Street
London W1U 4QS
+44 (0)20 7935 2077
www.skandium.com
Modern Scandinavian furniture.

West Elm
209 Tottenham Court Road
London W1T 7PN
+44 (0)20 7637 9150
www.westelm.co.uk
*Modern furniture plus home
accessories, curtains, rugs,
lighting and mirrors.*

The White Company
www.thewhitecompany.com
*High-quality bed- and bath linen
and other home accessories.*

WALLS AND UPHOLSTERY

Auro Organic Paints
www.auro.co.uk
*Natural emulsions, eggshells
and chalk paints in muted
colours, also floor finishes
and wood stains.*

Bennison Fabrics
16 Holbein Place
London SW1W 8NL
+44 (0)20 7730 8076
www.bennisonfabrics.com
*Classic hand-printed fabrics to
suit any scheme.*

Designers Guild
265–277 King's Road
London SW3 5EN
+44 (0)20 7893 7400
www.designersguild.com
*Fresh, pretty, modern designs for
curtains and upholstery.*

Fermoie
2 Pond Place
London SW3 6QJ
+44 (0)1672 513723
www.fermoie.com
Fine fabrics printed in England.

Fired Earth
www.firedearth.com
*Subtle, elegant paint colours as
well as wallpapers and tiles.*

Ian Mankin
269–271 Wandsworth Bridge Rd
London SW6 2TX
+44 (0)20 7722 0997
www.ianmankin.com
*Natural fabrics, including striped
tickings and plain and patterned
cottons.*

Lewis & Wood
www.lewisandwood.co.uk
*Interesting and eccentric range
of fabrics and wallpapers.*

Osborne & Little
308 King's Road
London SW3 5UH
+44 (0)20 8812 3123
www.osborneandlittle.com
*Stylish fabrics, wallpapers and
trimmings.*

Paint & Paper Library
3 Elystan Street
London SW3 3NT
+44 (0)20 7823 7755
www.paintlibrary.co.uk
*Paint and wallpaper, including
many shades of off-white.*

KITCHENS

Aga
www.agaliving.com
*Classic cast-iron range cookers
for both town and country.*

Alno
www.alnokitchens.co.uk
*Contemporary and elegant
kitchen designs from Germany.*

Bulthaup
37 Wigmore Street
London W1U 1PP
+44 (0)20 7495 3663
www.bulthaup.com
*High-quality contemporary and
high-tech kitchens, including
clever design features.*

deVOL
www.devolkitchens.co.uk
*Elegant and restrained
traditional-style wooden kitchens
handmade and handpainted in
the UK.*

Divertimenti
227–229 Brompton Road
London SW3 2EP
+44 (0)20 7581 8065
www.divertimenti.co.uk
*Complete range of cookware and
kitchen accessories.*

Summerill & Bishop
100 Portland Road
London W11 4LQ
+44 (0)20 7221 4566
www.summerillandbishop.com
*Inspirational collection of
tableware, utensils and
accessories.*

BATHROOMS

Aston Matthews
141–147a Essex Road
London N1 2SN
+44 (0)20 7226 7220
www.astonmatthews.co.uk
*Modern and traditional bathroom
fittings, including washbasins in
china, glass and stainless steel.*

Bathstore.com
www.bathstore.com
Sanitary ware in all styles.

C P Hart
Newnham Terrace
Hercules Road
London SE1 7DR
+44 (0)20 7902 5250
and branches
www.cphart.co.uk
*Bathroom designs by Philippe
Starck among others.*

Ideal Standard
www.ideal-standard.co.uk
Wide range of sanitary ware.

Stiffkey Bathrooms
89 Upper St Giles Street
Norwich NR2 1AB
+44 (0)1603 627850
www.stiffkeybathrooms.com
*Antique sanitary ware plus their
own range.*

LIGHTING

Artemide
106 Great Russell Street
London WC1B 3NB
+44 (0)20 7291 3853
www.artemide.com
Contemporary designer lighting.

John Cullen
561–563 King's Road
London SW6 2EB
+44 (0)20 7371 5400
www.johncullenlighting.co.uk
*Extensive range of contemporary
light fittings and bespoke lighting
design service.*

Holloways of Ludlow
115 & 121 Shepherd's Bush Road
London W6 7LP
+44 (0)20 7602 5757
www.hollowaysofludlow.com
*Classic, contemporary and
industrial-style lighting plus
bathrooms and radiators.*

The London Lighting Company
135 Fulham Road
London SW3 6RT
+44 (0)20 3507 1911
www.londonlighting.co.uk
Contemporary lighting.

FLOORING

Alternative Flooring
www.alternativeflooring.com
*Coir, seagrass, sisal, jute and
wool floor coverings, including
patterned carpets.*

Crucial Trading
www.crucial-trading.com
All types of natural floorings.

Junckers
www.junckers.co.uk
Solid hardwood flooring.

Limestone Gallery
583 King's Road
London SW6 2EH
+44 (0)20 7828 6900
www.limestonegallery.com
*A wide selection of limestone
flooring, also French ceramic
tiles and terracotta tiles.*

Roger Oates Design
1 Munro Terrace (off Riley Street)
London SW10 0DL
+44 (0)20 7351 2288
www.rogeroates.com
*Smart and simple 100% wool
flatweave rugs and runners in
chic stripes and checks.*

Sinclair Till Flooring
791–793 Wandsworth Road
London SW8 3JQ
+44 (0)20 7720 0031
www.sinclairtill.co.uk
*All kinds of flooring including
a range of linoleums.*

SOURCE LIST US

LARGE RETAILERS

ABC Carpet & Home
888 Broadway
New York, NY 10003
212 473 3000
www.abchome.com
An eclectic collection of accessories for the home. Stores in Manhattan, the Bronx, New Jersey and Florida.

Anthropologie
www.anthropologie.com
Vintage-inspired home accessories and decorative details.

Barneys New York
660 Madison Avenue
New York, NY 10021
212 826 8900
Visit www.barneys.com for details of their other stores High-quality home furnishings.

Canvas Home
www.canvashomestore.com
Elegant American-made sofas, loveseats and chaises as well as tableware, linens and decorative pieces.

Crate & Barrel
www.crateandbarrel.com
Furniture and home accessories for contemporary living.

Ethan Allen
www.ethanallen.com
Fine furniture for every room.

IKEA
www.ikea.com
Simple but well-designed flat-pack furniture, plus inexpensive storage and kitchenware.

Pier 1 Imports
www.pier1.com
Affordable home accessories and furniture from all over the world.

Pottery Barn
www.potterybarn.com
Contemporary furniture, lighting, linens, garden furniture and home accessories with a world beat.

R & Company
82 Franklin Street
New York, NY 10013
212 343 7979
www.r20thcentury.com
20th- and 21st-century furniture, lighting and accessories.

Restoration Hardware
www.restorationhardware.com
Fine hardware, including flooring, curtains and lighting, but also furniture and accessories for the home.

20C Design
1430 N. Riverfront Blvd
Dallas, TX 75207
214 939 1430
www.20cdesign.com
A carefully curated collection of classic Italian and Scandinavian Modern designs.

Bombay
www.bombaycompany.com
Reproductions of Colonial-style home furnishings and accessories.

California Closets
www.californiaclosets.com
Custom-designed and storage solutions for every room.

Charles P. Rogers
26 West 17th Street
New York, NY 10011
212 675 4400
www.charlesprogers.com
Brass, iron and wood bed frames, from classic to contemporary.

Country Farm Furniture
148 Front Street
Bath, ME 04530
207 443 2367
www.countryfarmfurniture.net
Finely designed and crafted country-style furniture.

Georgetown Flea Market
1819 35th St NW
Washington, D.C.
www.georgetownfleamarket.com
If you visit the nation's capital, this is a stop that's well worth making. Open Sundays year round.

Gump's
135 Post Street
San Francisco, CA 94108
1 800 284 8677
www.gumps.com
Elegant home furnishings.

Shaker Style
292 Chesham Road
Harrisville, NH 03450
603 827 3340
www.shakerstyle.com
Custom-built, beautifully simple Shaker-style furniture.

Swartzendruber Furniture Creations
574 536 0491
www.swartzendruber.com
Arts and Crafts and Prairie-style quality reproductions.

Urban Outfitters
www.urbanoutfitters.com.
Playful, affordable home details and furnishings that follow interior trends.

West Elm
www.westelm.com
Contemporary furniture and accessories featuring clean design.

Williams-Sonoma
www.williams-sonoma.com
Specializes in utensils, cookware, electrics, entertaining essentials and tableware.

WALLS AND UPHOLSTERY

Benjamin Moore Paints
www.benjaminmoore.com
Fine paints.

Calico Corners
www.calicocorners.com
Vast range of window treatments, furnishing fabrics and trims.

Clarence House Fabrics, Ltd.
979 Third Avenue, Suite 205
New York, NY 10022
212 752 2890
www.clarencehouse.com
Natural-fibre fabrics with prints based on 15th- to 20th-century documents.

Farrow & Ball
www.farrow-ball.com
Subtle paint colours, also wallpapers and varnishes.

Garnet Hill
www.garnethill.com
An online retailer of natural-fibre duvets, pillows and linens.

Gracious Home
www.gracioushome.com
Bedding, linens and fine fixtures.

The Old Fashioned Milk Paint Co.
www.milkpaint.com
These all-natural paints replicate the colour and finish of Colonial and Shaker antiques.

KITCHENS

Bosch
www.bosch-home.com
Kitchen appliances and fixtures.

Bulthaup
158 Wooster St,
New York, NY 10012
212 966 7183
www.bulthaup.com
High-quality contemporary and high-tech kitchens, including clever design features.

Fishs Eddy
889 Broadway
New York, NY 10003
212 420 9020
www.fishseddy.com
Eclectic selection of mugs, plates, bowls and other tableware.

Poggenpohl
www.poggenpohl-usa.com
Custom kitchen designs.

BATHROOMS

Bed Bath & Beyond
www.bedbathandbeyond.com
Everything for the bedroom and bathroom, plus kitchen utensils and storage.

Vintage Tub & Bath
www.vintagetub.com
Reproduction clawfoot tubs, pedestal and console sinks, copper double-ended tubs and more.

The Company Store
www.thecompanystore.com
Online retailer of quality bedding and other linens.

Waterworks
www.waterworks.com
Sleek bathroom fixtures, furniture and lights.

LIGHTING

Boyd Lighting
www.boydlighting.com
Classic and elegant lighting designs from uplighters to table lamps.

Brass Light Gallery
1101 W. St Paul Avenue
Milwaukee, WI 53233
800 243 9595
www.brasslight.com
Wide range of designs with many traditional styles.

Flos Inc.
www.flos.com
Cutting-edge lighting style, including designs by Philippe Starck.

Lighting Collaborative
121 W 27th St. Suite 404
New York, NY 10001
212 253 7220
www.lightingcollaborative.com
Supplier of high-end low-voltage lighting.

FLOORING

Anderson Hardwood Floors
www.andersonfloors.com
Large selection of hardwood flooring.

Country Floors
15 East 16th Street
New York, NY 10003
212 627 8300
www.countryfloors.com
American and imported ceramic, stone, tile and terracotta flooring.

Linoleum City
4849 Santa Monica Boulevard
Hollywood, CA 90029
323 469 0063
www.linoleumcity.com
Every kind of linoleum, from period to modern to high-tech, as well as cork and rubber flooring.

Native Tile and Ceramics
2317 Border Avenue
Torrance, CA 90501
310 533 8684
www.nativetile.com
Reproduction tiles made using traditional techniques.

Patina Old World Flooring
3927 North Southbank Road
Oxnard, CA 93036
800 501 1113
www.patinawoodfloors.com
Reproduction French-style parquet and rustic wide-plank flooring.

PICTURE CREDITS

Ph = photographer

Front endpaper The home of photographer Jake Curtis in London/ Ph. Polly Wreford; 1 Ph. Hans Blomquist; 2 An apartment designed by Stéphane Garotin and Pierre Emmanuel Martin of Maison Hand in Lyon/Ph. Rachel Whiting; 3 The home of the designer Yvonne Koné in Copenhagen/Ph. Anna Williams; 4 left & 5 below left The home of the decorator Bunny Turner of www.turnerpocock.co.uk/Ph. Polly Wreford; 4 right www.MIKinteriors.com/Ph. Polly Wreford; 5 above left Wynchelse, designed by Dave Coote and Atlanta Bartlett, available to hire for holiday lets and photography through www. beachstudios.co.uk/Ph. Polly Wreford; 5 above right The family home of Sacha Paisley in Sussex, designed by Arior Design/Ph. Polly Wreford; 6 The home of the interior decorator Caroline Van Thillo in Belgium/Ph. Polly Wreford; 8–9 The family home of Danielle de Lange of online shop Le Souk www.soukshop.com and lifestyle blog The Style Files www.style-files.com/Ph. James Gardiner; 10 Philip and Catherine Mould's house in Oxfordshire/Ph. Chris Tubbs; 11 above The home of the architect Joseph Dirand in Paris/Ph. Pia Ulin; 11 centre Pauline's apartment in Paris, designed by Marianne Evennou www.marianne-evennou.com; 11 below right Openview Barn at Foster House, designed by Atlanta Bartlett and Dave Coote and available to hire for photography through www.beachstudios.co.uk/ Ph. Polly Wreford; 12 above The home of Birgitte and Henrik Moller Kastrup in Denmark/Ph. Rachel Whiting; 12 below The Paris apartment of Audrey Chabert, designed by architect Sylvie Cahen/ Ph. Rachel Whiting; 13 A family home in west London by Webb Architects and Cave Interiors/Ph. Polly Wreford; 14 above The home of James Lynch and Sian Tucker of www.fforest.bigcartel.com and www.coldatnight.co.uk/Ph. James Gardiner; 14 below left Michael Giannelli and Greg Shano's home in East Hampton/Ph. Paul Massey; 14 below right Charlotte-Anne Fidler's home in London/Ph. Polly Wreford; 15 left The family home of Sarah and Mark Benton in Rye/ Ph. Polly Wreford; 15 right The home of George Lamb in London/ Ph. Debi Treloar; 16 above The home of fashion designer Mr Antoni Burakowski and hair stylist Mr Kerry Warn in London/Ph. Jan Baldwin; 16 below All items from Cote Jardin boutique/Ph. Paul Massey; 17 left The Brooklyn home of Helen Dealtry of wokinggirldesigns.com/Ph. James Gardiner; 17 above right Ylva Skarp www.ylvaskarp.se/Ph. James Gardiner; 17 below The London home of Adriana Natcheva/Ph. Pia Ulin; 18 The Paris apartment of Thierry Dreano, designed by the architect Sylvie Cahen/Ph. Rachel Whiting; 19 above www.sasaantic.com/Ph. Rachel Whiting; 19 below Designed by Stéphane Garotin and Pierre Emmanuel Martin of Maison Hand in Lyon/Ph. Rachel Whiting; 20 above The Grey House, the home of Paul Burgess and Karen Carter, designed by Dave Coote and Atlanta Bartlett and available for holiday lets and photography

through www.beachstudios.co.uk/Ph. Polly Wreford; 20 below The home of Guy and Natasha Hills in London/Ph. Debi Treloar; 21 Peri Wolfman and Charles Gold's New York Loft/Ph. Polly Wreford; 22 The Berlin home of designer Nadine Richter, co-owner of Noé & Zoë/Ph. Rachel Whiting; 23 above The family home of Ewa Solarz in Poland/Ph. Ben Robertson; 23 below A family home in west London by Webb Architects and Cave Interiors/Ph. Polly Wreford; 24 above Designed by Stéphane Garotin and Pierre Emmanuel Martin of Maison Hand in Lyon/Ph. Rachel Whiting; 24 below The home of Malene Birger in Copenhagen/Ph. Polly Wreford; 25 left /Ph. Rachel Whiting; 25 above right L'Atelier d'Archi – Isabelle Juy – www. latelierdarchi.fr/Ph. Polly Wreford; 25 below The home of Marie Worsaae of Aiayu/Ph. Pia Ulin; 26 The Hampstead home of the painter Henry Mee/Ph. Jan Baldwin; 27 above The apartment of Jacques Azagury in London/Ph. Winfried Heinze; 27 below The home of Grant and Sam, owners of Petite Violette in Malmö, Sweden/Ph. Rachel Whiting; 28 left The home of the architect Joseph Dirand in Paris/Ph. Pia Ulin; 28 right The home of the architect Jonas Bjerre-Poulsen of NORM Architects/Ph. Pia Ulin; 29 North London home/ Ph. Debi Treloar; 30 Wynchelse, designed by Dave Coote and Atlanta Bartlett, available to hire for holiday lets and photography through www.beachstudios.co.uk./Ph Polly Wreford; 31 above The London apartment of Adam Hills and Maria Speake, owners of Retrouvius (www.retrouvius.com)/Ph. Debi Treloar; 31 below Sara Schmidt, owner and creative director of Brandts Indoor/Ph. Katya de Grunwald; 32 above Dorthe Kvist, garden and interior designer, stylist, TV host, blogger and author/Ph. Katya de Grunwald; 32 below left The Paris apartment of Audrey Chabert, designed by architect Sylvie Cahen/ Ph. Rachel Whiting; 32 right The home of the architect Jonas Bjerre-Poulsen of NORM Architects/Ph. Pia Ulin; 33 The family home of Louise Kamman Riising, co-owner of hey-home.dk/Ph. Rachel Whiting; 34 Marco Lobina's home in Turin/Ph. Jan Baldwin; 35 above The home of Maaike Goldbach in the Netherlands/Ph. Katya de Grunwald; 35 below left The home of interior stylist and ceramic designer Silje Aune Eriksen of thisis-blogspot.com/Ph. Catherine Gratwicke; 35 below Pauline's apartment in Paris, designed by Marianne Evennou www.marianne-evennou.com; 36 left The home Leida Nassir-Pour of Warp & Weft in Hastings/Ph. Claire Richardson; 36 right The family home of Alison Smith in Brighton/Ph. Polly Wreford; 37 The family home of Camilla Ebdrup from LUCKYBOYSUNDAY/Ph. Rachel Whiting; 38 above left The home of Malene Birger in Copenhagen/Ph. Polly Wreford; 38 above right The home of designer and stylist Annaleena Leino Karlsson in Stockholm/ Ph. Pia Ulin; 38 below left The south London home of Carole Poirot of www.mademoisellepoirot.com/Ph. Rachel Whiting; 38 below right The home of James Lynch and Sian Tucker of www.fforest.bigcartel. com and www.coldatnight.co.uk/Ph. James Gardiner; 39 above Home of Tim Rundle and Glynn Jones/Ph. Debi Treloar; 39 below Michela Imperiali www.MIKinteriors.com/Ph. Polly Wreford; 40 left Giorgio and Ilaria Miani's Podere Buon Riposo in Val d'Orcia. Available for rent/Ph. Chris Tubbs 40 right Katrin Arens/Ph. Debi Treloar; 41 Wynchelse, designed by Dave Coote and Atlanta Bartlett, available to hire for holiday lets and photography through www.beachstudios.co.uk/Ph. Polly Wreford; 42 /Ph. Ngoc Minh Ngo; 43 left The home of the designer Myriam de Loor, owner of Petit Pan in Paris/Ph. Debi Treloar; 43 right The family home of the stylist Anja Koops and chef Alain Parry in Amsterdam/Ph. Polly Wreford; 44 The London home of one of the owners of Ochre, www.ochre.net/Ph. Debi Treloar; 45 The home of Virginie Denny, fashion designer, and Alfonso Vallès, painter/Ph. Debi Treloar; 46 The Grey House, the home of Paul Burgess and Karen Carter, designed by Dave Coote and Atlanta Bartlett, available for holiday lets and photography through www.beachstudios.co.uk/Ph. Polly Wreford; 47 above and centre Paul and Claire's beach house, East Sussex. Design www.davecoote.com; available to hire through www.beachstudios.co.uk/Ph. Polly Wreford; 47 below Beauty Point and Coast House available to hire as locations through www.beachstudios.co.uk/Ph. Polly Wreford; 48 Agata Hamilton www.my-home.com.pl/Ph. Ben Robertson; 49 The home of the founder/designer Sabien Engelenburg of engelpunt.com/Ph. Rachel Whiting; 50–51 The home of the designer Yvonne Koné in Copenhagen/Ph. Anna Williams; 52–53 above left The home of the interior decorator Caroline Van Thillo in Belgium/Ph. Polly Wreford; 53 above right The home of the textile designer Kim Schipperheijn in the Netherlands/Ph. Katya de Grunwald; 53 below The summerhouse of Helene Blanche and Jannik Martensen-Larsen, owner of Tapet Café in Copenhagen www.tapet-café.com/Ph. Earl Carter; 54 above The Brooklyn home of Helen Dealtry of wokinggirldesigns.com/Ph. James Gardiner; 54 below The London apartment of Adam Hills and Maria Speake, owners of Retrouvius (www.retrouvius.com)/Ph. Debi Treloar; 55 above left Rebecca Uth, creator of Ro/Ph. James Gardiner; 55 above right The home in Copenhagen of June and David/Ph. Polly Wreford; 55 below left The home of Giorgio DeLuca in New York/Ph. Pia Ulin; 55 below right Lucille and Richard Lewin's London House/Ph. Debi Treloar; 56 above Mark Hampshire and Keith Stephenson of Mini Moderns/Ph. James Gardiner; 56 below left The home of Marie Worsaae of Aiayu/Ph. Pia Ulin; 56 below right The London home of the interiors blogger Katy Orme (apartmentapothecary.com)/Ph. Rachel Whiting; 57 The Sussex home of Paula Barnes of www.elizabarnes.com/Ph. Polly Wreford; 58 above The family home of the designer Nina Nagel of byGraziela.com/Ph. Ben Robertson; 58 below The family home of Francesca Forcolini and Barry Menmuir, designers and co-founders of fashion label Labour of Love/Ph. Ben Robertson; 59 The Berlin home of designer Nadine Richter, co-owner of Noé and Zoë/Ph. Rachel Whiting; 60 The family home of Gina Portman of Folk at Home www.folkathome.com/Ph. Catherine Gratwicke; 61 left The home of stylist Emma Persson Lagerberg/Ph. Polly Wreford; 61 right The home of Maaike Goldbach in the Netherlands/Ph. Katya de Grunwald; 62 above The home of the artist Lou Kenlock, Oxfordshire/Ph. Catherine Gratwicke; 62 below The family home of Gina Portman of Folk at Home www.folkathome.com/

Ph. Catherine Gratwicke; 63 The home of James and Maria Backhouse in London/Ph. Debi Treloar; 64 above Kristina Dam Studio/Ph. James Gardiner; 64 below left The home of fashion designer Mr Antoni Burakowski and hair stylist Mr Kerry Warn in London/Ph. Jan Baldwin; 64 below right /Ph. Hans Blomquist; 65 above right Foster House, available to hire through www.beachstudios.co.uk/Ph. Polly Wreford; 65 below right Mark and Sally Bailey's home in Herefordshire www.baileyshome.com/Ph. Debi Treloar; 65 below left Hotel Endsleigh/Ph. Chris Tubbs; 66 above left The home of the interior designer Eva Gnaedinger in Switzerland/Ph. Jan Baldwin; 66 above right The home of fashion designer Mr Antoni Burakowski and hair stylist Mr Kerry Warn in London/Ph. Jan Baldwin; 66 below /Ph. Debi Treloar; 67 Designer Laure Vial du Chatenet from Maison Caumont Paris/Ph. Jan Baldwin; 68 New Cross – location to hire through www.beachstudios.co.uk/Ph. Polly Wreford; 69 left Sara Schmidt, owner and creative director of Brandts Indoor/Ph. Katya de Grunwald; 69 right This location (Varden Street) is available to hire through www.lightlocations.co.uk/Ph. Polly Wreford; 70 above The home of the stylist Ingeborg Wolf/Ph. Pia Ulin; 70 below The London home of Sam Robinson, co-owner of 'The Cross' and 'Cross the Road'/Ph. Debi Treloar; 71 The home of Elina Tripoliti and Mark Rachovides in London/Ph. Debi Treloar; 72 Christina and Allan Thaulow's home in Denmark/Ph. Debi Treloar; 73 left Elaine Tian of Studio Joo/Ph. James Gardiner; 73 right The home of Maaike Goldbach in the Netherlands/Ph. Katya de Grunwald; 74 above The home of the architect Joseph Dirand in Paris/Ph. Pia Ulin; 74 below left Ph Debi Treloar; 74 below right The home of the architect Jonas Bjerre-Poulsen of NORM Architects/Ph. Pia Ulin; 75 left The family home of Justina Blakeney in Los Angeles/Ph. Rachel Whiting; 75 right Garsington Manor, home of Mrs Rosalind Ingrams and her family/Ph. Jan Baldwin; 76 above Ylva Skarp www.ylvaskarp.se/Ph. James Gardiner; 76 below left The home of Marie Worsaae of Aiayu/Ph. Pia Ulin; 76 below right Charlotte-Anne Fidler's home in London/Ph. Polly Wreford; 77 Oliver Heath and Katie Weiner – sustainable architecture, interior and jewellery design/Ph. Catherine Gratwicke; 78 above Designed by Stephane Garotin and Pierre Emmanuel Martin of Maison Hand in Lyon/Ph. Pia Ulin; 78 below left The home of Hilary Robertson, interiors stylist, vintage and antiques buyer/Ph. Anna Williams; 78 below centre The Antwerp family home of Melanie Ireland, founder and creator of Simple Kids/Ph. Polly Wreford; 78 below right /Ph. Polly Wreford; 79 left /Ph. Hans Blomquist; 79 right Kvarngården, the home of photographer Nils Odier, stylist Sofia Odier, and their two daughters Lou and Uma. Skivarp, Sweden/Ph. Debi Treloar; 80 left The cabin of Hanne Borge and her family in Norway/Ph. Catherine Gratwicke; 80 right /Ph. Debi Treloar; 81 Oliver Heath and Katie Weiner – sustainable architecture, interior and jewellery design/Ph. Catherine Gratwicke; 82 The Norfolk family home of the designer Petra Boase/Ph. Debi Treloar; 83 above The home of fashion designer Mr Antoni Burakowski and hair stylist Mr Kerry Warn in London/Ph. Jan Baldwin; 83 below right The South

London home of designer Virginia Armstrong of roddy&ginger/ Ph. Polly Wreford; 83 below left The home and studio of Petra Janssen and Edwin Vollebergh of Studio Boot in the Netherlands www. studioboot.nl/Ph. Katya de Grunwald; 84 The home of photographer Jake Curtis in London/Ph. Polly Wreford; 85 above left The home of the architect Joseph Dirand in Paris/Ph. Pia Ulin; 85 above right The home of the interior designer Sarah Lavoine in Paris/Ph. Polly Wreford; 85 below Naja Munthe, owner of MUNTHE in Copenhagen/ Ph. Pia Ulin; 86 Charlotte-Anne Fidler's home in London/Ph. Polly Wreford; 87 Cecilia and Peter Granath's home in Copenhagen/Ph. Polly Wreford; 88 The home of Jonathan Sela and Megan Schoenbachler/Ph. Catherine Gratwicke; 89 The home of Marzio Cavanna in Milan/Ph. Pia Ulin; 90–91 The home of the architect Joseph Dirand in Paris/Ph. Pia Ulin; 92 The home and studio of the art & craft artist Nathalie Lete in Paris/Ph. Debi Treloar; 93 above Egford House, the home of Liddie and Howard Holt Harrison/Ph. Jan Baldwin; 93 below The home of Mary Martin and Carl Turner of Carl Turner Architects in London/Ph. Jan Baldwin; 94 above Kimberly Austin of Austin Press, San Francisco/Ph. Helen Cathcart; 94 below John Nicolson's house is available as a film and photographic location/Ph. Jan Baldwin; 95 The home of Sophie Lambert, owner of "Au Temps des Cerises", in France/Ph. Jan Baldwin; 96 above left The home of Virginie Denny, fashion designer, and Alfonso Vallès, painter/Ph. Debi Treloar; 96 above right L'Atelier d'Archi – Isabelle Juy – www.latelierdarchi.fr/Ph. Polly Wreford; 96 below left The home of Marzio Cavanna in Milan/Ph. Pia Ulin; 96 below right North London home/Ph. Debi Treloar; 97 above A Dutch farmhouse designed by Jan and Maud Steengracht van Oostcapelle-Noltes/Ph. Jan Baldwin; 97 below The Grey House, the home of Paul Burgess and Karen Carter, designed by Dave Coote and Atlanta Bartlett and available for holiday lets and photography through www.beachstudios.co.uk/Ph. Polly Wreford; 98 above left New Cross – location to hire through www. beachstudios.co.uk/Ph. Polly Wreford; 98 above right The home of photographer Jake Curtis in London/Ph. Polly Wreford; 98 below Judith Kramer, owner of webshop Juudt.com/Ph. Polly Wreford; 99 The home of Leida Nassir-Pour of Warp & Weft in Hastings/Ph. Claire Richardson; 100 Foster Cabin, designed by Dave Coote www. beachstudios.co.uk/Ph. Polly Wreford; 101 left /Ph. Rachel Whiting; 101 right Mark Hampshire and Keith Stephenson of Mini Moderns/ Ph. James Gardiner; 102 left "La Villa des Ombelles" the family home of Jean-Marc Dimanche, Chairman of V.I.T.R.I.O.L. agency www. vitriol-factory.com/Ph. Debi Treloar; 102 right /Ph. Claire Richardson; 103 The South London home of designer Virginia Armstrong of roddy&ginger/Ph. Polly Wreford; 104 above left Oliver Heath and Katie Weiner – sustainable architecture, interior and jewellery design/ Ph. Catherine Gratwicke; 104 above right Kvarngården, the home of photographer Nils Odier, stylist Sofia Odier, and their two daughters Lou and Uma. Skivarp, Sweden/Ph. Debi Treloar; 104 below The B&B Camellas-Lloret, designed and owned by Annie Moore near Carcassonne/Ph. Claire Richardson; 105 above The home of the

designer Yvonne Koné in Copenhagen/Ph. Anna Williams; 105 below Bruno et Michèle Viard: location-en-luberon.com/Ph. Polly Wreford; 106 left Foster House, the family home of Atlanta Bartlett and Dave Coote, available to hire for photography through www.beachstudios. co.uk/Ph. Polly Wreford; 106 right Designed by Stephane Garotin and Pierre Emmanuel Martin of Maison Hand in Lyon/Ph. Pia Ulin; 107 above The B&B Camellas-Lloret, designed and owned by Annie Moore near Carcassonne/Ph. Claire Richardson; 107 below Pauline's apartment in Paris, designed by Marianne Evennou www.marianne-evennou.com; 108 The home of the stylist Ingeborg Wolf/Ph. Pia Ulin; 109 above left The home of Rose Hammick and Andrew Treverton, www.marmoraroad.co.uk/Ph. Polly Wreford; 109 above right Designed by Stéphane Garotin and Pierre Emmanuel Martin of Maison Hand in Lyon/Ph. Rachel Whiting; 109 below The home of the designer Anne Geistdoerfer (and her family) of double g architects in Paris/Ph. Polly Wreford; 110 above Oliver Heath and Katie Weiner – sustainable architecture, interior and jewellery design/Ph. Catherine Gratwicke; 110 below Naja Munthe, owner of MUNTHE in Copenhagen/Ph. Pia Ulin; 111 above The home of Hilary Robertson, interiors stylist, vintage and antiques buyer/Ph. Anna Williams; 111 below centre The family home of architect Arash Nourinejad and artist Kristina Lykke Tønnesen in Copenhagen/Ph. Rachel Whiting; 111 below right Charlotte-Anne Fidler's home in London/Ph. Polly Wreford; 112 Foster Cabin designed by Dave Coote www. beachstudios.co.uk/Ph. Polly Wreford; 113 left Tracy Wilkinson www. twworkshop.com/Ph. Catherine Gratwicke; 113 right Foster Cabins, designed by Atlanta Bartlett and Dave Coote, available for hire through www.beachstudios.co.uk/Ph. Polly Wreford; 114 above Beauty Point and Coast House, available as locations from www. beachstudios.co.uk/Ph. ph Polly Wreford; 114 below New Cross – location to hire through www.beachstudios.co.uk/Ph. Polly Wreford; 115 The seaside home of designer Marta Nowicka, available to rent at www.martanowicka.com/Ph. Rachel Whiting; 116 The London home of the interiors blogger Katy Orme (apartmentapothecary.com)/Ph. Rachel Whiting; 117 above The White House, the home of Paul Burgess, designed by Dave Coote and Atlanta Bartlett and available for holiday lets and photography through wwww.beachstudios.co.uk/ Ph. Polly Wreford; 117 below The Norfolk home of Geoff and Gilly Newberry of Bennison Fabrics. All fabrics by Bennison, cabinet-maker, Victor Clark/Ph. Alan Williams; 118 left The home of the interior designer Eva Gnaedinger in Switzerland/Ph. Jan Baldwin; 118 right The home of Hilary Robertson, interiors stylist, vintage and antiques buyer/Ph. Anna Williams; 119 Manhattan home of designer Matthew Patrick Smyth/Ph. Chris Everard; 120 above left The designers Piet and Karin Boon's home near Amsterdam, www. pietboon.nl/Ph. Lisa Cohen; 120 above right Hèlène and Konrad Adamczewski, Lewes/Ph. Debi Treloar; 120 below The home of Jeanette Lunde/Ph. Debi Treloar; 121 left Robert Young, Robert Young Architecture & Interiors www.ryarch.com/Ph. Earl Carter; 122–123 Marco Lobina's home in Turin/Ph. Jan Baldwin; 124 The B&B

Camellas-Lloret, designed and owned by Annie Moore near Carcassonne/Ph. Claire Richardson; 125 above centre The home of Elina Tripoliti and Mark Rachovides in London/Ph. Debi Treloar; 125 above right www.stylexclusief.nl/Ph. Catherine Gratwicke; 125 below Beauty Point and Coast House are available to hire as locations from www.beachstudios.co.uk/Ph. Polly Wreford; 126 above left The South London home of designer Virginia Armstrong of roddy&ginger/Ph. Polly Wreford; 126 above right The family home of Gina Portman of Folk at Home www.folkathome.com/Ph. Catherine Gratwicke; 126 below The family home of Sacha Paisley in Sussex, designed by Arior Design/Ph. Polly Wreford; 127 New York family home designed by Shamir Shah/Ph. Chris Everard; 128 The home of Nici Zinell, designer of Noé & Zoë in Berlin, and Knut Hake, film editor/Ph. Rachel Whiting; 129 above The family home of Louise and Garth Jennings in London/Ph. Rachel Whiting; 129 below The family home of Janneke van Houtum of www.liefsvanmaantje.nl in Eindhoven/Ph. James Gardiner; 130 above left /Ph.Debi Treloar; 130 above right www.stylexclusief.nl/Ph. Catherine Gratwicke; 131 above left and below right The Antwerp family home of Melanie Ireland, founder and creator of Simple Kids/Ph. Polly Wreford; 131 above right The home of the designer Agnès Emery of Emery & Cie in the Medina in Marrakech/Ph. Katya de Grunwald; 131 below left Mark Hampshire and Keith Stephenson of Mini Moderns/Ph. James Gardiner; 132 The family home of Fiona and Alex Cox of www.coxandcox.co.uk/ Ph. Polly Wreford; 133 above The Brooklyn home of Helen Dealtry of wokinggirldesigns.com/Ph. James Gardiner; 133 below The family home of Sacha Paisley in Sussex, designed by Arior Design/Ph. Polly Wreford; 134 left The Paris apartment of Thierry Dreano, designed by the architect Sylvie Cahen/Ph. Rachel Whiting; 134 right The home of the Voors family in the Netherlands designed by Karin Draaijer/Ph. Polly Wreford; 135 The home of Birgitte and Henrik Moller Kastrup in Denmark/Ph. Rachel Whiting; 136 Judith Kramer, owner of webshop Juudt.com; the art of living; living and art/Ph. Polly Wreford; 137 above left The Kent home of William Palin of SAVE Britain's Heritage/ Ph. Jan Baldwin; 137 above right Ben Pentreath's London flat/Ph. Jan Baldwin; 137 below Kristin Krogstad Interior Architect, www. thedrawingroom.no/Ph. Jan Baldwin; 138 left The designer Nina Hartmann's home in Sweden, www.vintagebynina.com/Ph. Lisa Cohen; 138 right The cabin of Hanne Borge and her family in Norway/ Ph. Catherine Gratwicke; 139 The home of Victoria and Stephen Fordham, designed by Sarah Delaney, in London/Ph. Polly Wreford; 140 above left Bruno et Michèle Viard: location-en-luberon.com/Ph. Polly Wreford; 140 below left The home of Victoria and Stephen Fordham, designed by Sarah Delaney, in London/Ph. Polly Wreford; 140 right Lykkeoglykkeliten.blogspot.com/Ph. Debi Treloar; 141 www.stylexclusief.nl/Ph. Catherine Gratwicke; 142 above left The family home of Sacha Paisley in Sussex, designed by Arior Design/ Ph. Polly Wreford; 142 above right Sara Schmidt, owner and creative director of Brandts Indoor/Ph. Katya de Grunwald; 142 below The home of Victoria and Stephen Fordham, designed by Sarah Delaney,

in London/Ph. Polly Wreford; 143 The family home of Gina Portman of Folk at Home www.folkathome.com/Ph. Catherine Gratwicke; 144 The Brooklyn loft of Alina Preciado, owner of lifestyle store dar gitane www.dargitane.com/Ph. Anna Williams; 145 left The seaside home of designer Marta Nowicka, available to rent at www.martanowicka. com/Ph. Rachel Whiting; 145 centre Foster House, available to hire through www.beachstudios.co.uk/Ph. Polly Wreford; 145 right The home of Elina Tripoliti and Mark Rachovides in London/Ph. Debi Treloar; 146 New Cross – location to hire through www.beachstudios. co.uk/Ph. Polly Wreford; 147 above left The family home of Sarah and Mark Benton in Rye/Ph. Polly Wreford; 147 above right John Nicolson's house is available as a film and photographic location/ Ph. Jan Baldwin; 147 below Country house, Suffolk/Ph. Debi Treloar; 148 left Openview Barn at Foster House, designed by Atlanta Bartlett and Dave Coote and available to hire for photography through www. beachstudios.co.uk/Ph. Polly Wreford; 148 right The family home in Denmark of Tine Kjeldsen and Jacob Fossum, owners of www. tinekhome.dk/Ph. Polly Wreford; 149 Kimberly Austin of Austin Press, San Francisco/Ph. Helen Cathcart; 150 above left 'La Maison du College Royal'/Ph. Jan Baldwin; 150 above right The family home of Fiona and Alex Cox of www.coxandcox.co.uk/Ph. Polly Wreford; 150 below right The home of James Russell and Hannah Plumb, the artists behind JAMESPLUMB www.jamesplumb.co.uk/Ph. Debi Treloar; 150 below centre The family home in Denmark of Tine Kjeldsen and Jacob Fossum, owners of www.tinekhome.dk/Ph. Polly Wreford; 150 below left The home of James and Maria Backhouse in London/Ph. Debi Treloar; 151 Bea B&B owned by Bea Mombaers in Knokke-Le Zoute, Belgium www.bea-bb.com/Ph. Anna Williams; 152 left A family home in west London by Webb Architects and Cave Interiors/Ph. Polly Wreford; 152 right The home of the architect Joseph Dirand in Paris/Ph. Pia Ulin; 153 The home of Jonathan Sela and Megan Schoenbachler/Ph. Catherine Gratwicke; 154–155 A family home in North London designed by Sally Mackereth of Wells Mackereth Architects/Ph. Winfried Heinze; 156 above left The family home of architect Arash Nourinejad and artist Kristina Lykke Tønnesen in Copenhagen/Ph. Rachel Whiting 156 above right The family home of Danielle de Lange of online shop Le Souk www. soukshop.com and lifestyle blog The Style Files www.style-files.com/ Ph. James Gardiner; 156 below right The home of Maaike Goldbach in the Netherlands/Ph. Katya de Grunwald; 156 below left The home of the textile designer Kim Schipperheijn in the Netherlands/Ph. Katya de Grunwald; 157 The family home of the designer Nina Nagel of byGraziela.com/Ph. Ben Robertson; 158 above The family home of architect Arash Nourinejad and artist Kristina Lykke Tønnesen in Copenhagen/Ph. Rachel Whiting; 158 below The home of Britt, Jurgen and Mascha/Ph. Rachel Whiting; 159 The home of Jeanette Lunde www.byfryd.com/Ph. Catherine Gratwicke; 160 Cathie Curran Architects/Ph. Polly Wreford; 161 above left Victoria Andreae's house in London/Ph. Debi Treloar; 161 above right A family home in Holland designed by Jasper Jansen of i29 design/Ph. Winfried Heinze; 161

below Monika of kaszkazmlekiem.com, co-founder of girlsontiptoes. com/Ph. Ben Robertson; 162 left The Collette's home in Holland, designed by architect Pascal Grosfeld/Ph. Winfried Heinze; 162 right The home of the textile designer Kim Schipperheijn in the Netherlands/Ph. Katya de Grunwald; 163 The home of interior journalist and blogger Jill Macnair in London/Ph. Rachel Whiting; 164 Ashlyn Gibson, founder of children's concept store Olive Loves Alfie, interior stylist/writer and children's fashion stylist/Ph. Rachel Whiting; 165 above left The home of Nici Zinell, designer of Noé & Zoë in Berlin, and Knut Hake, film editor/Ph. Rachel Whiting; 165 above right Dorthe Kvist, garden and interior designer, stylist, TV host, blogger and author/Ph. Katya de Grunwald; 165 below Karine Köng, founder and Creative Director of online concept store BODIE and FOU www.bodieandfou.com/Ph. Rachel Whiting; 166 above The family home of the designer Nina Nagel of byGraziela.com/Ph. Ben Robertson; 166 below The home of Susanne Brandt and her family in Copenhagen/Ph. Rachel Whiting; 167 The home of Jonathan Sela and Megan Schoenbachler/Ph. Catherine Gratwicke; 168 & 169 left The home and studio of designer Erika Harberts of mikodesign from the Netherlands/Ph. Helen Cathcart; 169 right Niki Brantmark of My Scandinavian Home/Ph. Rachel Whiting; 170 & 171 below The Clapton Laundry photographic location and creative workshop space/ Ph. Ben Robertson; 171 above left The Fried family home in London/ Ph. Winfried Heinze; 171 above right The family home of the interiors stylist and author Emily Henson in London/Ph. Katya de Grunwald; 172 Family Ponsa-Hemmings home, xo-inmyroom.com/Ph. Rachel Whiting; 173 above The home of Emma Donnelly, photographer www.takeapicturelady.com in Leigh-on-Sea/Ph. Ben Robertson; 173 below The family home of Francesca Forcolini and Barry Menmuir, designers and co-founders of fashion label Labour of Love/Ph. Ben Robertson; 174 above left The home of Anne Bjelke, hapelbloggen. blogspot.no/Ph. Catherine Gratwicke; 174 above right Agata Hamilton www.my-home.com.pl/Ph. Ben Robertson ; 174 below right The family home of Paola Sells of www.sugarkids.es in Barcelona/Ph. Rachel Whiting; 175–176 The family home of the designer Nina Nagel of byGraziela.com/Ph. Ben Robertson; 177 above The family home of Janneke van Houtum of www.liefsvanmaantje.nl in Eindhoven/Ph. James Gardiner; 177 below Anki Wijnen and Casper Boot from www. zilverblauw.nl and www.jahallo.nl/Ph. Rachel Whiting; 178 above The family home of Ewa Solarz in Poland/Ph. Ben Robertson; 178 below The Clapton Laundry photographic location and creative workshop space/Ph. Ben Robertson; 179 above centre The family home of Janneke van Houtum of www.liefsvanmaantje.nl in Eindhoven/Ph. James Gardiner; 179 above right The family home of the designer Nina Nagel of byGraziela.com/Ph. Ben Robertson; 179 below Anki Wijnen and Casper Boot from www.zilverblauw.nl and www.jahallo. nl/Ph. Rachel Whiting; 180 The home in Glasgow of textile designer Fiona Douglas of bluebellgray/Ph. Debi Treloar; 181 above The family home of Rebecca Proctor in Cornwall www.futurusticblog.com/Ph. Rachel Whiting; 181 below Emma Cassi's home in London/Ph.

Winfried Heinze; 182 L'Atelier d'Archi – Isabelle Juy – www. latelierdarchi.fr/Ph. Polly Wreford; 183 above The family home of Louise and Garth Jennings in London/Ph. Rachel Whiting; 183 below The family home of the interior designer Larissa van Seumeren in the Netherlands/Ph. Catherine Gratwicke; 184 The home of the founder/ designer Sabien Engelenburg of engelpunt.com/Ph. Rachel Whiting; 185 above The family home of Louise and Garth Jennings in London/ Ph. Rachel Whiting; 185 below The London home of Louise Scott-Smith of www.lovelylovely.co.uk/Ph. Debi Treloar; 186 above The family home of the architects Jeanette and Rasmus Frisk of www. arkilab.dk/Ph. Ben Robertson; 186 below The family home of the designer Nina Nagel of byGraziela.com/Ph. Ben Robertson; 187 above The home and studio of designer Erika Harberts of mikodesign from the Netherlands/Ph. Helen Cathcart; 187 below right The family home of the interior designer Larissa van Seumeren in the Netherlands/Ph. Catherine Gratwicke; 187 below left The family home of Janneke van Houtum of www.liefsvanmaantje.nl in Eindhoven/ Ph. James Gardiner; 188–189 Naja Munthe, owner of MUNTHE in Copenhagen/Ph. Pia Ulin; 190 The home of the decorator Bunny Turner of www.turnerpocock.co.uk/Ph. Polly Wreford; 191 above centre Foster House, the family home of Atlanta Bartlett and Dave Coote, available to hire for photography through www.beachstudios. co.uk/Ph. Polly Wreford; 191 above right Armando Elias, Hugo D'Enjoy. Craft Design/Ph. Rachel Whiting; 191 below The Brooklyn loft of Alina Preciado, owner of lifestyle store dar gitane www. dargitane.com/Ph. Anna Williams; 192 above The home of Virginie Denny, fashion designer, and Alfonso Vallès, painter/Ph. Debi Treloar; 192 below Home of the designer Anne Geistdoerfer (and her family) of double g architects in Paris/Ph. Polly Wreford; 193 The family home of Danielle de Lange of online shop Le Souk www.soukshop. com and lifestyle blog The Style Files www.style-files.com/Ph. James Gardiner; 194 The home in Provence of Carolyn Oswald/Ph. Polly Wreford; 195 above left The home of Marie Worsaae of Aiayu/Ph. Pia Ulin; 195 above right The London home of the interiors blogger Katy Orme (apartmentapothecary.com)/Ph. Rachel Whiting; 195 below The home of the stylist Ingeborg Wolf/Ph. Pia Ulin; 196 above left The family home of Alison Smith in Brighton/Ph. Polly Wreford; 196 above right The London apartment of Adam Hills and Maria Speake, owners of Retrouvius (www.retrouvius.com)/Ph. Debi Treloar; 196 below The home of Anne Bjelke hapelbloggen.blogspot.no/Ph. Catherine Gratwicke; 197 The home of designer and stylist Annaleena Leino Karlsson in Stockholm/Ph. Pia Ulin; 198 The home in Provence of Carolyn Oswald/Ph. Polly Wreford; 199 left Home of writer and director Tannaz Hazemi/Ph. Debi Treloar; 199 right Kvarngården, the home of photographer Nils Odier, stylist Sofia Odier, and their two daughters Lou and Uma. Skivarp, Sweden/Ph. Debi Treloar; 200 above Anki Wijnen and Casper Boot from www.zilverblauw.nl and www.jahallo.nl/Ph. Rachel Whiting; 200 below centre Mark and Sally Bailey's home in Herefordshire, www.baileyshome.com/Ph. Debi Treloar; 200 below left The Brooklyn home of Asumi and Kuni of

Kanorado Shop/Ph. James Gardiner; 201 /Ph. Claire Richardson; 202 Foster House, available to hire through www.beachstudios.co.uk/Ph. Polly Wreford; 203 left The home of the architect Jonas Bjerre-Poulsen of NORM Architects/Ph. Pia Ulin; 203 right Mark and Sally Bailey's home in Herefordshire, www.baileyshome.com/Ph. Debi Treloar; 204 left The home and studio of Petra Janssen and Edwin Vollebergh of Studio Boot in the Netherlands www.studioboot.nl. Katya de Grunwald; 204 right The home of Malene Birger in Copenhagen/Ph. Polly Wreford; 205 Jeska and Dean Hearne www.thefuturekept.com/Ph. James Gardiner; 206 The home of Maria and Frank in Southern Germany, with interior design by Barbara G/Ph. Jan Baldwin; 207 above /Ph. Simon Brown; 207 below The apartment of Yancey and Mark Richardson in New York, Architecture and Interior Design by Steven Learner Studio /Ph. Winfried Heinze; 208 above The home of antiques dealer and interior designer Oliver Gustav in Copenhagen/Ph. Debi Treloar; 208 below The family home of Gina Portman of Folk at Home www.folkathome.com/Ph. Catherine Gratwicke; 209 The Brooklyn home of Helen Dealtry of wokinggirldesigns.com/Ph. James Gardiner; 210–211 /Ph. Rachel Whiting; 212 Wynchelse, designed by Dave Coote and Atlanta Bartlett, available to hire for holiday lets and photography through www.beachstudios.co.uk/Ph. Polly Wreford; 213 above and below right The home and studio of Petra Janssen and Edwin Vollebergh of Studio Boot in the Netherlands www.studioboot.nl/Ph. Katya de Grunwald; 213 below left The home of Birgitte and Henrik Moller Kastrup in Denmark/Ph. Rachel Whiting: 214 above The home and studio of Petra Janssen and Edwin Vollebergh of Studio Boot in the Netherlands www.studioboot.nl/Ph. Katya de Grunwald; 214 below Photographer Joanna Vestey and her husband Steve Brooks' home in Cornwall/Ph. Jan Baldwin; 215 The home of the illustrator Kate Bingaman-Burt in Portland/Ph. Helen Cathcart; 216 Wynchelse, designed by Dave Coote and Atlanta Bartlett, available to hire for holiday lets and photography through www.beachstudios.co.uk/Ph. Polly Wreford; 217 above The home of Giorgio DeLuca in New York/Ph. Pia Ulin; 217 below Simon and Antonia Johnson's home in Somerset/Ph. Chris Tubbs; 218 The home of Virginie Denny, fashion designer, and Alfonso Vallès, painter/Ph. Debi Treloar; 219 an apartment in Bath designed by Briffa Phillips Architects/Ph. Andrew Wood; 220 above Designed by Steve Schappacher and Rhea White of SchappacherWhite Ltd www.schappacherwhite.com/Ph. Earl Carter; 220 below The home and studios of the artists Freddie Robins and Ben Coode-Adams in Essex. Designed by Anthony Hudson of Hudson Architects. Built by Ben Coode-Adams and Nick Spall (NS Restorations); 221 The London home of the artist Bobby Petersen/Ph. Katya de Grunwald; 222 left Armando Elias, Hugo D'Enjoy. Craft Design/Ph. Rachel Whiting; 222 right Stansfield Road, designed by Dave Coote and Atlanta Bartlett. Available to hire for photography through www.beachstudios.co.uk/Ph. Polly Wreford; 223 Abigail Ahern's home in London/Ph. Polly Wreford; 224–225 The home of Cary Tamarkin and Mindy Goldberg on Shelter Island/Ph. Earl Carter;

226 above Stenhuset Antikhandel shop, café and B&B in Stockamollan, Sweden/Ph. Polly Wreford; 226 below left The family home of Sarah and Mark Benton in Rye/Ph. Polly Wreford; 226 below right The home of the interior designer Eva Gnaedinger in Switzerland/Ph. Jan Baldwin; 227 left The home of Jonathan Sela and Megan Schoenbachler/Ph. Catherine Gratwicke; 227 right The home of the designer Agnès Emery of Emery & Cie in the Medina in Marrakech/Ph. Katya de Grunwald; 228 above The B&B Camellas-Lloret, designed and owned by Annie Moore near Carcassonne/Ph. Claire Richardson; 228 below The garden of Viktoria Johansson of www.lillagrona.se/Ph. Rachel Whiting; 229 /Ph. Rachel Whiting; 230 The garden of Viktoria Johansson of www.lillagrona.se/Ph. Rachel Whiting; 231 above The summerhouse of Tine Kjeldesen of www.tinekhome.com in Denmark/Ph. Earl Carter; 231 below The home and shop of Katarina von Wowern of www.minaideer.se/Ph. Rachel Whiting; 232 /Ph. Rachel Whiting; 233 above left www.lightlocations.com/Ph. Debi Treloar; 233 above right Ph Rachel Whiting; 233 below right Ph Peter Cassidy; 233 below left Robert Young Architecture & Interiors www.ryarch.com/Ph. Earl Carter; 234 above left www.shootspaces.com/Ph. Debi Treloar; 234 above right Ph Debi Treloar; 234 below right The family home of the stylist and writer Katrine Martensen-Larsen in Zealand, Denmark/Ph. Earl Carter; 234 below left Designed by Steve Schappacher and Rhea White of SchappacherWhite Ltd www.schappacherwhite.com/Ph. Earl Carter; 235 above The home of Jeanette Lunde www.byfryd.com. Catherine Gratwicke; 235 below The home of Anne Bjelke hapelbloggen.blogspot.no/Ph. Catherine Gratwicke; 236 left The home of Velasco Vitali, designed by Arturo Montanelli. All paintings and sculptures © Velasco Vitali. www.velascovitali.com. www.arturomontanelli.com/Ph. Debi Treloar; 236 right Marina Ferrara Pignatelli's home in Val d'Orcia, Tuscany/Ph. Chris Tubbs; 237 /Ph. Peter Cassidy; 238 The home of the author/stylist Selina Lake/Ph. Rachel Whiting; 239 left Helen and Andrew Fickling. www.helenfickling.com/Ph. Debi Treloar; 239 right Barbara Bestor, www.bestorarchitecture.com/Ph. Catherine Gratwicke; 243 The home of Rose Hammick and Andrew Treverton www.mamoraroad.co.uk/Ph. Polly Wreford; 244 The home of Jonathan Sela and Megan Schoenbachler/Ph. Catherine Gratwicke; 249 The Linen Shed, boutique B&B near Whitstable, Kent, UK www.linenshed.com/Ph. Catherine Gratwicke; 256 The home of Birgitte and Henrik Kastrup in Denmark/Ph.Rachel Whiting; back endpaper the home of Oliver Heath and Katie Weiner – sustainable architecture, interior and jewellery design/Ph. Catherine Gratwicke.

ARCHITECTS, DESIGNERS AND BUSINESSES FEATURED IN THIS BOOK

Aiayu
Dampfaergevej 2A
2100 Copenhagen
Denmark
T: +45 33 32 32 80
E: mw@aiayu.com
www.aiayu.com
Pages 25 below, 56 below left, 76 below left.

Alfonso Vallès
www.alfonsovallès.fr
Pages 45, 96 above left, 192 above, 218.

Annaleena Leino Karlsson
Sånga-säbyvägen 178
17996 Svartsjö
Sweden
T: +46 73 6004626
E: info@annaleena.se
www.annaleena.se
Pages 38 above right, 197.

Antoni Burakowski
The Antoni & Alison Shop
43 Rosebery Avenue
London EC1R 4SH
T: +44 (0)20 7833 2141
www.antoniandalison.co.uk
Pages 16 above, 64 below left, 66 above right, 83 above.

Katrin Arens
E: info@katrinarens.it
www.katrinarens.it
Page 40 right.

Ashlyn Gibson
Olive Loves Alfie
84 Stoke Newington Church Street
London N16 0AP
T: +44 (0)20 7241 4212
www.olivelovesalfie.co.uk
www.ashlyngibson.co.uk
Pages 164, 170, 171 below, 178 below.

Atlanta Bartlett and Dave Coote
www.beachstudios.co.uk
www.paleandinteresting.com
www.paleandinterestingholidays.com
www.atlantabartlett.com
www.davecoote.com
Pages 4 above left, 11 below right, 20 above, 30, 41, 46, 47 above and centre, 65 above, 68, 97 below, 98 above left, 100, 106 left, 112, 113 right, 114 below, 117 above, 145 centre, 146, 148, 191 above right, 202, 212, 216, 222 above.

Baileys
Whitecross Farm
Bridstow
Ross-on-Wye
Herefordshire HR9 6JU
T: +44 (0)1989 561931
www.baileyshome.com
Pages 65 below right, 200 below right, 203 above right.

Eliza Barnes Architectural Salvage and Design
T: +44 (0)7977 234896
www.elizabarnes.com
Pages 57.

Pentreath & Hall
17 Rugby Street
Bloomsbury
London WC1N 3QT
T: +44 (0)20 7430 2526
info@benpentreath.com
www.benpentreath.com
Page 137 above right.

Brandts Indoor
Lindeallé 31
DK-5230 Odense M
Denmark
T: +45 6614 5343
E: info@brandtsindoor.dk
www.brandtsindoor.dk
Pages 31 below, 69 left, 142 above right.

Camellas-Lloret
Maison d'Hote
Rue de l'angle
11290 Montréal
France
T: +33 6 45 73 96 42
E: annie@camellaslloret.com
www.camellaslloret.com
Pages 104 below, 107 above, 124, 228.

Caroline von Thillo
Interior Decorator
MJL Interiors
Bredabaan 158
2930 Brasschaat
Belgium
T: +32 3 653 55 96
Facebook: MJL-Interiors by Caroline von Thillo
Pages 6, 52, 53 above left.

Cave interiors
www.caveinteriors.com
Pages 13, 23 below, 152 left.

Danielle de Lange
Le Souk
www.soukshop.com
and
www.style-files.com
Pages 8–9, 193.

Joseph Dirand Architecture
51 rue Saint Georges
75009 Paris
France
T: +33 1 44 69 04 80
E: jd@josephdirand.com
www.josephdirand.com
Pages 11 above, 28 left, 74 above, 85 above left, 90–91, 152 right.

ENGEL. celebrate for life
www.engelpunt.com
Pages 49, 184.

Eva Gnaedinger
www.evagnaedinger.com
Pages 66 above left, 118 left, 226 below centre.

Fforest General Store
www.fforest.bigcartel.com
and
E: info@coldatnight.co.uk
www.coldatnight.co.uk
Pages 14 above, 38 below right.

Folk at Home
www.folkathome.com
Pages 60, 62 below right, 126 above right, 143, 208 below.

Hans Blomquist
www.agentbauer.com
Pages 1, 64 below right, 79 left.

Helen Dealtry
www.helendealtry.com
and
www.wokinggirldesigns.com
Pages 17 above left, 54–55 above, 133 above, 209.

Hilary Robertson
T: +1 917 971 7081
E: hilaryrobertsona@gmail.com
www.hilaryrobertson.com
Pages 78 left, 111 above, 118 right.

Melanie Ireland
www.simplekids.be
Pages 78 centre, 131 above left, 131 below right.

Isabelle Juy
L'Atelier d'Archi
www.latelierdarchi.fr
Page 25 above right.

Jill Macnair
www.myfriendshouse.co.uk
www.jillmacnair.com
Page 163.

Kim Schipperheijn
E: kimschipperheijn@hotmail.com
Pages 53 above right, 156 below left, 162 right.

Kristina Dam
www.kristinadam.dk
Page 64 above.

Louise Kamma Riising
www.heyhome.dk
Page 33.

**Stéphane Garotin and
Pierre Emmanuel Martin**
MAISON HAND
E: info@maison-hand.fr
www.maison-hand.com
*Pages 2, 19 below, 24 above, 78
above, 106 right, 109 above right.*

By Malene Birger
Head Office
Rahbeks Allé 21
1801 Frederiksberg
Copenhagen
Denmark
T: +45 3326 9620
www.bymalenebirger.com
*Pages 24 below, 38 above left, 204
above right.*

Marco Lobina
www.rezina.it
www.uda.it
Pages 34, 123–124.

Marianne Evennou
www.marianne-evennou.com
*Pages 11 below left, 35 below
right, 107 below.*

**Marzio Cavanna
& Cristiana Giva Architects**
MC2 Studio
www.mc2studio.com
Pages 88–89, 96 below left.

**Megan Schoenbachler
Photography**
www.meganschoenbachler.com
and
Architects:
Marmol Radziner Architecture
www.marmol-radziner.com
*Pages 88 left, 153, 167, 226–227,
244.*

Michela Imperiali
www.MIKinteriors.com
Pages 4 right, 39 below.

Mini Moderns
www.minimoderns.com
*Pages 56 above, 101 above,
131 below left.*

Munthe
www.munthe.com
*Pages 85 below, 110 below,
188–189.*

Adriana Natcheva
Groves Natcheva Architects
6 Kensington Mews
London W8 5DR
T: +44 (0)20 7937 7772
E: info@grovesnatcheva.com
Page 17 below.

Nina Nagel
www.byGraziela.com
*Pages 157, 166 above, 175, 176,
179 above right, 186 below.*

Noé & Zoë
Berlin
T: +49 1736843736
E: info@noe-zoe.com
www.noe-zoe.com
Pages 22, 59, 128, 165 above left.

Jonas Bjerre-Poulsen
NORM Architects
Snaregade 14
1205 Copenhagen
Denmark
E: info@normcph.com
www.normcph.com
*Pages 28 right, 32 below right, 74
below right, 203 above left.*

Oliver Heath
www.oliverheath.com
and
Katie Weiner
www.katieweiner.com
*Pages 77, 81, 104 above left, 110
above.*

Petite Violette
Online shop, retail space and
prop hire business
Davidshallstorg 1
211 45 Malmö
Sweden
T: +46 (0)709 487 929
E: info@petiteviolette.com
www.petiteviolette.com
Page 27 below.

Petra Boase
www.petraboase.com
www.cliffbarns.com
Page 82.

Retrouvius
2A Ravensworth Road
London NW10 5NR
T: +44 (0)20 8960 6060
E: design@retrouvius.com
www.retrouvius.com
*Pages 15 right, 20 below, 31
above, 54 below left, 74 below
left, 80 above, 96 below right,
130, 147 below, 196 above right.*

Saša Antic
www.sasaantic.com
sasaantic.tumblr.com
Page 19 above.

Selina Lake
www.selinalake.co.uk
www.selinalake.blogspot.co.uk
Instagram and Pinterest: @
selinalake
Page 238.

Studio Boot
workshop for image & type
Van Tuldenstraat 2
5211 TG's-Hertogenbosch
The Netherlands
T: +31 (0)7361 43593
+31 (0)6 5111 5618
E: info@studioboot.nl
www.studioboot.nl
*Pages 83 below left, 204, 213
above, 213 below right, 214.*

Architect:
Tamarkin Co.,
www.tamarkinco.com
and
Associate Architect:
Techler Design Group
www.techlerdesign.com
and
Interior Design:
Suzanne Shaker interiors
www.suzanneshaker.com
Pages 224–225.

Bunny Turner
Turner Pocock Interior Design
Unit 18A
First Floor Parsons Green Depot
Parsons Green Lane
London SW6 4HH
T: +44 (0)20 3463 2390
Pages 4 left, 5 below, 190.

Yvla Skarp
E: info@yvlaskarp.se
www.yvlaskarp.se
Pages 17 above right, 76 above.

Yvonne Koné
E: info@yvonnekone.com
www.yvonnekone.com
Pages 3, 50–51, 105 above.

INDEX

Page numbers in *italic* refer to the captions

A

Aarnio, Eero *83*
appliances, kitchen 26–7
artwork
    bedrooms 110
    children's rooms 181
    living rooms *65*, *65*, *79*, 84
    teen bedrooms *171*

B

babies' rooms 160–3, *181*
barbecues 231
basins, in bathrooms *126*, 129,
    130–1, *130*, *152*
bathrooms 122–53
    bathtubs and basins 130–1
    colour 134, 136–7
    design and decoration 124–5
    family bathrooms 128–9
    finishing touches 144–5
    flooring 140–1
    hotel glamour 152–3
    lighting 138–9
    natural bathrooms 150–1
    open-plan living 218, *218–19*
    planning 126–7
    small bathrooms 134–5
    storage 134, 142–3
    traditional style 146–7
    wet rooms 132–3
    white schemes 148–9
bathtubs *126*, 130–1, *130*, *137*,
    146, *147*, 152
bedrooms 90–121
    bedding and mattresses 100–1
    clothes storage 108–9
    colours 96–7, 118, 121
    design and decoration 92–3
    finishing touches 110–11
    flooring 106–7
    furniture 98–9, 118
    grown-up glamour 118–19
    lighting 104–5
    modern country 112–13
    open-plan living *214*, 218,
        218–19
    planning 94–5
    romantic florals 116–17
    simple retreats 120–1
    white schemes 114–15
    windows 102–3
    see also children's rooms
beds 98, *98*, 101, *101*, 113, 118,
    121
    children's rooms 169, 170, *183*
benches *62*, *232*
blankets 101
blinds/shades
    bathrooms 145
    bedrooms 102
    children's rooms 179
    kitchens 32
    living rooms 57, 70, *70*
book shelves *52*, *76*, 77, 166, 177,
    198

boys' rooms 166–7, 181
breakfast bars *25*
bunk beds 169, *169*

C

cabinets, displays in *65*
candles 105, *105*, *138*, 227, 235,
    235
carpets
    bedrooms 106, 107
    children's rooms 174, *174–5*,
        175
    living rooms 75, *75*
chairs
    babies' rooms 162
    kitchens 24, *25*
    living rooms 62, 69
    see also seating; sofas
chalkboards *23*, 158
chandeliers 73, 105, *138*
children
    family bathrooms 128–9
    family kitchens 23, *23*, 48
    living rooms 58–9
children's rooms 154–87
    action stations 186–7
    babies' rooms 160–3, *181*
    boys' rooms 166–7, 181
    dens and hideaways 182–3
    design and decoration 156–7
    flooring 174–5
    gender neutral bedrooms
        180–1
    girls' rooms 164–5, 181
    lighting 172–3
    planning 158–9
    print and pattern 184–5
    shared bedrooms 168–9
    storage 158, *161*, 162–3, *166*,
        176–7, 186–7
    teen bedrooms 170–1
    white and bright 178–9
clothes, storage 108–9
collections *see* displays
colour
    bathrooms 134, 136–7
    bedrooms 96–7, 118, 121
    children's rooms 165, *165*, 166,
        178–9, 181, 185
    kitchens 39, 40, 43
    living rooms 66–7, 69, 83, 84
    see also monochrome
        schemes; white schemes
computers *61*, 187, *195*, 196, 203
concrete floors 34, 44, 75, *75*, *140*
conservatories 228–9
cooker hoods 19
cookers *26*, 27, 40, *47*
cots/cribs *161*, 162
country style
    bedrooms 112–13
    kitchens 40–1
    living rooms 80–1
cupboards
    bathrooms 142, *142*
    bedrooms 94

fitted versus unfitted kitchens
    16–17
    home offices 199
    kitchens 15, *15*, *20*, 31, *31*, 36
    living rooms 76, *76*, 77, *77*
    under-stairs 183
    see also storage
curtains
    bathrooms 145
    bedrooms 102, 118
    home offices 203
    kitchens 32
    living rooms 57, 70, *70*, 80
cushions
    bedrooms *101*, 118
    children's rooms 183
    living rooms 69, *69*, 80
    outdoor living 235, 236

D

decks 238–9
dens and hideaways 182–3
desks
    children's rooms *158*, 170, 186,
        186, 187
    home offices 191–209
dimmers, lighting 33, 73, 105,
    161, 173
dining areas
    kitchens 24–5, 31, 34
    outdoor living 230–1, *235*
dishwashers 28
displays
    bedrooms 111, *111*
    children's rooms *165*, *166*, 176,
        186, *186*
    home offices *204*, 208
    kitchens *39*, 40, 48
    living rooms 64–5, 79, *79*
doors
    bathrooms *134*
    living rooms 57
    sliding *227*
drawers, in kitchens *36*
dressers/hutches *15*
duvets 101

E

eclectic style
    kitchens 42–3
    open-plan living 220–1
elegant living rooms 84–5

F

fabrics
    bedrooms *93*, 113
    floral patterns 117
    living rooms 68–9, 80
family-friendly kitchens 22–3,
    48–9
fireplaces 54
fitted kitchens 16–17
flooring
    bathrooms 140–1

bedrooms 106–7
children's rooms 174–5
kitchens 34–5
living rooms 74–5, 84
open-plan living *223*
outdoor living 227
floral patterns 116–17
flowers
    bathrooms 145
    bedrooms 111, 115
    floral patterns 116–17
    home offices 204
    kitchens 39, *39*
    living rooms 84
focal points, living rooms 54
freezers 27
furniture
    babies' rooms 162–3
    bedrooms 98–9, 118
    living rooms 54, 62–3, 82–3
    outdoor living *226*, 232–3, 236
    see also chairs, seating, tables
        etc

G

galley kitchens 16, 19
garden rooms 228–9
gardens *see* outdoor living
girls' rooms 164–5, 181
glamour
    bathrooms 152–3
    bedrooms 118–19
glass, toughened 31

H

heating
    babies' rooms 161
    bathrooms 126, 129, 141, 145
    living rooms 80
    underfloor 35, 80, 126, 129, 141
Hicks, David 79
hideaways 182–3
hobs 26, 27, 36
home offices 188–209
    corner offices 196–7
    design and decoration 190–1
    finishing touches 204–5
    freeform offices 208–9
    lighting 202–3
    planning 192–3
    purpose-built offices 206–7
    storage 192, 198–201, 207
    workstations 194–5

I

induction hobs 26
industrial kitchens 44–5
island units, kitchens *11*, *12*, *15*,
    16, *17*, 20, *23*, 217

K

Kidston, Cath 117
kitchens 9–49

adapting existing kitchens 14–15
country kitchens 40–1
dining areas 24–5, 31, 34
eclectic kitchens 42–3
family-friendly kitchens 22–3, 48–9
finishing touches 38–9
fitted versus unfitted 16–17
flooring 34–5
galley kitchens 16, 19
industrial kitchens 44–5
large appliances 26–7
large kitchens 20–1, 23
lighting 32–3, 48
materials 30–1
open-plan living *214*, 217, *217*
planning 12–13
plumbing 28–9
storage 36–7
white kitchens 46–7

L

ladders, storage on *36*
lamps *see* lighting
large spaces
  kitchens 20–1, 23, 44
  living rooms *54*
  open-plan living 211–23
LED lighting *32*, 105
lighting
  babies' rooms 161
  bathrooms 138–9
  bedrooms 104–5
  children's rooms 172–3
  dimmers 33, 73, 105, 161, 173
  home offices 202–3
  kitchens 25, 32–3, 48
  living rooms 72–3, 79, 84, 87, 89
  work areas 187
  see also natural light
linoleum 34, 35, 75, 141
living rooms 50–89
  adapting existing rooms 56–7
  collections and displays 64–5
  colour 66–7
  corner offices 196–7
  design and decoration 52–3
  elegant rooms 84–5
  family rooms 58–9
  finishing touches 78–9
  flooring 74–5, 84
  furniture 62–3, 82–3
  lighting 72–3, 79, 84, 87, 89
  masculine monochrome 88–9
  modern country 80–1
  planning 54–5
  soft furnishings 68–9, 80
  storage 76–7, 84
  technology 60–1
  vintage-inspired style 82–3
  white schemes *84*, 86–7
  windows 70–1
  see also open-plan living

M

mantelpieces *111*
mattresses 98, *98*, 100–1, 162
Mediterranean style, outdoor living 236–7

mirrors
  in bathrooms *125*, 134
  in bedrooms 110, *111*, 118
  in kitchens *19*
  in living rooms *79*
  outdoor living 235
modern country style
  bedrooms 112–13
  living rooms 80–1
monochrome schemes
  bathrooms 137
  bedrooms *120*
  living rooms *85*, 88–9
  see also white schemes
mood boards 185

N

natural light
  home offices 203
  living rooms *53*
  see also lighting
noticeboards *23*, 158, 200
nurseries 160–3, *181*

O

offices *see* home offices
open-plan living 211–23
  cooking, living and eating 216–17
  eclectic style 220–1
  pros and cons 214–15
  sleeping, dressing and bathing 218–19
  slick and streamlined 222–3
  storage 222, *222*
outdoor living 225–39
  accessories 234–5
  decks 238–9
  dining areas 230–1, *235*
  furniture 232–3, 236
  garden rooms and conservatories 228–9
  Mediterranean style 236–7
  planning 226–7
ovens 26, *26*, 27, 36

P

pattern, in children's rooms 184–5
pendant lights
  bedrooms 105, *105*
  children's rooms 173
  home offices 203, *203*
  kitchens 25, *32*, 33, *33*
  living rooms *73*, *85*
pictures *see* artwork
plants
  outdoor living 236
  see also flowers
plumbing, kitchens 28–9
porches 239

R

range cookers *26*, 27, 40, *47*
refrigerators 26, 27
roller blinds/shades 70, 102, 113, 179, 228
Roman blinds/shades 70, 102, *102*, 113

room dividers *54*, *158*, 169
rubber flooring 34, 35, 75, 174, 187
rugs 75, *75*, 80, 106, *106*, 175, *238*

S

safety
  babies' rooms 161
  bathrooms 138, 139, 141
seating
  family-friendly kitchens 23, 48
  living rooms 53, 62, *62*
  outdoor living 232, *232*
  see also chairs; sofas
shelving
  book shelves *52*, *76*, 77, 166, 177, *198*
  children's rooms 169, 186
  clothes storage *109*
  home offices *198*, 199, *204*, *207*
  kitchens *15*, *20*, *36*, 39
  living rooms *52*, *54*, 57, *76*, *76*
showers *126*, 129, 132–3, 134, 152, *219*
shutters 70, 102, *102*, 148
sideboards/credenzas 77, *77*
sinks, kitchens 28, *28*
sitting rooms *see* living rooms
small rooms
  bathrooms 134–5
  kitchens 19, *19*
sofas *54*, 57, 62, *82*, *217*
soft furnishings *see* curtains; cushions; fabrics
splashbacks, kitchens *28*, *39*
spot lights *32*
stairs, cupboards under 183
steel, in kitchens 31, 44, *44*
stone floors 35, *35*, 40, 75, 141, *141*
storage
  bathrooms 129, *129*, 134, 142–3
  bedrooms *94*, 98
  children's rooms 158, *161*, 162–3, *166*, 176–7, 186–7
  clothes 108–9
  family-friendly kitchens 23, 48
  home offices 192, 198–201, 207
  kitchens 19, 36–7
  living rooms 58, 76–7, 84
  open-plan living 222, *222*
  teen bedrooms 170
  see also cupboards
studies *see* home offices

T

tables
  kitchens 24, *25*
  living rooms 62
  'tablescapes' 79
  see also dining areas
taps/faucets
  bathrooms 129
  kitchens 28, *28*
task lighting
  bedrooms 105, *105*
  children's rooms 173, *173*
  home offices 203, *203*
  kitchens 32, *32*, 33
  living rooms 73, 89

technology
  home offices 192
  living rooms 60–1
teen bedrooms 170–1
televisions 54, *54*, 61, *61*
tents 182, *183*
terracotta tiles, flooring 35
throws 80, *101*, 113
tiles
  bathrooms *129*
  flooring 35, *75*, *140*, 141
toilets 130
toys 58, *59*, *157*, 176, 177, *179*, 181
trolleys *15*

U

underfloor heating 35, 80, 126, 129, 141
unfitted kitchens 16–17
uplighters 73

V

Venetian blinds/shades 102
ventilation, kitchens 19
vintage-inspired style, living rooms 82–3

W

wallpaper
  bathrooms *145*, 146, 147
  bedrooms 117, *117*
  children's rooms 179, *185*, *187*
wardrobes/closets 98, 108, 109, *162*, 177
water, plumbing kitchens 28–9
wet rooms 132–3
white schemes
  bathrooms *125*, 148–9
  bedrooms 114–15, *120*
  children's rooms 178–9
  kitchens *11*, *31*, 46–7
  living rooms *84*, 86–7
windows
  bathrooms 145
  bedrooms 102–3
  living rooms 57, 70–1
wood
  bathrooms 151, *151*
  decks 239
  flooring 35, *35*, 75, 89, 106, *106*, *140*, 141, 148, 174, *174*, 175
  kitchens 31, *31*, 40, *40*, 47
  panelling *147*
wood-burning stoves 57
workstations 194–5
  children's rooms 186–7
  lighting 187
  in living rooms *61*
  see also home offices
work triangle, kitchens 16
worktops, kitchens 28, 31